HEALTHY
PLEASURES

HEALTHY PLEASURES

Great Tastes from
Canadian Dietitians and Chefs

The Canadian Dietetic Association
in collaboration with
the Canadian Federation of Chefs and Cooks

Macmillan Canada
Toronto

Canadian Cataloguing in Publication Data
Main entry under title:

Healthy Pleasures : great tastes from Canadian dietitians and chefs

Includes index.
ISBN 0-7715-7362-6

1.   Cookery – Canada.   I.   Canadian Dietetic Association.

TX714.H43 1995   641.5'63   C95–931505–5

Macmillan Canada wishes to thank the Canada Council, the Ontario Arts Council and the Ontario Ministry of Culture and Communications for supporting its publishing program.

Macmillan Canada
A Division of Canada Publishing Corporation
Toronto, Canada

1 2 3 4 5   99 98 97 96 95

Cover and Book Design: Gillian Tsintziras/The Brookview Group
Photographs: Fred Bird
Typeset in Gill Sans by Archetype
Cover Photo: Grilled Chicken Breast with Mediterranean Dried Fruit Salsa
(page 161)

Printed in Canada

*The Canadian Dietetic Association wishes to recognize
the efforts of Langdon Starr,
without whose commitment and financial support,
Healthy Pleasures would not have moved from
the idea stage to reality.
Many thanks to the public relations team of
Jane Langdon, Linda Wirkowski, Suzanne Ross
and Murray Luening.*

Acknowledgments

Healthy Pleasures is truly the result of a team effort.

Credit for the idea goes to Helen Haresign, RD, director of communications and marketing for The Canadian Dietetic Association.

Susan Fyshe, RD, CDA's manager of public awareness, was instrumental in the "Celebrating the Pleasure of Healthy Eating" Nutrition Month campaign that first paired dietitians and chefs, and was a strong supporter of this project.

Thanks to Julius Pokomandy, national president of the Canadian Federation of Chefs and Cooks, for his support; immediate past president Arthur Rayner, who first opened the door to a joint project; and a special thanks to Claire Forester, executive assistant of the CFCC, for her invaluable assistance liaising with branch presidents and chefs.

Healthy Pleasures project manager was Mary Margaret Laing, RD, whose enthusiasm and efficiency was a key factor in meeting the publishing deadlines, and who tasted virtually every one of the recipes!

Of course, there wouldn't be a cookbook without the fabulous recipes created by our chef/dietitian partnerships, all of whom are identified throughout the cookbook. These teams really proved that healthy eating does taste great.

Each of the recipes was tested for home use, and modified if necessary, by home economist Sue Bailey and her assistants, Shirley Ann Holmes and Elaine Duffy.

The nutrient analysis was conducted by Barbara Selley, RD and Beverley Bell-Rowbotham of Info Access (1988) Inc.

The nutrition information was written by dietitians Mary Margaret Laing, RD, Susie Langley, RD, Vesanto Melina, RD, Elizabeth Shears, P.Dt., Susan Sutherland, RD, and Ellen Vogel, RD. Copy was reviewed by a group of very capable reviewers: Suzanne Hendricks, RD, Mary Ann Rangam, RD, Carol Poduch, RD, and Helen Hale Tomasik, RD, who provided excellent input and feedback.

A picture is worth a thousand words, and Healthy Pleasures benefited from the skill and expertise of Fred Bird, photographer extraordinaire, stylist Jennifer McLagan, a magician in the studio, and Debbie Boyden, who found perfect props for every shot.

And finally, thanks to Denise Schon and Nicole de Montbrun for sharing their knowledge of cookbooks and helping make the process so painless.

Contents

Can great taste and nutrition go hand in hand?

The answer is a resounding yes and it's the reason why—for the first time ever—The Canadian Dietetic Association and the Canadian Federation of Chefs and Cooks teamed up to show Canadians that eating well tastes great.

In March 1995, the relationship between taste and nutrition was the focus for CDA's Nutrition Month campaign—"Celebrating the Pleasure of Healthy Eating." The goal was to focus attention on the enjoyment of eating while following a healthy eating pattern.

This cookbook features more than 200 recipes, developed by 75 dietitian and chef partnerships. Together, they have created a great cookbook that will tempt you to explore the variety of flavors and styles of food we can enjoy in Canada.

On behalf of the two associations, we invite you to enjoy healthy eating at its best. Nutritious is delicious, and thanks to the efforts of dietitians and chefs from coast to coast, you too can Celebrate the Pleasure of Healthy Eating.

Bon appétit!

Carollyne Conlinn
President (1994–95)
The Canadian Dietetic Association

Julius Pokomandy
President (1994–95)
Canadian Federation of Chefs and Cooks

The Canadian
Dietetic Association

The Canadian Dietetic Association is the national voice of dietitians, working to achieve health through food and nutrition. Representing more than 5,000 dietitians across Canada, CDA is the third largest national dietetic association in the world.

Dietitians are the ideal source of up-to-date, reliable nutrition advice. If you have any questions concerning nutrition, contact a dietitian at your local hospital, health department, university, in private consulting or industry.

Canadian Federation
of Chefs and Cooks

The Canadian Federation of Chefs and Cooks, headquartered in Ottawa, is the national association representing 1,400 professional chefs and cooks across Canada. The CFCC recognizes the importance of partnering dietitians and chefs to educate consumers about the pleasure of healthy eating and the diversity of food that Canada offers.

How to Use
This Cookbook

Healthy Pleasures was created to show how good taste and nutrition go hand in hand. Our chefs were asked to consider all levels of cooking skills and to develop recipes that would inspire, not intimidate, the home cook.

Our dietitian partners then worked with the chefs to ensure each recipe followed the principles of Canada's Guidelines for Healthy Eating: using a variety of foods; emphasizing cereals, breads, other grain products, vegetables and fruits; and choosing lower fat dairy products, leaner meats and foods prepared with little or no fat. Salt, alcohol and caffeine were used in moderation.

The 75 teams did a fabulous job of combining taste and nutrition. Within this book, you'll find that most of the recipes use local ingredients, reflecting regional cooking styles and multicultural influences. You'll also find a copy of "Canada's Food Guide to Healthy Eating," which will help you determine how much of which foods you should be eating each day.

The goal in a healthy eating pattern is to choose a variety of foods that will provide the nutrients and energy you need each day. Most of the energy (calories) should come from complex carbohydrates such as grains, fruits and vegetables (55%) with the remainder coming from proteins (12% to 15%) and fats (30% or less).

So how do you keep your total fat intake to 30 percent of calories? To begin, look at your normal eating pattern over a week, not during one particular day. The average woman who eats 2,000 calories a day should try to limit fat intake to 65 grams daily. That might mean on some days she eats 50 grams of fat while on others, she eats 80. The bottom line is that over the week she averages 65 grams of fat a day. By comparison, a teenage boy might need 3,000 calories a day, so his fat intake should average out to 90 grams of fat.

In keeping with the "total diet approach," not every recipe in this book had to meet all the guidelines (choosing one food for its high or low fat content does not make or break a healthy meal). Each recipe includes a nutrient analysis that will give you information about how much fat, fibre, protein, carbohydrate and calories it contains. With this nutrient information, you can figure out the fat percentage of each recipe by multiplying the number of grams of fat it contains by nine. Divide the answer by the total number of calories for the per cent of total calories from fat. In this way, you can balance your fat intake by aiming for 30 percent of total calorie intake from fat, over time.

Many of the recipes include comments from the dietitian partner to help you make nutritious choices. Moderation, as always, is the key to healthy eating. Enjoy the food you do eat and tempt your taste buds with the recipes on the pages that follow.

Celebrating the Pleasure of Healthy Eating

Enjoying delicious food is one of life's pleasures and, in Canada, we have lots to celebrate in the way of good food and healthy eating. From coast to coast, we enjoy a wide range of foods and eating styles that reflect our many ethnic, cultural and regional influences...from Figgy Duff and fiddleheads to B.C. salmon and bannock bread.

Although taste is still the main reason we choose to eat particular foods, more and more of us are also considering the role that nutrition and health play.

That's good news. But sometimes we lose the "pleasure" of food because of conflicting messages about what is "good for you" or "bad for you." The fear that certain foods may be bad for us can cause guilt rather than enjoyment. Always restricting your favorite foods, however, may be equally harmful because when you feel deprived of eating enjoyment, your eating patterns suffer. It's not so much what you eat, as how much and how frequently you eat it.

At last!

Congratulations to all the chefs and dietitians across Canada who joined efforts to promote healthy eating. The result of our partnership is this cookbook, and we hope that it will tempt you to challenge your taste buds and discover that delicious is nutritious.

In keeping with "Canada's Food Guide to Healthy Eating," The Canadian Dietetic Association provided guidelines for each chef and dietitian team. Chefs used local ingredients, which are easy to find and readily available, and foods that are native to their area.

Variety was strongly encouraged, with emphasis on whole grains, vegetables and fruits. Lower fat dairy products and leaner meats were used where appropriate, and moderation was the rule when recipes called for salt, alcohol and caffeine. All the techniques of healthy cooking were employed—encouraging the use of little fat, while emphasizing flavor and visual appeal.

What is healthy eating, anyway?

Healthy eating is the result of all food choices made over time. It is the overall "pattern" of foods eaten and not any one food, meal or even a day's meals that determines if an eating pattern is healthy. All foods can fit into a healthy diet with a little planning. Our overall diet can include foods high, moderate and low in fat and still meet Canada's Guidelines for Healthy Eating.

"Canada's Food Guide to Healthy Eating" provides the framework to help make healthy and delicious choices both at home and when eating out. The Food Guide arranges the food you eat into four food groups, as well as foods called "Other Foods."

It's important to choose from each food group the number of servings appropriate for your age, size, sex, and activity level. These factors affect how much and what kinds of foods you choose. The bar side of the Food Guide gives you the range of daily servings for each food group. Most adults will be somewhere in the middle of the range. The lower end of the range is for children and inactive older adults. The higher end is for male teens and more active people. This pattern gives the best guarantee for adequate nutrient intake.

Variety is the key in all food choices—emphasizing grain products, vegetables and fruit, and choosing lower fat foods more often. Variety ensures an adequate intake of essential nutrients, improving overall diet quality. Canada provides an abundance of food from the whole spectrum of the Food Guide (which is important nutritionally and economically), from the bountiful grains of the western prairie provinces to the seafood of the Atlantic and Pacific coasts.

Trying new flavors and developing a taste for new foods is as important as knowing the sources of hidden fat. When was the last time you shared the experience of enjoying a completely new food with family or friends?

Moderation is an important healthy-eating watchword. Practicing moderation means accepting *all* foods as pleasurable and life-giving, at the same time understanding that there are foods we should eat only "every now and again." Setting your own course of moderation can have a considerable effect on the quality of your life—in terms of taste, health and overall enjoyment.

And keep moderation in mind when consuming caffeine, alcohol, salt and foods from the "Other Foods" category in the Food Guide. Although these foods are not bad for you, do take care in limiting the serving size and frequency of them.

And there's more . . .

The Vitality message of "Canada's Food Guide to Healthy Eating" also encourages a renewed emphasis on the enjoyment of food, which affects not only our physical but also our psychological and emotional well-being:

Eating well means enjoying a wide variety of Canada's local and regional foods and exploring the taste of our diverse multicultural, ethnic and regional cuisines.

Being active means not only participating in regular physical activity but having fun too. More and more research is finding that we can derive health benefits from all kinds of physical activity. It's not so much what you do as long as you just do it!

Feeling good about ourselves means accepting who we are and how we look, deciding to treat ourselves to the pleasure of healthy, great-tasting foods without feelings of deprivation and guilt.

To be effective, nutrition guidelines must be translated in terms of what and how people like to eat. Dietary recommendations by themselves are not enough to change the way we eat, because they do not address why we eat.

We eat for many reasons. Besides taste, there are psychological, social, cultural, ethnic, economic and emotional influences that help shape our food preferences. Our taste preferences and eating patterns start to form early in life and are determined by many factors.

Children acquire attitudes about food first and foremost at home. Positive attitudes develop when food preparation and mealtimes are pleasant and fun experiences. Getting children involved in shopping and cooking is one way to increase their familiarity with foods and educate their taste buds! Family tables are the backbone of our ethnic and cultural heritage and form the foundation of "food memories" that children will carry with them all life long.

Try not to think of nutritious foods as low in fat, high in carbohydrate or eaten just for health. Instead, enjoy foods simply for being delicious! Pleasure, relaxation and a sense of well-being are key to a healthy lifestyle.

Enjoy!

When it comes right down to it, there is no one definition of Canadian cooking. Our cultural mosaic is influenced by a multitude of cuisines and unlimited culinary delights, which clearly demonstrate that a diversity of eating styles can be not only tasty but healthy and nutritious. Many different eating styles can be a part of a healthy lifestyle.

Dietitians play a key role in advising individuals and families about healthy eating. They are the recognized leaders in nutrition and health. Chefs are the recognized "taste" leaders who help shape today's food trends. The formation of a "health and taste" partnership is a powerful alliance for translating the message of healthy eating to all Canadians and can make a positive contribution to the future health of our country.

In our celebration of Canada's culinary traditions, we need to consider both taste and nutrition when choosing our food. Throughout this cookbook you will find both traditional and innovative recipes—a fusion of culinary statements—featuring taste and nutrition with a health-conscious twist.

Come and join with us in our adventure into taste and nutrition, as we celebrate the pleasure of healthy eating.

Susie Langley, M.S., RD
Toronto, Ontario

Appetizers

Spinach-Stuffed Mushrooms with Walnuts

Spinach and Chèvre Phyllo Triangles

Fruit and Cheese Bundles

Eggplant and Olive Antipasto

Steamed Mussels with Julienne Vegetables

Pickerel and Basmati Rice Crepes

Ham Roulades "Forestière"

Scallops with Pepper Coulis and Polenta

Hummus with Parmesan and Pimiento

Warm Cornbread and Quinoa Timbales with Tomato Coulis and Zucchini Purée

Fazool

Tiger Shrimp with Dill-Roasted Plum Tomatoes

Mediterranean Eggplant Spread

For Starters, There's Milk

Many of the recipes in this book, particularly the appetizers and soups, provide an opportunity to include a serving of milk and milk products. From Cream of Butternut Squash Soup to Spinach and Chèvre Phyllo Triangles, milk makes our choices not just tasty and enjoyable, but rich in nutrients as well.

It may seem that milk products have fallen into some disfavor in recent years because they contain saturated fat. But they are also a rich source of many important nutrients: calcium, protein, riboflavin and vitamins A and D. In fact, milk is among the most economical sources of nutrients available to Canadians today.

The good news is you can economize on fat without losing the nutrients found in milk and milk products! Simply choose two per cent, one per cent, skim milk or buttermilk. Products such as cheese, yogurt and cottage cheese all have labels that clearly tell you how much butterfat (B.F.) or milk fat (M.F.) they contain. All you have to do is compare products and choose the ones that are lower in fat.

We're fortunate to have an abundance of milk products to choose from. In addition to milk itself, we can enjoy a nearly limitless array of cheeses — hard and soft, flavored and plain, high or lower fat — in almost any shape and size. Yogurt and cottage cheese also come in many flavors, sizes and fat levels. Although cream cheese, sour cream, ice cream and whipping cream are higher fat choices, they too have a place. Choose them in moderation as they fit into the healthy eating pattern you create for yourself and your family.

You'll notice that some recipes in *Healthy Pleasures* do call for a higher fat dairy product because substituting a lower fat alternative would take away from the taste or appearance of the dish. Other recipes use "light" or lower fat alternatives, and in those where the fat level of dairy products is not specified, choose the lower fat option more often.

We need two to four servings from this food group daily, each serving being equal to 125 mL (1/2 cup) of milk, yogurt or cottage cheese, or approximately 30 grams (one ounce) of cheese.

Although appetizers and soups frequently contain milk and milk products, look for other recipes throughout the book to select flavorful milk servings. From Meatless Meals containing cheese, to salads with yogurt dressings and even Aphrodite's Pasta, there are lots of different ways to choose and enjoy milk and milk products. What a great way to start or round out your meal!

Mary Margaret Laing, RD
Cambridge, Ontario

Spinach-Stuffed Mushrooms with Walnuts

White mushrooms are available year round. Choose large ones for this easy-to-make appetizer.

Chef:

Hans Hartmann, CCC,
Instructor, Cook Training
Okanagan University
College,
Kelowna
British Columbia

18	jumbo mushrooms	18
2 tbsp	olive oil	25 mL
2 tbsp	lemon juice	25 mL
2 cups	chopped spinach	500 mL
1	small onion, chopped	1
1/2 lb	tofu	250 g
1	egg	1
1-1/2 tsp	ground cumin	7 mL
1/4 tsp	each salt and pepper	1 mL
18	walnut halves	18

Dietitian:

Donna Antonishak, RDN
Community Nutritionist
North Okanagan
Health Unit
Vernon, British Columbia

Tofu is a low-fat, high-protein alternative to cream cheese in this appetizer. Spinach and walnuts add iron, fibre and lots of flavor.

Clean mushrooms. Remove stems and chop; set aside. In skillet over medium heat, heat oil and 1 tbsp (15 mL) of the lemon juice. Add mushroom caps; cover and steam for 2 to 3 minutes, turning once. Drain on paper towels.

To pan juices, add chopped mushroom stems, spinach and onion; cook, stirring, for 2 minutes. Drain off excess moisture; cool.

In food processor or blender, purée tofu until smooth. Combine with egg, cumin, salt, pepper, remaining lemon juice and spinach mixture. Spoon into mushrooms. Place walnut half on top. Place in 13- x 9-inch (3.5 L) baking dish. Bake at 375°F (190°C) for 20 to 25 minutes or until heated through. Serve warm.

Makes 6 servings.

Per serving:

147 Calories
7 g protein
11 g fat
7 g carbohydrate
3 g fibre

Spinach and Chèvre Phyllo Triangles

Phyllo dough is available in the frozen section of most supermarkets and makes a delicious wrap for these Greek-style spinach and cheese appetizers.

Chef:

Albert Cipryk, CCC
Chef/Instructor
Niagara College
Niagara Falls, Ontario

Dietitian:

Cynthia Paul, RD
Manager
Clinical Nutrition
St. Catharines
General Hospital,
St. Catharines, Ontario

You can brush the phyllo sheets with olive oil rather than butter without sacrificing flavor.

1/2 cup	olive oil, divided	125 mL
1/2 cup	finely chopped onion	125 mL
1	pkg (10 oz/300 g) frozen chopped spinach, thawed and squeezed to remove moisture	1
1/4 lb	chèvre cheese, crumbled	125 g
1 tsp	salt	5 mL
1/4 tsp	pepper	2 mL
1/4 tsp	nutmeg	2 mL
1 lb	phyllo dough (about 20 sheets)	500 g

Sauce:		
1/4 cup	1% plain yogurt	50 mL
1/4 cup	light sour cream	50 mL
1/4 cup	finely diced seeded peeled cucumber	50 mL
1	clove garlic, minced	1

In small skillet, heat 1 tbsp (15 mL) of the oil; cook onion, stirring, until softened. Remove from heat. Mix in spinach, cheese, salt, pepper and nutmeg until combined.

Place one sheet phyllo on work surface, keeping remaining phyllo covered with damp tea towel to prevent drying; brush sheet lightly with oil and top with second sheet; brush with oil.

With sharp knife or pizza cutter, cut phyllo lengthwise into 6 equal strips.

Place about 1 tsp (5 mL) filling 1 inch (2.5 cm) from bottom end of strip; fold one corner to opposite side, forming triangle that covers filling. Continue folding from side to side up entire length of strip. Place seam side down on baking sheet; repeat with remaining phyllo.

Brush tops lightly with oil. Cover with plastic wrap and refrigerate for up to 12 hours or freeze in airtight containers.

Sauce: In small bowl, mix yogurt, sour cream, cucumber and garlic. Cover and chill at least 1 hour before serving.

Bake triangles at 425°F (220°C) for about 10 minutes or until golden (frozen ones may take a little longer). Serve with sauce.

Makes 60 hors d'oeuvres.

Tip: Substitute 1 pkg (10 oz/284 g) fresh spinach for frozen and add to onion mixture; stir and cook 4 to 5 minutes or until wilted. Cool and chop finely.

Per hors d'oeuvre:

48 Calories
1 g protein
2 g fat
5 g carbohydrate
trace fibre

Fruit and Cheese Bundles

You can substitute cantaloupe or honeydew for canary melon in this recipe.

Chef:

*Gary Heaney
E.C. Drury School
for Deaf
Milton, Ontario*

8	sheets phyllo dough	8
2 tbsp	butter, melted	25 mL
Half	canary melon, peeled and thinly sliced	Half
Half	sweet red pepper, thinly sliced	Half
1/2 cup	shredded Havarti cheese (2 oz/50 g)	125 mL

Dietitian:

*Vicki Poirier, RD
Halton Healthy
Lifestyles Coalition
Oakville, Ontario*

**Canary melons —
a wonderful new fruit
experience —
are large, bright yellow
football-shaped
melons with very
sweet flesh. Canada's
Food Guide
encourages you to
choose orange-
colored fruits and
vegetables more
often.**

Place one sheet of phyllo on work surface, keeping remaining phyllo covered with damp cloth to prevent drying out. Brush sheet lightly with butter and top with second sheet. Continue brushing and layering, making stack of 6 sheets.

Arrange melon slices in single layer covering centre third of length of phyllo sheets. Top with red pepper; sprinkle with Havarti. Fold one side of phyllo over fruit. Brush lightly with butter. Fold other side over and brush again.

Brush one of remaining phyllo sheets with butter; top with final sheet and brush again. Invert prepared roll and place diagonally on phyllo. Fold in ends and sides to enclose fruit bundle. Brush with remaining butter and place on large ungreased baking sheet. With serrated knife, score top layers of pastry into 8 portions, cutting just through to fruit. Bake at 400°F (200°C) for 12 to 14 minutes or until richly golden. Serve warm.

Makes 8 servings.

Per serving:

138 Calories
4 g protein
6 g fat
17 g carbohydrate
1 g fibre

Eggplant and Olive Antipasto

Here's a recipe that will feed a crowd and is ideal on the buffet table. For a more elaborate antipasto add canned tuna chunks, salmon flakes and baby clams, or cooked shrimp. Serve on lettuce and garnish with Italian parsley and lemon wedges.

Chef:

Alex Clavel, Chef/Owner
Restaurant Chez
la vigne
Wolfville, Nova Scotia

Dietitian:

Heather Cutler, P.Dt.
Clinical Dietitian
Camp Hill Hospital
Halifax, Nova Scotia

This antipasto is a colorful and tasty alternative to the traditional "chip and dip" or meat-based appetizers—a great addition to any party!

1	medium eggplant, diced (or 2 Japanese-type eggplants)	1
2	medium onions, chopped	2
4	stalks celery, sliced	4
2	small zucchini, sliced	2
3	cloves garlic, sliced	3
1	can (14 oz/398 mL) chick-peas, drained	1
1	can (14 oz/398 mL) tomatoes, drained and sliced	1
1/2 cup	green or black pitted olives, halved	125 mL
4	sun-dried tomatoes, softened and sliced	4
3 tbsp	capers, drained	50 mL
2 tbsp	balsamic vinegar	25 mL
2 tbsp	olive oil	25 mL
1 tbsp	granulated sugar	15 mL
1/4 tsp	pepper	1 mL

On greased baking sheet, bake eggplant at 400°F (200°C) for 5 minutes. Turn eggplant with lifter and cook 5 minutes longer. Spoon into bowl.

In saucepan with steamer, steam onions for 5 minutes. Add celery; steam for 3 minutes. Add zucchini and garlic; cover, remove from heat and let stand 2 minutes. Add to eggplant in bowl.

Add chick-peas, tomatoes, olives, sun-dried tomatoes, capers, vinegar, oil, sugar and pepper; toss well. Cover and refrigerate until chilled.

Makes 10 to 12 servings.

Tips: You can add steamed mussels (shelled) and/or sliced squid lightly cooked in lemony water for 1 minute. To soften sun-dried tomatoes, soak in boiling water for 5 minutes; drain.

Per each of 12 servings

94 Calories
3 g protein
4 g fat
14 g carbohydrate
3 g fibre

Steamed Mussels with Julienne Vegetables

If you enjoy mussels when eating out but have never made them at home, here's your chance to experiment with a fabulous one-pot dish! Serve with crusty French bread to mop up the juices.

Chef:

John Halloran
Chef de Partie
The Inn Restaurant
Jasper, Alberta

3 lb	fresh mussels	1.5 kg
1 tbsp	olive or vegetable oil	15 mL
1/4 cup	finely chopped shallots or onions	50 mL
1/4 cup	julienned sweet red and green pepper	50 mL
1/4 cup	minced garlic	50 mL
2	medium tomatoes, diced	2
1 cup	beef stock	250 mL
1 cup	dry white wine (optional)	250 mL
Pinch	saffron (optional)	Pinch

Dietitian:

Janice Yeaman, RD
Consulting Dietitian
Jasper, Alberta

By cooking mussels, which are a good source of protein, in this tasty sauce, you can enjoy a hearty appetizer with little added fat.

Wash mussels, cutting off beards and discarding any that are open.

In 8-cup (2 L) saucepan, heat oil over medium heat; cook shallots, red and green peppers, garlic and tomatoes, stirring, 2 to 3 minutes. Add mussels, stock, then wine and saffron if using; increase heat to high. Cover and bring to boil; cook about 5 minutes or until mussels have opened. Discard any that have not opened. Serve in wide soup plates or soup tureen.

Makes 4 servings.

Per serving:

155 Calories
14 g protein
6 g fat
12 g carbohydrate
2 g fibre

Pickerel and Basmati Rice Crepes

These crepes, which will dazzle guests, can be made ahead of time and refrigerated for up to three days.

Chef:

Don Pattie, CCC
Executive Chef
Niakwa Country Club
Winnipeg, Manitoba

1/2 cup	mango chutney	125 mL
1/2 cup	water	125 mL
	Fresh parsley, starfruit slices or other fruit	
	Filling:	
12 oz	boneless, skinless pickerel	375 g
1/2 cup	white wine	125 mL
1 cup	cooked Basmati rice	250 mL
1 tbsp	minced fresh parsley	15 mL
1 tsp	light margarine	5 mL
Pinch	each salt and pepper	Pinch
	Crepes:	
2	eggs	2
2 tsp	light margarine, melted	10 mL
1 cup	skim milk	250 mL
1/2 cup	all-purpose flour	125 mL

Dietitian:

Joan Rew, RD
Co-op Coordinator,
Community Cooking,
Nutrition Instructor
Red River
Community College
Winnipeg, Manitoba

This recipe highlights a lower fat crepe batter complemented by a chutney sauce to keep the fat content low and the flavor high.

Filling: Cut pickerel into 3- x 1-1/2-inch (8 x 4 cm) strips; marinate in wine for 15 minutes. Remove pickerel and reserve wine. Mix rice with parsley, margarine, salt and pepper. Set aside.

Crepes: In small bowl, whisk together eggs, margarine, milk and flour until smooth. Heat nonstick 6-7-inch (15-18 cm) crepe or omelette pan over medium-low heat. Pour about 3 tbsp (50 mL) batter into pan, swirling to cover bottom. Cook until bottom is lightly browned; flip crepe onto wire rack to cool. Repeat with remaining batter to make 12 crepes. (Recipe uses 8 crepes; extra crepes may be wrapped and frozen.)

Spoon about 2 tbsp (25 mL) rice mixture in centre of each crepe; place pickerel strip on rice. Fold in ends of crepe and roll up. Place crepes, seam side down, in lightly greased 9-inch (2.5 L) square baking pan. Pour reserved wine over crepes. Cover with foil. Bake at 350°F (180°C) for 10 to 12 minutes or until heated through.

In blender, purée chutney and water; warm in small saucepan over medium-low heat. Place crepe on each salad plate; top each with spoonful of sauce. Garnish with parsley and fruit.

Makes 8 servings.

Tip: If nonstick pan isn't available, spray pan with cooking spray or lightly brush with oil. To check if pan is hot enough, sprinkle a few drops of water on it and they should sizzle.

Ham Roulades "Forestière"

You can substitute smoked turkey, roast beef or prosciutto for these make-in-advance appetizers. The filling is also great as a spread for crackers or as a filling for tortillas.

Chef:

Gerald Philippe, CCC
Cuisinier
Centre Hospitalier de
Gatineau
Gatineau, Québec

1 tbsp	soft margarine	15 mL
1 cup	finely chopped mushrooms	250 mL
1/4 cup	chopped green onions	50 mL
1/4 lb	light cream cheese, softened	125 g
1/2 cup	chopped fresh parsley	125 mL
2 tsp	Dijon mustard	10 mL
1 tsp	lemon juice	5 mL
Pinch	cayenne	Pinch
6	slices cooked lean ham	6

Dietitian:

Debra Reid, Ph.D., RD
Ottawa–Carleton
Health Dept.
Ottawa, Ontario

These "roll-ups" are so simple to make even young children can help. Kids love to cook and your encouragement is great for their self-esteem!

In skillet, melt margarine over medium heat; cook mushrooms and green onions for 3 to 5 minutes or until tender. Cool.

In bowl, blend together cheese, parsley, mustard, lemon juice and cayenne; stir in mushroom mixture. Spread evenly over ham slices and roll up. Wrap in plastic wrap. Refrigerate at least 2 hours or until chilled. Cut each roll into 4 pieces. Serve with frilled toothpick.

Makes 24 hors d'oeuvres.

Per hors d'oeuvre:

29 Calories
2 g protein
2 g fat
1 g carbohydrate
trace fibre

Scallops with Pepper Coulis and Polenta

This starter tastes as good as it looks! The pepper coulis and polenta may be prepared ahead, then reheated at serving time.

Chef:

Philippe Guiet,
Master Chef/Professeur
Le Cordon Bleu Paris
Cooking School
Ottawa, Ontario

Dietitian:

Dawn Palin, Ph.D., RD
Consulting Dietitian
Gloucester, Ontario

Using the marinade from the scallops for cooking the onions controls the fat content in this colorful and nutritious dish.

2	medium sweet red peppers	2
2	medium sweet yellow peppers	2
12 oz	scallops	375 g
3 tbsp	olive oil	50 mL
1/4 cup	chopped fresh dill	50 mL
1	medium onion, chopped	1
1	clove garlic, minced	1
	Salt and pepper	
8	cherry tomatoes	8
1 tsp	olive oil	5 mL
	Dill sprigs	
	Polenta:	
2 cups	water	500 mL
1/2 tsp	salt	2 mL
1/2 cup	cornmeal	125 mL

Cut red and yellow peppers in half; remove all stems and seeds. Place, cut side down, on greased baking sheet. Bake at 400°F (200°C) for 30 minutes or until browned. Place in plastic bag and cool 10 minutes. Remove skins.

Meanwhile, marinate scallops in oil and dill for 30 minutes.

Polenta: Meanwhile, in saucepan, bring water and salt to boil; gradually add cornmeal, whisking constantly. Cook over low heat, stirring occasionally, for 15 minutes. Pour into small greased loaf pan. Cool.

Reserving scallops, drain oil into small skillet; add onion and garlic and sauté for 5 minutes. In food processor or blender, purée red peppers. Add half of the onion mixture; blend until smooth. Set aside. Repeat with yellow peppers and remaining onion mixture. Season both mixtures with salt and pepper to taste. Keep warm (or reheat in microwave oven).

Cut tomatoes in half. Place on baking sheet; drizzle with 1 tsp (5 mL) oil. Bake at 400°F (200°C) for 10 to 15 minutes or until tender. In skillet, sauté scallops until golden, 3 to 5 minutes.

To serve, cut polenta into 8 servings; place in centre of serving plate. Arrange yellow pepper coulis on one side of polenta and red pepper coulis on other side. Place scallops on red pepper coulis and cherry tomatoes on yellow pepper coulis. Garnish with dill sprigs.

Makes 8 servings.

Per serving:

144 Calories
9 g protein
6 g fat
14 g carbohydrate
2 g fibre

Hummus with Parmesan and Pimiento

Hummus, a Middle Eastern dip made with chick-peas, takes on a new twist with the addition of Parmesan cheese and bottled red pimiento. Serve as dip for vegetables, or as a spread for breads or crackers.

Chef:

Rainer Schindler, CCC
Spa Cuisine®,
St. Clair College
Windsor, Ontario

I	clove garlic	I
Half	small onion	Half
I	can (19 oz/540 mL) chick-peas, drained and rinsed	I
1/4 cup	bottled pimientos, drained	50 mL
3 tbsp	freshly grated Parmesan cheese	50 mL
I tsp	slightly toasted sesame seeds	5 mL
I tsp	lemon juice	5 mL
1/2 tsp	salt	2 mL

Dietitian:

Monica Stanton, RD
Windsor Regional
Hospital
Windsor, Ontario

In food processor, mince garlic and onion Add chick-peas, pimientos, Parmesan, sesame seeds, lemon juice and salt; process until blended. Chill.

Makes 2 cups (500 mL).

Great for entertaining, this low-fat mix is nutritious and versatile. It also stores well *and* is easy on the budget.

Per 1/3 cup (75 mL):

105 Calories
6 g protein
2 g fat
16 g carbohydrate
2 g fibre

Warm Cornbread and Quinoa Timbales with Tomato Coulis and Zucchini Purée

Quinoa (pronounced KEEN-wah) was a staple grain of the ancient Incas and takes half the cooking time of regular rice. Petite squash pearls, tiny cherry tomatoes and fresh herbs would add even more flourish to the presentation.

Chef:

Bernard Casavant, CCC
Executive Chef
Château Whistler Resort
Whistler, British Columbia

Dietitian:

Jane Thornthwaite, RDN
Nutrition Consultant
Fresh Choice Restaurant
Program
Vancouver, British
Columbia

Skim milk, part-skim mozzarella and vegetable spray control the fat in this delicious gourmet dish.

Per serving:

133 Calories
8 g protein
4 g fat
17 g carbohydrate
2 g fibre

Timbales:

1/4 cup	uncooked quinoa	50 mL
1/2 cup	water	125 mL
1-1/2 cups	cubed (1/2 inch/1 cm) day-old cornbread	375 mL
1/4 cup	chopped shallots	50 mL
1/4 cup	each diced sweet red and green pepper	50 mL
3	cloves roasted garlic (See page 97)	3
1/3 cup	shredded part-skim mozzarella cheese	75 mL
1/2 tsp	crushed dried thyme	2 mL
2/3 cup	skim milk	150 mL
1/4 cup	2% evaporated milk	50 mL
1	egg	1
1	egg white	1

Tomato Coulis:

1 tbsp	sliced shallots	15 mL
2	plum tomatoes, peeled and seeded	2
1/4 tsp	salt	1 mL
Pinch	pepper	Pinch
8-10 drops	liquid smoke	8-10 drops

Zucchini Purée:

1 cup	sliced (unpeeled) zucchini	250 mL
1/4 cup	spinach leaves	50 mL
1	clove garlic, roasted	1
2 tbsp	tofu	25 mL
Pinch	salt	Pinch
Pinch	pepper	Pinch

Timbales: In small saucepan, bring quinoa and water to boil; reduce heat and simmer 10 to 15 minutes or until water is absorbed. In bowl, combine quinoa, cornbread, shallots, red and green peppers, garlic, cheese and thyme.

In separate bowl and using electric mixer, beat together skim milk, evaporated milk, egg and egg white; gently blend into quinoa mixture. Spray six 1/2 cup (125 mL) ramekins with vegetable oil spray; evenly spoon filling into ramekins.

Place ramekins in baking dish; pour in boiling water to depth of 1 inch (2.5 cm). Bake at 350°F (180°C) for 25 minutes or until knife inserted in centre comes out clean.

Tomato Coulis: Meanwhile, in food processor, mince shallots. Add tomatoes, salt, pepper, and liquid smoke to taste; process until smooth. Remove and set aside.

Zucchini Purée: In saucepan of boiling water, simmer zucchini until wilted; drain well. In food processor, purée zucchini, spinach, garlic and tofu; season with salt and pepper.

Unmold hot timbales and place each in centre of each plate. Drizzle tomato coulis around timbales. Pipe zucchini purée decoratively over coulis.

Makes 6 servings.

Fazool

Fazool is great spread on crackers or can be used as a substitute for butter or margarine.

Chef:

Hans Anderegg
Chef/Instructor
Culinary Institute of
Canada
Charlottetown
Prince Edward Island

1 cup	dried white beans	250 mL
1	medium onion, chopped	1
3 tbsp	chopped gingerroot	50 mL
	Salt	
3 tbsp	olive oil	50 mL
2 tbsp	balsamic vinegar	25 mL
1/4 tsp	hot pepper sauce	1 mL
Pinch	pepper	Pinch

Dietitian:

Cheryl Turnbull-Bruce,
P.Dt.
Nutrition Consultant
Charlottetown
Prince Edward Island

This spread is a great tasty alternative to high-fat spreads and it has fibre too. Go ahead and indulge!

Cover beans in water; let soak overnight. Drain and rinse.

In large saucepan, combine beans, onion, ginger, 1/2 tsp (2 mL) salt and enough water to cover; bring to boil. Reduce heat and simmer, uncovered, until beans are tender, 35 to 40 minutes. Drain well.

In food processor, purée beans with oil, vinegar, hot pepper sauce, 1/4 tsp (1 mL) salt and pepper. Chill.

Makes about 2-1/4 cups (550 mL).

Per 1 tbsp (15 mL):

30 Calories
1 g protein
1 g fat
4 g carbohydrate
1 g fibre

Tiger Shrimp with Dill-Roasted Plum Tomatoes

Add a pinch of cayenne to the cornmeal if you like your shrimp spicy.

Chef:

James McLean
Sous Chef
Benjamin's Restaurant
St. Jacobs, Ontario

Dietitian:

Jane Curry, RD
Community Dietitian
Woolwich Community
Health Centre
St. Jacobs, Ontario

4	medium plum tomatoes, cored and quartered	4
2 tbsp	olive oil	25 mL
I tsp	dried dillweed	5 mL
	Salt and pepper	
12	jumbo tiger shrimp, peeled and deveined (about 8 oz/250 g)	12
2 tbsp	lemon juice	25 mL
1/3 cup	cornmeal	75 mL
4	small green onions, sliced	4
	Lemon rind twist and fresh dill (optional)	

In medium bowl, toss tomatoes with I tbsp (15 mL) of the oil, dill, and salt and pepper to taste. Place on baking sheet, skin side down. Roast at 350°F (180°C) for 10 to 12 minutes or until skins slightly sear and tomatoes are soft and hot. Set aside and keep warm.

Toss shrimp with lemon juice, and salt and pepper to taste; dip into cornmeal to coat. In medium skillet, heat remaining oil over medium-high heat; cook shrimp about 1 to 1-1/2 minutes on each side or until lightly browned and shrimp are pink.

Toss warm tomatoes with green onions. Arrange one whole tomato and 3 shrimp on each salad plate. Garnish with lemon rind and dill if using.

Makes 4 servings.

Per serving:

165 Calories
10 g protein
8 g fat
14 g carbohydrate
2 g fibre

Mediterranean Eggplant Spread

Make this creamy spread when eggplant and tomatoes are in season for maximum flavor and minimum cost. Serve with melba toast and bread sticks.

Chef:

Louis Rodriguez
Executive Chef
Norwood Hotel
Winnipeg, Manitoba

Dietitian:

Joan Rew, RD
Co-op Coordinator,
Community Cooking,
Nutrition Instructor
Red River Community
College
Winnipeg, Manitoba

Substituting yogurt for sour cream in this delicious appetizer reduces the fat.

2	medium eggplants	2
2 cups	low-fat plain yogurt	500 mL
2 tbsp	lemon juice	25 mL
I	clove garlic, minced	I
I tbsp	red wine vinegar	15 mL
I tbsp	olive oil	15 mL
1/2 tsp	crumbled dried oregano	2 mL
1/2 tsp	salt	2 mL
2	medium tomatoes, seeded and diced	2
1/2 cup	diced celery	125 mL

Cut eggplants in half lengthwise. Place on greased baking sheet, cut side down; cut 2 or 3 slits in skin. Cover with foil; bake at 375°F (190°C) for 35 to 45 minutes or until tender. Cool. Remove stalk, peel and seeds; finely chop eggplants.

In bowl, combine eggplant, yogurt, lemon juice, garlic, vinegar, oil, oregano, salt, tomatoes and celery, mixing well. Cover and chill for at least 30 minutes.

Makes about 5 cups (1.25 L).

Per 3 tbsp (50 mL):

21 Calories
I g protein
I g fat
3 g carbohydrate
trace fibre

Soups

Cream of Butternut Squash Soup

Purée of Carrot Soup with Yogurt Raita

Country Vegetable Chowder

Oriental Mushroom Soup

Hot and Sour Chicken Soup

Hot Smoked Salmon Chowder

Chilled Pink Cucumber Soup

Cranberry Beet Soup

Gingered Prawn Wonton Soup with Vegetables

Cream of Potato and Sausage Soup

White Bean Soup

Creole Tomato Soup

Chilled Ginger Lime Melon Soup

Creamy Roasted Sweet Pepper Soup

Cappuccino Curry Soup

Curried Fiddlehead Soup

Purée of Fennel Soup

Cream of Butternut Squash Soup

Colorful, easy-to-make and delicious to eat—what else can you say about this fabulous soup? For a variation, use pumpkin instead of squash.

Chef:

John Higgins
Executive Chef
King Edward Hotel
Toronto, Ontario

2 tbsp	vegetable oil	25 mL
1	large onion, chopped	1
4 cups	coarsely chopped butternut squash	1 L
4 cups	chicken broth	1 L
1/2 tsp	salt	2 mL
1/2 tsp	pepper	2 mL
1/2 cup	whipping cream or half-and-half	125 mL

Dietitian:

Susan Iantorno, M.H.Sc.,
RD
Food and Nutrition
Communications
Specialist
NutriQuest
Toronto, Ontario

In large saucepan, heat oil over medium heat; cook onion, stirring often, until translucent, 3 to 5 minutes. Add squash; cook, stirring, for 5 minutes.

Add broth and bring to boil. Cover and simmer over low heat 25 to 30 minutes or until squash is tender. Purée soup in batches in blender; return to saucepan. Add salt, pepper and cream; heat through but do not let boil.

Makes 6 servings.

This great fall or winter soup is a good source of vitamin A, but take note that it does include a higher fat dairy ingredient.

Per serving:

178 Calories
5 g protein
13 g fat
13 g carbohydrate
3 g fibre

Purée of Carrot Soup with Yogurt Raita

The sweetness of harvest-fresh carrots really comes through in this light-tasting soup.

Chef:

James McLean
Sous Chef
Benjamin's Restaurant
St. Jacobs, Ontario

Dietitian:

Jane Curry, RD
Community Dietitian
Woolwich Community
Health Centre
St. Jacobs, Ontario

The array of colors and abundance of vitamin A make this light soup appealing for more than one reason.

1 tbsp	olive oil	15 mL
1	medium onion, chopped	1
4 cups	coarsely chopped carrots	1 L
5 cups	vegetable or chicken broth	1.25 L
1/2 tsp	salt	2 mL
1/4 tsp	pepper	1 mL

	Raita:	
1 cup	low-fat plain yogurt	250 mL
2/3 cup	grated English cucumber	150 mL
1/4 cup	minced red onion	50 mL
1 tbsp	lemon juice	15 mL
1 tsp	ground cumin	5 mL

Raita: In small bowl, mix together yogurt, cucumber, onion, lemon juice and cumin; chill until serving time.

In saucepan, heat oil over medium heat; cook onion, stirring, 2 to 3 minutes or until softened. Add carrots; cook, stirring, 1 to 2 minutes. Add broth; bring to boil. Reduce heat and simmer, uncovered, for 25 to 30 minutes or until carrots are tender.

In blender or food processor, purée soup in batches until smooth. Strain, if desired. Return to saucepan and heat until hot; add salt and pepper. Serve soup in bowls with two spoonfuls of raita on top.

Makes 5 servings.

Per serving:

127 Calories
5 g protein
5 g fat
18 g carbohydrate
3 g fibre

Scallops with Pepper Coulis and Polenta (page 17)

Country Vegetable Chowder

A lighter chowder, serve this with whole grain bread for lunch or a light dinner. You can substitute green peas for beans; add them with the broccoli.

Chef:

Yvonne C. Levert
Cordon Bleu Chef
Instructor, Hospitality
Administration
University College of
Cape Breton Island
Sydney, Nova Scotia

Dietitian:

Nanette Porter-
MacDonald, P.Dt.
Clinical Dietitian
Glace Bay Healthcare
Corporation
Glace Bay, Nova Scotia

This recipe can be reheated without loss of quality as well as frozen for later use.

1 tbsp	margarine	15 mL
1	medium onion, chopped	1
3 cups	vegetable stock or water	750 mL
2 cups	cubed peeled potatoes	500 mL
1-1/2 cups	parsnip strips	375 mL
1 cup	turnip strips	250 mL
1 cup	cut green beans	250 mL
1/2 cup	thickly sliced carrots	125 mL
1/2 tsp	each dried thyme, oregano and salt	2 mL
1/4 tsp	white or black pepper	1 mL
1	bay leaf	1
2 cups	broccoli florettes and sliced peeled stem	500 mL
2 cups	2% milk	500 mL

In 4-quart (4 L) saucepan, melt margarine over medium heat; cook onion, stirring, until softened, about 2 minutes.

Add vegetable stock, potatoes, parsnip, turnip, beans, carrots, thyme, oregano, salt, pepper and bay leaf; bring to boil. Cover and reduce heat to simmer; cook 5 to 10 minutes or until vegetables are tender-crisp.

Add broccoli; cook until vegetables are tender. Stir in milk; heat until hot, but do not boil. Discard bay leaf.

Makes 6 servings.

Per serving:

166 Calories
6 g protein
4 g fat
28 g carbohydrate
4 g fibre

Purée of Fennel Soup (page 41)

Oriental Mushroom Soup

Using a mixture of different mushrooms and cutting tofu into stars with cookie cutters makes this a mushroom soup with a difference.

Chef:

Samuel Glass, CWC
Executive Chef
Caterers York
Toronto, Ontario

5 cups	chicken broth	1.25 L
4 tsp	finely chopped gingerroot	20 mL
1/2 lb	sliced mushrooms (shiitake, oyster, portobello or a combination), about 2 cups (500 mL)	250 g
1/2 lb	firm tofu	250 g
1	green onion, thinly sliced	1
2 tbsp	sodium-reduced soy sauce	25 mL
1 tsp	sesame oil	5 mL

Dietitian:

Rosie Schwartz, RD
Consulting Dietitian
Nutrition Guidance
Services Inc.
Toronto, Ontario

In large saucepan, combine broth, gingerroot and mushrooms; bring to boil. Reduce heat and simmer, uncovered, for 15 minutes.

Cut tofu into small cubes or use small decorative cutters to cut into different shapes. Place tofu and green onion in individual soup bowls or soup tureen.

Stir soy sauce and sesame oil into soup; pour into prepared bowls.

Makes 6 servings.

For those concerned about weight control, a steaming bowl of hot soup is a perfect way to take the edge off a hearty appetite.

Per serving:

107 Calories
11 g protein
5 g fat
5 g carbohydrate
2 g fibre

Hot and Sour Chicken Soup

You've had it in a restaurant or for Chinese take-out; now you can impress friends and family with your own version!

Chef:

Raymond Colliver, CCC
Chef/Instructor
Southern Alberta
Institute of Technology
Calgary, Alberta

Dietitian:

Dani Flowerday, RD
Consulting Dietitian
Calgary, Alberta

Serve this spicy soup with a refreshing salad and crusty roll for a light meal.

6	dried Chinese mushrooms	6
5 cups	chicken broth	1.25 L
2 cups	shredded cooked chicken (7oz/200 g)	500 mL
1 tbsp	finely chopped gingerroot	15 mL
1	fresh red chili, chopped (or 1/2 tsp/2 mL crushed chili flakes)	1
1 cup	diced tofu	250 mL
2 tbsp	white wine vinegar	25 mL
1 tbsp	sodium-reduced soy sauce	15 mL
1 tbsp	dry sherry	15 mL
1 tbsp	cornstarch	15 mL
1 tbsp	cold water	15 mL
3	egg whites, lightly beaten	3
2	shallots, thinly sliced (optional)	2

Cover Chinese mushrooms with hot water and soak 10 minutes. Drain, discard stems and slice caps.

In large saucepan, bring broth to boil; add mushrooms, chicken, gingerroot and red chili. Reduce heat and simmer, covered, for 5 minutes. Add tofu, vinegar, soy sauce and sherry; simmer 2 minutes.

Stir cornstarch with water until smooth; gradually stir into soup and simmer 2 to 3 minutes until thickened slightly. Remove from heat; immediately swirl egg whites through soup. Garnish with shallots, if desired.

Makes 6 servings.

Per serving:

145 Calories
18 g protein
5 g fat
6 g carbohydrate
1 g fibre

Hot Smoked Salmon Chowder

'Hot' refers to the method of smoking the fish, not the heat of the dish. If you want it hotter, sprinkle in crushed chili flakes to taste.

Chef:

Dean Mitchell, CCC
Executive Chef
Canyon Meadows Golf
and Country Club
Calgary, Alberta

I	small onion	I
I	medium potato	I
I	large carrot	I
Quarter	stalk celery	Quarter
I	medium sweet green pepper, quartered and seeded	I
2 cups	fish or chicken broth	500 mL
1/2 tsp	crumbled dried thyme	2 mL
1/4 tsp	crumbled dried basil	I mL
2 cups	1% milk	500 mL
1/4 cup	all-purpose flour	50 mL
4 oz	non-salted hot smoked salmon or smoked whitefish	125 g
3/4 cup	frozen corn kernels	175 mL
Pinch	salt	Pinch
	Pepper	

Dietitian:

Suzanne Journault-
Hemstock, RD
Food Production
Dietitian
Nutrition and Food
Services
Foothills Hospital
Calgary, Alberta

This method of cooking vegetables maintains the nutritional value, while minimizing the fat content

Peel and cut onion and potato into 1/4-inch (0.5 cm) thick slices. Peel and cut carrot lengthwise into 1/4-inch (0.5 cm) thick slices.

Place onion, potato, carrot, celery and green pepper on hot barbecue grill or under broiler; cook, turning occasionally, until distinct grill marks are visible and pepper skins are blackened. Place vegetables in plastic bag; seal and let stand 20 minutes.

Peel skins off peppers; dice peppers. Dice remaining roasted vegetables and place in large saucepan. Add 1 cup (250 mL) of the broth, thyme and basil; bring to boil. Add remaining broth and 1-1/2 cups (375 mL) of the milk; bring just to simmer. Stir flour with remaining milk until smooth; gradually stir into soup. Simmer over low heat for 5 minutes.

Remove skin and any bones from fish; cut into 1/4-inch (0.5 cm) cubes. Add to soup along with corn; cook 10 minutes. Season with salt, and pepper to taste. Serve hot.

Makes 5 servings.

Tip: If salmon is unavailable, smoked whitefish may be substituted.

Per serving:

169 Calories
13 g protein
2 g fat
25 g carbohydrate
2 g fibre

Chilled Pink Cucumber Soup

The pink color comes from the beets, and this cold soup marries them with cucumbers for a taste that's unique.

Chef:

Bruno Marti, CCC
Owner
La Belle Auberge
Restaurant
Ladner, British Columbia

Dietitian:

Laura Cullen, RDN
Director, Dietetic and
Purchasing Services
Chantelle Management
Ltd.
Vancouver,
British Columbia

Using light sour cream does not compromise the taste of this colorful, refreshing soup.

2	cucumbers	2
I tsp	salt	5 mL
I tsp	butter or margarine	5 mL
I tsp	vegetable oil	5 mL
I	large Granny Smith apple, peeled, cored and chopped	I
I	small onion, chopped	I
2-1/2 cups	chicken broth	625 mL
1-1/2 cups	chopped cooked beets (or 14 oz/398 mL can, drained)	375 mL
1/3 cup	dry vermouth or dry white wine	75 mL
3 tbsp	dry sherry	50 mL
3 cups	shredded Boston lettuce	750 mL
1/4 tsp	salt	I mL
Pinch	white pepper	Pinch
I cup	light sour cream (or 1/2 cup/125 mL each light sour cream and 1% plain yogurt)	250 mL
	Chopped chives	

Peel cucumbers and cut in half lengthwise; scoop out seeds. Shred cucumbers and sprinkle with salt; drain in colander 30 minutes. Squeeze out as much liquid as possible. Set aside.

In large saucepan or Dutch oven, heat butter and oil over medium heat; cook apple and onion, without browning, until softened, about 10 minutes. Add broth, beets, vermouth and sherry; bring to boil. Add lettuce and cucumbers; cover and simmer 2 minutes. Cool.

In food processor, purée cold mixture until smooth. Season with salt and pepper. Blend in sour cream. Refrigerate until chilled. Garnish each serving with chopped chives.

Makes 4 servings.

Per serving:

216 Calories
10 g protein
6 g fat
25 g carbohydrate
4 g fibre

Cranberry Beet Soup

You may never have thought of combining beets and cranberries but the result is delightful. For an elegant clear soup, serve without the pulp.

Chef:

Peter Ochitwa
Executive Chef/Owner
Mad Apples Restaurant
Toronto, Ontario

3	large beets	3
1-1/2 cups	cranberries (fresh or frozen)	375 mL
2/3 cup	granulated sugar	150 mL
1 tbsp	lemon juice	15 mL
1	cinnamon stick	1
4 tsp	cornstarch	20 mL
2 tbsp	cold water	25 mL
2 tbsp	1% plain yogurt	25 mL

Dietitian:

Susie Langley, M.S., RD
Nutrition Consultant
Toronto, Ontario

Cranberries add a unique touch to this version of Borscht... inspired by the chef's Ukrainian roots.

Peel beets and shred in food processor to make about 4 cups (1 L). Finely chop cranberries in food processor; set aside 1/4 cup (50 mL) for garnish.

In large saucepan, bring 5 cups (1.25 L) water to boil; remove from heat. Add beets and cranberries; cover and let stand 20 minutes.

Strain into large heat-proof bowl, reserving pulp. Return liquid to saucepan. Add sugar, lemon juice and cinnamon stick; bring to boil. Reduce heat and simmer, uncovered, for 5 minutes.

Stir cornstarch with water until smooth; gradually stir into soup until slightly thickened. Return reserved pulp to soup; heat through. Garnish with dollop of yogurt and reserved cranberries.

Makes 5 servings.

Per serving:

139 Calories
1 g protein
trace fat
35 g carbohydrate
2 g fibre

Gingered Prawn Wonton Soup with Vegetables

Ginger is the 'secret' ingredient inside the wontons and flavors this soup. If the soup thickens after standing, add more stock as needed.

Chef:

Alfred Fan
Executive Chef
Bridges Restaurant
Vancouver,
British Columbia

1/2 lb	shrimp, peeled and deveined	250 g
Half	can (8 oz/227 mL) sliced water chestnuts, drained	Half
1 tbsp	sodium-reduced soy sauce	15 mL
1 to 1-1/2 tsp	grated gingerroot	5 to 7 mL
	Salt and pepper	
42	wonton wrappers	42
5 cups	chicken broth	1.25 L
1 cup	each thinly sliced carrots, leeks and celery	250 mL

Dietitian:

Leah Hawirko, RDN
Leah Hawirko Nutrition
Consulting and
The Vancouver Health
Department
Vancouver,
British Columbia

In food processor, finely chop shrimp and water chestnuts with soy sauce, gingerroot and pinch each of the salt and pepper (or finely chop by hand and mix well).

Put 1 tsp (5 mL) shrimp mixture in middle of each wonton; bring outer edges of wrapper together over filling and squeeze firmly to form pouch.

In 8-cup (2 L) saucepan, bring chicken stock to boil; add 1/4 tsp (1 mL) salt, 1/8 tsp (0.5 mL) pepper, carrots, leeks, celery and wontons. Return to boil; cook 2 minutes. Serve in wide soup bowls.

Makes 6 servings.

The fat rather than the cholesterol content of food affects blood cholesterol levels the most. Rejoice and enjoy this lower fat prawn soup!

Per serving:

242 Calories
18 g protein
3 g fat
34 g carbohydrate
2 g fibre

Cream of Potato and Sausage Soup

Our creamy soup uses leaner turkey sausage that still delivers all the traditional sausage taste.

Chef:

Larry DeVries
Chef/Instructor
Crocus Plains Secondary
School
Brandon, Manitoba

Dietitians:

Jackie Kopilas, RD
Rachel Barkley, RD
Brandon and Westman
Area Dietitians
Heather Duncan,
P.H.Ec.
Manitoba Association of
Home Economists—
Southwest Branch
Brandon, Manitoba

This recipe uses potato as a thickener rather than a roux of fat and flour. Ask your butcher for lean garlic sausage or look for minimal amount of marbling in the meat.

3 cups	chicken broth	750 mL
2 cups	diced peeled russet potatoes (2 large)	500 mL
I	large onion, chopped	I
4 oz	diced turkey kielbasa sausage	125 g
I cup	2% evaporated milk	250 mL
1/4 tsp	dried dillweed	I mL
	White pepper	

In 8-cup (2 L) saucepan, bring chicken broth to boil. Add potatoes; cook until tender, about 10 minutes. Remove from heat and remove half of the potatoes with slotted spoon; reserve.

In a small nonstick skillet, cook onions with sausage, stirring, until lightly browned.

In blender or food processor, purée remaining potatoes with broth; return to saucepan. Add reserved potatoes, sausage mixture, milk and dillweed. Heat over medium-low heat until hot, but do not boil. Season with pepper to taste.

Makes 4 servings.

Per serving:

217 Calories
15 g protein
5 g fat
29 g carbohydrate
2 g fibre

White Bean Soup

A great make-ahead soup that's practically a meal in itself, this soup uses inexpensive dried white beans, which are also called pea beans.

Chef:

Tyrone Miller, CCC
Chef
Kitchener-Waterloo
Hospital
Kitchener, Ontario

Dietitian:

Karen Jackson, RD
Patient Food Service
Manager
The Mississauga Hospital
Mississauga, Ontario

By using purées of ingredients such as grains, legumes and starchy vegetables instead of a fat-based roux, you can achieve a creamy texture without rich ingredients. This recipe highlights beans as a meat alternative and is an excellent source of protein.

1 cup	dried white navy beans	250 mL
1 tbsp	butter or margarine	15 mL
2	medium onions, chopped	2
1	large potato, peeled and diced	1
1/2 cup	chopped celery	125 mL
4 cups	chicken broth	1 L
1	clove garlic, minced	1
1 tsp	crushed dried oregano	5 mL
1/2 cup	half-and-half	125 mL
1/2 cup	diced cooked ham	125 mL
1/4 tsp	pepper	1 mL
	Chopped fresh parsley	

Cover beans with 2-1/2 cups (625 mL) water; let stand overnight. Drain. In small saucepan, combine half of the beans with 1-1/4 cups (300 mL) water; bring to boil. Reduce heat and simmer, uncovered, for 30 minutes or until softened. Drain and set aside.

In large saucepan, melt butter over medium heat; cook onions, potato and celery for 5 minutes. Add chicken broth, garlic, oregano and remaining beans; bring to boil. Cover, reduce heat and simmer about 30 minutes or until beans are softened.

Purée soup in food processor or blender; pass through sieve back into saucepan. Add cooked beans, half-and-half, ham and pepper; heat through. Serve garnished with parsley.

Makes 6 servings.

Per serving:

238 Calories
14 g protein
6 g fat
32 g carbohydrate
7 g fibre

Creole Tomato Soup

A potpourri of color and flavor, this soup will appeal to kids and adults alike. You can use other small pasta, such as maca- roni, in place of the pasta shells.

Chef:

Tyrone Miller, CCC
Chef
Kitchener-Waterloo
Hospital
Kitchener, Ontario

1 tbsp	vegetable oil	15 mL
1	small onion, chopped	1
1	clove garlic, minced	1
1/4 cup	finely sliced celery	50 mL
1	can (19 oz/540 mL) tomatoes, drained and diced	1
2 cups	chicken broth	500 mL
1/2 tsp	crushed dried thyme	2 mL
1/4 tsp	paprika	1 mL
1/4 tsp	red pepper flakes	1 mL
1/4 tsp	black pepper	1 mL
1 cup	cubed cooked chicken	250 mL
3/4 cup	frozen corn kernels	175 mL
1/3 cup	baby pasta shells	75 mL
	Sliced green onions and chopped fresh parsley (optional)	

Dietitian:

Karen Jackson, RD
Patient Food Service
Manager
The Mississauga Hospital
Mississauga, Ontario

Emphasize soups based on vegetables to enhance color, taste and nutrient content. If you make your own stock, refrigerate then skim off all traces of fat.

In saucepan, heat oil over medium heat; cook onion, garlic and celery, stirring often, for 3 to 5 minutes or until softened. Stir in tomatoes, broth, thyme, paprika, red pepper flakes and black pepper; bring to boil. Cover, reduce heat and simmer for 10 minutes.

Stir in chicken, corn and pasta. Simmer, uncovered and stirring occasionally, for about 10 minutes, until pasta is tender.

Serve garnished with green onions and parsley if desired.

Makes 4 servings.

Per serving:

208 Calories
16 g protein
7 g fat
21 g carbohydrate
3 g fibre

Chilled Ginger Lime Melon Soup

The soup may be chilled but the ginger provides lots of heat! The first time you make it, you may want to reduce the ginger slightly. It looks delightful served garnished with edible flower petals and grated lime rind.

Chef:

Kenneth Peace, CCC
Chef de Cuisine
O'Keefe Centre for the
Performing Arts
Toronto, Ontario

2 cups	white wine	500 mL
1/4 cup	grated lime rind	50 mL
2 tbsp	lime juice	25 mL
3 tbsp	grated gingerroot	50 mL
2 tbsp	liquid honey	25 mL
1	large honeydew melon, peeled, seeded and cut in chunks	1

Dietitian:

Maye Musk, RD
Maye Musk Nutrition
Consultants
Toronto, Ontario

In saucepan, combine wine, lime rind and juice, gingerroot and honey; bring to boil. Reduce heat and simmer, uncovered, until reduced by half. Cool to room temperature. Strain through cheesecloth-lined sieve into bowl.

In food processor or blender, purée melon to make about 4 cups (1 L). Add to wine mixture. Refrigerate for at least 30 minutes or for up to 1 day.

Makes 6 servings.

This tangy summer soup is an innovative way to offer a serving of fruit.

Per serving:

97 Calories
1 g protein
trace fat
22 g carbohydrate
1 g fibre

Creamy Roasted Sweet Pepper Soup

Take advantage of local peppers when they are in season and this soup will be inexpensive to make. The creamy texture actually comes from tofu!

Chef:

Margaret Carson
Chef/Instructor/Owner
Bonne Cuisine School of
Cooking
Halifax, Nova Scotia

Dietitians:

Pam Lynch, P.Dt.
Consultant Dietitian-
Nutritionist
Nutrition Counselling
Services & Associates
Judy Fraser-Arsenault
Research Associate
Mount Saint Vincent
University
Halifax, Nova Scotia

A "cream soup" that is lighter in fat! Tofu (soybean curd) is a very good source of protein, low in fat, and contains no cholesterol.

I	each large red, yellow and green pepper, halved and seeded	I
2 tsp	olive oil	10 mL
I	medium onion, chopped	I
I	clove garlic, minced	I
2 cups	chicken broth	500 mL
I	can (10 oz/284 mL) regular or seasoned tomatoes, drained	I
2 tbsp	tomato paste	25 mL
I tsp	ground cumin	5 mL
6 oz	soft tofu	170 g
1/2 tsp	salt	2 mL
1/4 tsp	white pepper	I mL
	Black sesame seeds or toasted white sesame seeds	

Place halved peppers on greased baking sheet, cut side down. Bake at 400°F (200°C) for 25 to 30 minutes until skin chars. Cool slightly; peel and coarsely chop.

In large saucepan, heat oil over medium heat; cook onion and garlic, stirring, 2 to 3 minutes or until softened. Add peppers, broth, tomatoes, tomato paste and cumin; bring to boil. Cover, reduce heat, and simmer for 30 minutes. Cool slightly.

In blender, purée pepper mixture with tofu, in batches. Strain through sieve into saucepan; season with salt and pepper. Reheat over low heat. Garnish with sesame seeds.

Makes 4 servings.

Per serving:

140 Calories
8 g protein
6 g fat
17 g carbohydrate
4 g fibre

Cappuccino Curry Soup

Sweetened condensed milk contributes the creamy texture and sweetness to the recipe, a nice balance to the hot curry.

Chef:

Thomas Pitt, CCC
Chef de Cuisine
Larters at St. Andrews
Golf and Country Club
Winnipeg, Manitoba

2 tbsp	soft margarine	25 mL
2 tbsp	all-purpose flour	25 mL
2 cups	chicken broth	500 mL
1/4 cup	sweetened condensed milk	50 mL
1 tbsp	curry powder	15 mL
	Paprika	

In saucepan, melt margarine over medium heat. Stir in flour to blend; simmer for 30 seconds. Stir in chicken broth until smooth.

Stir in condensed milk and curry powder; bring to boil. Reduce heat and simmer, uncovered, for 20 minutes, stirring occasionally. Pour into blender and process until frothy. Serve sprinkled with paprika.

Makes 4 servings.

Dietitian:

Joan Rew, RD
Co-op Coordinator,
Community Cooking
Nutrition Instructor
Red River Community
College
Winnipeg, Manitoba

This soup has the texture of cappuccino, which gives it the unusual name.

Per serving:

151 Calories
5 g protein
8 g fat
15 g carbohydrate
trace fibre

Curried Fiddlehead Soup

Fiddleheads are a spring delicacy. If you have access to a supply, freeze some for use later in the year and you can enjoy this soup year round.

Chef:

Darren Meredith, Chef
Garden Breeze
Restaurant
Dieppe, New Brunswick

1 lb	fresh or frozen fiddleheads	500 g
2 cups	chicken broth	500 mL
2 cups	1% milk	500 mL
2 tsp	margarine	10 mL
2 tsp	curry powder	10 mL
1/4 cup	gin (optional)	50 mL

Dietitian:

Johanne Thériault, RD
Public Health
Nutritionist
Department of Health
and Community Services
Moncton,
New Brunswick

In large saucepan, cook fiddleheads in chicken broth for 15 to 20 minutes; don't overcook or they will go brown. Remove fiddleheads with slotted spoon and purée in food processor; return to broth. Stir in milk; simmer until hot.

In small skillet, heat margarine over low heat; stir in curry powder and cook, stirring, 2 to 3 minutes. Add to soup. Stir in gin, if desired.

Makes 5 servings.

Containing vitamin C and iron, fiddleheads are a distinctive-tasting alternative to an old favorite such as asparagus.

Per serving:

91 Calories
8 g protein
4 g fat
9 g carbohydrate
trace fibre

Purée of Fennel Soup

Fennel, with its distinct licorice-like flavor, is available throughout the year at specialty produce stores and in many supermarkets.

Chef:

Ron Glover
Chef/Instructor
Southern Alberta
Institute of Technology
Edmonton, Alberta

1/4 cup	olive oil	50 mL
3	leeks (white part only), sliced	3
1 cup	chopped fennel bulb	250 mL
1/4 cup	diced red onion	50 mL
Pinch	each nutmeg and cayenne	Pinch
6 cups	chicken broth	1.5 L
2 tbsp	lemon juice	25 mL
2	medium potatoes, peeled and diced	2
1 cup	1% milk	250 mL

Garnish (optional):

8	large shrimp	8
1 tbsp	olive oil	15 mL
1/3 cup	chicken broth	75 mL
	Fennel sprigs	

Dietitian:

Mary Sue Waisman, RD
Nutrition Coordinator
Nutrition and Food
Services
Calgary Regional Health
Authority
Calgary, Alberta

One per cent milk helps control the fat as flavorful fennel teams up with vegetables and spices to make a rich-tasting soup.

Garnish (if using): In small skillet, sauté shrimp in olive oil for 1 minute. Add chicken broth; simmer 5 minutes or until pink. Reserve cooking liquid to add to soup. Peel and devein shrimp when cool.

In large saucepan, heat oil over medium heat; cook leeks, fennel, onion, nutmeg and cayenne, stirring often, for about 5 minutes or until softened. Add chicken broth, lemon juice and potatoes; bring to boil. Reduce heat, cover and simmer 30 minutes.

In blender or food processor, purée in batches; return to saucepan. Stir in milk and heat through. Garnish with shrimp and fennel sprigs.

Makes 8 servings.

Per serving:

150 Calories
6 g protein
8 g fat
14 g carbohydrate
1 g fibre

Salads

Black-Eyed Pea Salad with Cajun Chicken

Warm Duck Salad

Marinated Vegetable Salad

"Fire and Ice" Shrimp Salad

Mango, Strawberry and Cucumber Salad

Orange Mushroom Salad

Chop Chop Romaine Toss with Smoked Turkey,
Mozzarella Cheese and Basil Balsamic Dressing

Warm Chicken Salad with Fruit

Tomato Mozzarella Salad on Crisp Greens
with Vinaigrette

Warm Thai Chicken Salad

Spinach and Grapefruit Salad

Basil Marinated Tomatoes

Winter Vegetable Salad with Apple

Spicy Bean Salad

Lamb and Grilled Vegetable Salad with
Roasted Garlic Sauce

Fruits & Vegetables: Plenty to Celebrate

"Canada's Food Guide to Healthy Eating" is a new approach to the way we eat, which gives new emphasis to vegetables and fruits. The message is clear: we need to eat more of them! Fortunately, there are lots to choose from and an endless variety of ways to eat them.

The Guide recommends that we eat anywhere from five to 10 servings from this food group daily. Why such a range? When it comes to food and nutrition needs, no two people are exactly alike. We differ according to age, body size, sex, activity level and natural individual differences. Generally speaking, a serving from this category is equal to a medium-sized piece of fruit or vegetable, 1 cup (250 mL) of salad, 1/2 cup (125 mL) of fruit juice, mixed fruit or cooked vegetable, or 1/4 cup (50 mL) dried fruit.

Fruits and vegetables really are the "spice of life." As well as giving color, texture and flavor to meals, they are our most important source of many vitamins, minerals and fibre. Antioxidants, such as beta-carotene, may be protective substances for the body, and fruits and vegetables that are yellow, orange and deep green are a good source of these substances. All of these nutrients play a vital role in maintaining good health.

Also, our choice of fruits and vegetables enables us to experiment with our food, learning not only about different regions, but also about the cultures of fellow Canadians. Where would we be without fabulous fiddle-heads from the Maritimes, beautiful berries from Saskatchewan, crisp apples from British Columbia, perfect peaches from Niagara, or the bountiful potatoes from Prince Edward Island? Potatoes are a good example of a vegetable that lost favor in our mistaken belief that we should reduce carbohydrates to control weight. Good news! Potatoes are a great source of vitamin C, and are a great, economical way to increase our intake of complex carbohydrate. Try Garlic Herb Potato Purée — you'll love this new take on a favorite food!

In order to get the best flavor, value and nutrition from fruits and vegetables, there are some important things to keep in mind when purchasing and preparing them. When you buy fruits and vegetables in season, you get terrific value for their nutrition content. Choose produce that has not been damaged, and in general, the richer the color, the more nutrients there are.

If fresh produce is not available, or is difficult to get, Canadian produce that is frozen or canned at the peak of its growing season is as good a choice nutritionally and economically as fresh produce that is imported from afar.

Fruits and vegetables are naturally low in fat, so try not to add too much fat when cooking. Season with herbs to vary the flavor. Eat them raw as well as cooked, for great crunch and taste. Dark green and orange vegetables and orange fruit should be chosen often to ensure adequate intake of vitamins A and C as well as folic acid.

Produce should be well washed under running water. Avoid soaking, as many valuable nutrients will be lost. Leave peels on if you can — they are a great source of fibre. Vegetables should be steamed, microwaved or stir-fried, just until tender-crisp, to preserve their nutrition as well as their fabulous flavor and color. If you do have to boil, use as little water as possible, and make the cooking time as short as you can.

Whether you choose raw or cooked, fresh, canned or frozen, green, orange, red or white, steamed or baked, the message is clear: eat lots and enjoy!

Susan Sutherland, RD
Ottawa, Ontario

Black-Eyed Pea Salad with Cajun Chicken

Both black-eyed peas and black beans, popular in southern-style recipes, are now available canned in many supermarkets, as are several brands of Cajun seasoning.

Chef:

Rainer Schindler, CCC
Spa Cuisine®
St. Clair College
Windsor, Ontario

1	can (14 oz/398 mL) black-eyed peas or black beans	1
3	green onions, chopped	3
1	small bunch watercress	1
1	medium carrot, grated	1
1	medium apple (unpeeled), cored and cubed	1
2/3 cup	bottled no-fat vinaigrette salad dressing	150 mL
8 oz	boneless skinless chicken breasts	250 g
1 tsp	olive oil	5 mL
1-2 tsp	Cajun seasoning	5-10 mL
	Russian rye bread (optional)	

Dietitian:

Monica Stanton, RD
Windsor Regional
Hospital
Windsor, Ontario

This salad is almost a meal in one dish and delivers a whopping 7 grams of fibre in one serving! The nutrition score can be raised even further by using spinach.

Drain and rinse peas. In bowl, combine peas, green onions, watercress, carrot and apple; toss with dressing. Cover and chill for 30 minutes.

Slice chicken breasts lengthwise into 8 thin strips. Coat with oil and Cajun seasoning. In hot skillet, cook chicken until browned and no longer pink inside, about 5 minutes.
Serve with salad, and bread, if desired.

Makes 4 servings.

Tip: Instead of watercress, you can use 2 cups (500 mL) shredded spinach or romaine.

Per serving:

211 Calories
21 g protein
3 g fat
27 g carbohydrate
7 g fibre

Warm Duck Salad

Warm salads—which usually include some meat, poultry or seafood—have become very popular in restaurants yet are easy to make at home. Duck is a higher fat poultry so put a pan of cold water under the broiler rack to prevent spattering and flare-ups.

Chef:

Bruno Marti, CCC
Owner
La Belle Auberge
Restaurant
Ladner, British Columbia

Dietitian:

Laura Cullen, RDN
Director, Dietetic and
Purchasing Services
Chantelle Management
Ltd.
Vancouver,
British Columbia

Although high in fat, this salad plate provides a nutritious gourmet alternative for summer entertaining. Removing the skin from the duck will reduce the fat content of the recipe.

Per serving:

282 Calories
17 g protein
20 g fat
11 g carbohydrate
3 g fibre

1/2 cup	soy sauce	125 mL
1	clove garlic, minced	1
2 tsp	minced shallots	10 mL
1/2 tsp	crushed dried thyme	2 mL
1/4 tsp	pepper	1 mL
2	whole boneless duck breasts (about 12 oz/375 g each)	2

Dressing:

2 tbsp	olive oil	25 mL
2 tbsp	water	25 mL
4 tsp	red wine vinegar	20 mL
1 tbsp	minced shallots	15 mL
2 tsp	Dijon mustard	10 mL
1	clove garlic, minced	1
Dash	hot pepper sauce	Dash
Pinch	each salt and pepper	Pinch

Salad:

2 tbsp	butter or margarine	25 mL
2 cups	sliced shiitake, chanterelle or crimini mushrooms	500 mL
2 tbsp	minced shallots	25 mL
1/4 tsp	crushed dried thyme	1 mL
8 oz	green beans (2 cups/500 mL)	250 g
8	leaves red leaf lettuce	8
4	leaves butter or Boston lettuce	4
12	cherry tomatoes, quartered	12

In shallow dish, combine soy sauce, garlic, shallots, thyme and pepper. Add duck; cover and marinate in refrigerator, turning occasionally, for 24 hours.

Dressing: In small jar or bowl, mix together oil, water, vinegar, shallots, mustard, garlic, hot pepper sauce, salt and pepper; cover and refrigerate.

Remove duck from marinade; pat dry. Score skin in crisscross pattern with sharp knife. Broil or grill about 5 minutes each side or until cooked through. Drain on paper towels. Discard skin; thinly slice meat diagonally.

Salad: In skillet, melt 1 tbsp (15 mL) of the butter over medium-high heat; cook mushrooms, shallots and thyme, stirring, for 2 minutes. Remove and set aside. Melt remaining butter in skillet; cook beans, stirring, until tender-crisp. Remove from heat.

Arrange red leaf and butter lettuce leaves on one side of plate; arrange tomatoes on top. Fan duck slices on other side of plate. Spoon mushrooms and beans around duck in middle of plate. Spoon dressing evenly over salad greens.

Makes 4 servings.

Marinated Vegetable Salad

Marinated salads have been popular for years, but you can use specialty vinegars, such as tarragon, wine, champagne or balsamic, to spice up the flavor.

Chef:

Beth Van Arenthals
Food Service
Supervisor/Chef
Fiddick's Nursing and
Retirement Home
Petrolia, Ontario

Dietitian:

Connie Mallette, RD
Nutrition Educator
Lambton County Health
Unit
Point Edward, Ontario

**This recipe
has everything going
for it — color, flavor,
texture and taste!**

1/2 cup	broccoli florettes	125 mL
1/2 cup	cauliflower florettes	125 mL
1/2 cup	sliced carrots	125 mL
1/2 cup	chopped sweet green pepper	125 mL
1/2 cup	diagonally sliced celery	125 mL
1/2 cup	coarsely chopped English cucumber	125 mL
1/4 cup	diced red or Spanish onion	50 mL
1	small tomato, cut in wedges	1

	Dressing:	
3 tbsp	white vinegar	50 mL
1 tbsp	olive oil	15 mL
2 tsp	granulated sugar	10 mL
1-1/2 tsp	dried oregano or tarragon	7 mL
pinch	pepper	pinch

In large saucepan of boiling water, blanch broccoli, cauliflower and carrots. Drain and plunge into ice water; drain again and place in medium bowl. Add green pepper, celery, cucumber and onion.

Dressing: In small bowl or measuring cup, mix together vinegar, oil, sugar, oregano and pepper; pour over vegetables. Marinate at room temperature for 2 to 3 hours, stirring occasionally to ensure vegetables are well coated. Serve garnished with tomato wedges.

   Makes 4 servings.

Per serving:

69 Calories
1 g protein
4 g fat
9 g carbohydrate
2 g fibre

"Fire and Ice" Shrimp Salad

Your taste buds will wake up with this attractive, make-in-advance salad.

Chef:

David Nicolson
Executive Chef
Gourmet Goodies
Catering
Edmonton, Alberta

5	medium oranges	5
2 tbsp	lime juice	25 mL
2 tsp	fish sauce	10 mL
2	large cloves garlic, minced	2
1 tsp	crushed chili flakes	5 mL
1 lb	shrimp, peeled, deveined, cooked and cooled	500 g
1/4 cup	chopped fresh mint	50 mL
2-1/2 oz	rice vermicelli, soaked and drained (or Chinese egg noodles, cooked, chilled and drained)	70 g
	Mint sprigs	

Dietitian:

Leslie Maze, RD
Diabetes Outpatient
Clinic
Royal Alexandra
Hospital
Edmonton, Alberta

The combination of chilled orange, lime and mint is very refreshing (hence the name "ice") and balances the spark of red chilies.

With sharp knife, peel oranges, removing all pith. Cut into segments between membranes, reserving 3 tbsp (50 mL) juice for dressing and discarding any seeds.

In medium bowl, combine reserved orange juice, lime juice, fish sauce, garlic and chili flakes. Add orange segments and shrimp; toss gently. Cover and chill at least 1 hour or up to 4 hours.

At serving time, stir in chopped mint. Serve over rice vermicelli; garnish with mint sprigs.

Makes 8 appetizer or 4 entrée servings.

Per appetizer serving:
123 Calories
10 g protein
1 g fat
18 g carbohydrate
2 g fibre

Mango, Strawberry and Cucumber Salad

The strawberry season never seems to last long enough! This recipe combines strawberries with mango slices and cucumber cubes on top of crisp salad greens.

Chef:

John Scott
Executive Chef
D'Arcy Ranch Golf Club
Okotoks, Alberta

Dietitian:

Suzanne Journault-
Hemstock, RD
Food Production
Dietitian
Nutrition and Food
Services
Foothills Hospital
Calgary, Alberta

Vitamins C and A abound—even more so when you use spinach. Try easing up on the dressing for a lower fat option.

2 cups	strawberries, sliced	500 mL
1	medium English cucumber, cut in 1/4 inch (5 mm) cubes (about 4 cups/1 L)	1
1	large mango, peeled and cut into 1/4 inch (5 mm) cubes (about 1/2 lb/250 g)	1
8 cups	mixed torn greens	2 L
	Vinaigrette:	
1/3 cup	rice wine vinegar	75 mL
3 tbsp	walnut or olive oil	50 mL
1 tbsp	granulated sugar	15 mL
1 1/2 tsp	coarsely chopped fresh mint	7 mL
1/4 tsp	each salt and pepper	1 mL

Vinaigrette: In large bowl, whisk together vinegar, oil, sugar, mint, salt and pepper. Add strawberries, cucumber and mango; toss gently.

Divide greens among 8 plates. Top with strawberry mixture. Makes 8 servings.

Tip: Garnish each plate with a mint leaf and sliced strawberry.

Per serving:

97 Calories
2 g protein
6 g fat
12 g carbohydrate
3 g fibre

Orange Mushroom Salad

You may not have combined oranges and mushrooms before, but this quick and easy salad could start a trend! You can also use the dressing on other vegetables like blanched carrots or broccoli with slivered peppers.

Chef:

Vern Dean, Chef
Inlet Bistro/Blue Horizon
Hotel
Vancouver,
British Columbia

I tsp	vegetable oil	5 mL
1/4 cup	diced onion	50 mL
1/3 cup	frozen orange juice concentrate, thawed	75 mL
1/4 cup	1% plain yogurt	50 mL
I tsp	lemon juice	5 mL
1/4 tsp	salt	I mL
2 cups	quartered fresh mushrooms	500 mL
2	medium oranges	2
	Chopped green onions (optional)	

Dietitian:

Jane Thornthwaite, RDN
Nutrition Consultant
Fresh Choice Restaurant
Program
Vancouver,
British Columbia

In small skillet, heat oil over medium heat; cook onions, stirring, for 3 minutes or until tender.

In bowl, combine orange juice concentrate, yogurt, lemon juice and salt; stir in onions. Add mushrooms and toss to coat. Peel oranges and slice thinly crosswise; arrange on 4 salad plates. Top with mushroom mixture. Garnish with green onions, if desired. Serve immediately.

Makes 4 servings.

The oranges and yogurt in this salad not only add a tangy flavor, they boost the calcium and vitamin C content too.

Per serving:

98 Calories
3 g protein
2 g fat
20 g carbohydrate
2 g fibre

Chop Chop Romaine Toss with Smoked Turkey, Mozzarella Cheese and Basil Balsamic Dressing

Here's a tasty salad that does double duty—either as a side salad or served with whole grain bread or rolls as a main dish.

Chef:

Alfred Fan
Executive Chef
Bridges Restaurant
Vancouver,
British Columbia

Dietitian:

Leah Hawirko, RDN
Leah Hawirko Nutrition
Consulting and
The Vancouver Health
Department
Vancouver,
British Columbia

Lean turkey breast and mozzarella cheese make the difference here. This is a lovely salad especially in the summer when fresh herbs are available.

1/4 cup	extra-virgin olive oil	50 mL
2 tbsp	balsamic vinegar	25 mL
1 tbsp	chopped fresh parsley	15 mL
1 tsp	liquid honey	5 mL
1 tsp	dried basil (or 1 tbsp/15 mL chopped fresh)	5 mL
Pinch	each salt and pepper	Pinch
8 cups	thinly sliced romaine lettuce	2 L
4 oz	thinly sliced smoked or cooked turkey breast	125 g
	(about 2 slices), cut in strips	
4 oz	part-skim mozzarella cheese, cut in cubes	125 g

In small bowl or measuring cup, mix together oil, vinegar, parsley, honey, basil, salt and pepper. Chill.

In large bowl, toss together lettuce, turkey and cheese; cover and refrigerate until chilled. Pour dressing over top; toss to mix thoroughly.

Makes 6 side-salad servings or 4 main-course servings.

Per side-salad serving:

178 Calories
10 g protein
14 g fat
4 g carbohydrate
1 g fibre

Warm Chicken Salad with Fruit

You can use any favorite fresh fruit in this salad that is pretty as a picture and delicious to eat.

Chef:

Dean Mitchell, CCC
Executive Chef/Owner
Canyon Meadows Golf
and Country Club
Calgary, Alberta

4	boneless skinless chicken breasts (3 oz/90 g each)	4
I lalf	each head butter or Boston lettuce and romaine	Half
Half	medium cantaloupe, peeled	Half
2 cups	strawberries, halved	500 mL
I cup	blueberries or blackberries	250 mL
	Dressing:	
I cup	fresh or thawed unsweetened raspberries	250 mL
1/2 tsp	grated orange rind	2 mL
1/4 cup	orange juice	50 mL
I tsp	grated lemon rind	5 mL
I tbsp	lemon juice	15 mL
I tbsp	chopped fresh mint	15 mL
I tsp	liquid honey	5 mL
1/4 tsp	salt	I mL

Dietitian:

Suzanne Journault-
Hemstock, RD
Food Production
Dietitian
Nutrition and Food
Services
Foothills Hospital
Calgary, Alberta

Here it is: a salad dressing with no fat! Serve with a muffin and glass of milk for a complete meal.

Dressing: In food processor or blender, purée raspberries; press through sieve to remove seeds and return to food processor. Add orange rind and juice, lemon rind and juice, mint, honey and salt; process until well blended. Pour into jar; refrigerate for up to 24 hours. Shake well before serving.

Broil or barbecue chicken until no longer pink inside. Cut into strips.

Meanwhile, tear lettuce and romaine into bite-sized pieces; arrange on 4 large plates. Slice cantaloupe into 8 wedges; cut wedges in half crosswise. Arrange on greens along with strawberries and blueberries. Place chicken on top. Drizzle with dressing. Serve immediately.

Makes 4 servings.

Per serving:

192 Calories
22 g protein
2 g fat
23 g carbohydrate
4 g fibre

Tomato Mozzarella Salad on Crisp Greens with Vinaigrette

Use local beefsteak tomatoes when they are in season for this salad with an Italian touch.

Chef:

Yvonne C. Levert
Cordon Bleu Chef
Instructor, Hospitality
Administration
University College of
Cape Breton Island
Sydney, Nova Scotia

Dietitian:

Nanette Porter-
MacDonald, P.Dt.
Clinical Dietitian
Glace Bay Healthcare
Corporation
Glace Bay, Nova Scotia

This easy vinaigrette is loaded with flavor and adds taste; especially when vegetables are in season.

3	large tomatoes	3
12	leaves romaine or Boston lettuce	12
1/2 cup	cubed part-skim mozzarella cheese	125 mL
6	green onions, sliced	6

	Vinaigrette:	
1/4 cup	vegetable or olive oil	50 mL
2 tbsp	white vinegar	25 mL
1 tbsp	chopped fresh parsley	15 mL
2 tsp	Dijon mustard	10 mL
1 tsp	granulated sugar	5 mL
2	cloves garlic, minced	2
1/2 tsp	dried basil	2 mL
1/2 tsp	pepper	2 mL
1/4 tsp	salt	1 mL
2 tbsp	water	25 mL

Vinaigrette: In jar with tight-fitting lid, shake together oil, vinegar, parsley, mustard, sugar, garlic, basil, pepper, salt and water; chill. Shake before using.

Cut tomatoes in half; cut each half crosswise into slices. Arrange 2 lettuce leaves on each of 8 salad plates. Arrange tomato slices on lettuce; sprinkle with cheese and green onion.

At serving time, pour vinaigrette over each salad.

Makes 8 servings.

Per serving:

106 Calories
3 g protein
8 g fat
6 g carbohydrate
1 g fibre

Warm Thai Chicken Salad

Thai cuisine, with its use of coriander and peanut butter, is a popular addition to the menu of many restaurants across Canada. This delicious salad is partially made the day before then 'cooked' on the grill. Garnish the plates with red onion rings, green onions and cherry tomatoes if desired.

Chef:

John Cordeaux

Chef Exécutif

des Cuisines

Hôtel le Reine Elizabeth

Montréal, Québec

Dietitian:

Kim Arrey, P.Dt.

Consulting Dietitian

Montréal, Québec

To increase the nutrient value, use a variety of salad greens such as dandelion, spinach or beet greens. Remember, the greener the leaves, the more nutrients in the salad.

1 cup	1% plain yogurt	250 mL
1/4 cup	skim milk	50 mL
1 tbsp	chopped fresh coriander	15 mL
1 tsp	curry powder	5 mL
1 tsp	ginger	5 mL
1 tsp	lemon juice	5 mL
	Pepper	
6	boneless skinless chicken breasts (about 1-1/2 lb/750 g)	6
6	medium red-skinned potatoes, cooked	6
6 cups	mixed torn salad greens	1.5 L

Peanut Dressing:		
1/3 cup	chicken broth	75 mL
1/4 cup	light peanut butter	50 mL
1/4 cup	sliced green onions	50 mL
3 tbsp	rice vinegar	50 mL
2 tbsp	sesame oil	25 mL
2 tbsp	grated gingerroot	25 mL
1 tbsp	sherry	15 mL
1 tbsp	granulated sugar	15 mL
1	clove garlic, minced	1
1 tbsp	soy sauce	15 mL
1/4 tsp	salt	1 mL

Per serving:

399 Calories

35 g protein

11 g fat

42 g carbohydrate

4 g fibre

In shallow glass dish, combine yogurt, milk, coriander, curry powder, ginger, lemon juice, and pepper to taste. Add chicken and turn to coat. Cover and refrigerate overnight.

Peanut Dressing: In food processor or blender, process chicken broth, peanut butter, onions, vinegar, oil, gingerroot, sherry, sugar, garlic, soy sauce and salt until smooth. Pour into jar; cover and refrigerate.

Remove chicken from marinade; cook on greased grill or broil 7 to 8 minutes on each side or until no longer pink inside.

Quarter potatoes; place on grill and brown for last 6 to 8 minutes.

Slice each chicken breast crosswise into strips. Arrange salad greens on plates; top with chicken and potatoes. Drizzle with peanut dressing.

Makes 6 servings.

Tip: To cook potatoes, pierce skin with fork in several places and microwave at High for 10 to 12 minutes, turning once halfway through cooking.

Spinach and Grapefruit Salad

Segments of grapefruit with slices of red onion are a perfect color and taste contrast to spinach. You can prepare the dressing in advance, then cover and refrigerate until ready to use.

Chef:

Stephen Ashton
Head Chef/Instructor
Picasso Café
Vancouver,
British Columbia

Dietitian:

Leah Hawirko, RDN
Leah Hawirko Nutrition
Consulting and
The Vancouver Health
Department
Vancouver,
British Columbia

Spinach is high in beta-carotene and folacin, while pink grapefruit provides vitamin C. Because vitamin C helps in the absorption of iron, this salad is a nutritional powerhouse.

2 tsp	poppy seeds	10 mL
Half	red onion, thinly sliced	Half
4	cloves garlic	4
3	medium red grapefruit	3
3 tbsp	olive oil	50 mL
2 tbsp	white wine vinegar	25 mL
2 tbsp	chopped fresh parsley	25 mL
1 tbsp	grainy mustard	15 mL
1/2 tsp	liquid honey	2 mL
1/2 tsp	salt	2 mL
1/4 tsp	pepper	1 mL
1	bunch spinach, washed and torn into bite-sized pieces	1

Heat small skillet over medium heat; toast poppy seeds for 1 to 2 minutes, stirring constantly. Remove from heat.

In small bowl, cover onion with cold water; let stand for 10 minutes, then drain. In small saucepan, cover garlic with cold water and bring to boil; simmer for 3 minutes, then drain.

Remove skin and white pith from grapefruit; cut fruit into segments, catching juice in small bowl.

In blender or food processor, combine garlic, oil, vinegar, parsley, mustard, honey, salt, pepper and 2 tbsp (25 mL) reserved grapefruit juice; blend until creamy.

In large bowl, combine spinach, onions and grapefruit; toss with dressing. Garnish with poppy seeds.

Makes 8 side salads.

Per serving:

99 Calories
2 g protein
6 g fat
12 g carbohydrate
3 g fibre

Basil Marinated Tomatoes

This is a great summer salad to include in suppers on the deck.

Chef:

Barb Armstrong
Chef/Instructor
Spectrum Community
School
Victoria,
British Columbia

4	*medium tomatoes*	*4*
1/4 cup	*chopped fresh parsley*	*50 mL*
3 tbsp	*olive oil*	*50 mL*
1 tbsp	*white wine vinegar*	*15 mL*
1 tbsp	*red wine vinegar*	*15 mL*
1 tbsp	*chopped fresh basil (or 1 tsp/5 mL dried)*	*15 mL*
3/4 tsp	*granulated sugar*	*4 mL*
1/4 tsp	*each salt and pepper*	*1 mL*

Dietitian:

Marianna Fiocco, RDN
Consulting Dietitian
Westcoast Dietetics Ltd.
Victoria,
British Columbia

Remove seeds from tomatoes, if desired. Slice tomatoes and arrange on flat serving plate. Sprinkle with parsley.

Whisk together oil, white and red wine vinegars, basil, sugar, salt and pepper; pour over tomatoes. Cover and refrigerate about 1 hour before serving.

Makes 8 servings.

Fresh tomatoes from the garden are a source of vitamin C. Removing the tomato seeds will eliminate any bitterness.

Per serving:

81 Calories
1 g protein
7 g fat
5 g carbohydrate
1 g fibre

Warm Chicken Salad with Fruit (page 53)

Winter Vegetable Salad with Apple

This simple salad combines inexpensive fall vegetables with apples tossed in a creamy mustard dressing.

Chef:

Julius Pokomandy, CCC
Chef/Instructor
South Delta Secondary
School
Delta, British Columbia

Dietitian:

Leah Hawirko, RDN
Leah Hawirko Nutrition
Consulting and
The Vancouver Health
Department
Vancouver,
British Columbia

For optimum nutrition, taste and economy, whenever possible choose locally grown seasonal produce. You'll be supporting the local businesses as well.

3	medium carrots	3
2	medium potatoes, peeled if desired	2
1	medium parsnip	1
3/4 cup	frozen peas	175 mL
2/3 cup	diced dill pickle	150 mL
1	medium apple (unpeeled), diced	1
1/3 cup	light mayonnaise	75 mL
1/3 cup	1% plain yogurt	75 mL
2 tbsp	honey mustard	25 mL
1/4 tsp	each salt and pepper	1 mL
	Orange slices	
	Toasted slivered almonds	

Dice carrots, potatoes and parsnip into 1/2-inch (1 cm) cubes. In saucepan of boiling water, or in microwave, cook individually just until tender; drain well. Pour hot water over peas just to thaw; drain well. In large bowl, combine carrots, potatoes, parsnips, peas, pickle, apple, mayonnaise, yogurt, honey, salt and pepper; cover and refrigerate about 8 hours before serving. Garnish with orange slices and almonds.

Makes 8 servings.

Per serving:

128 Calories
3 g protein
4 g fat
21 g carbohydrate
3 g fibre

Spinach and Grapefruit Salad (page 57)

Spicy Bean Salad

Beans are now in vogue and for good reason: they're high in fibre and pick up the flavor of herbs and spices in recipes. Make this salad the day before serving so the flavors have a chance to blend together.

Chef:

Chris Klugman
Executive Chef
Wayne Gretzky's
Restaurant
Toronto, Ontario

Dietitian:

Susie Langley, M.S., RD
Nutrition Consultant
Toronto, Ontario

Smoking the spices — heating in a pan without oil — to intensify the flavor and aroma makes this colorful combination of complex carbohydrates a sure winner!

2 tsp	ground cumin	10 mL
1 tsp	curry powder	5 mL
1	can (14 oz/398 mL) kidney beans (or 2 cups/500 mL cooked dried beans)	1
Half	medium Spanish or red onion, diced	Half
2	tomatoes, chopped	2
2	stalks celery, chopped	2
2	green onions, sliced	2
2 tbsp	lime juice	25 mL
1 tbsp	olive oil	15 mL
1/4 cup	chopped fresh coriander	50 mL

In small dry skillet, heat cumin and curry powder over high heat until fragrant and smoking.

Drain and rinse kidney beans; place in large bowl. Stir in onion, tomatoes, celery and green onions.

Mix lime juice and olive oil with roasted cumin and curry powder; pour over bean mixture. Stir in coriander. Cover and chill for up to 24 hours, stirring occasionally.

Makes 6 servings.

Per serving:

105 Calories
5 g protein
3 g fat
16 g carbohydrate
6 g fibre

Lamb and Grilled Vegetable Salad with Roasted Garlic Sauce

Fall vegetables and boneless lamb loin are grilled with seasoned oil in this recipe. Roasted garlic has a milder taste than fresh garlic and is also easier on the digestive system.

Chef:

Philippe Guiet
Master Chef/Professeur
Le Cordon Bleu Paris
Cooking School
Ottawa, Ontario

Dietitian:

Dawn Palin, Ph.D., RD
Consulting Dietitian
Gloucester, Ontario

The subtle flavor of roasted garlic blends perfectly with the warm vegetable salad and thinly sliced lamb in this "two-food-group" combination.

2	stalks celery, cut in 1-inch (2.5 cm) thick slices	2
1	medium sweet red pepper, cut in strips	1
1	medium zucchini, sliced	1
1	medium eggplant, cut in 1/4-inch (5 mm) thick slices	1
1 tsp	crushed dried thyme	5 mL
2	bulbs garlic	2
1/4 cup	olive oil	50 mL
2 tbsp	white wine vinegar	25 mL
1/4 tsp	each salt and pepper	1 mL
1	pkg (400 g) frozen boneless lamb loins, thawed	1
	Fresh thyme	

In bowl, combine celery, red pepper, zucchini, eggplant and thyme; let stand for 1 hour.

Cut top off garlic bulbs; place in small baking dish or custard cups. Cover with oil. Bake at 400°F (200°C) for 30 to 35 minutes or until cloves come out of their skins. (Do not burn.) Set 1 tbsp oil aside to grill lamb. Remove garlic from skins and mash with fork. Stir in vinegar, salt and pepper. Keep warm (or reheat in microwave for 15 seconds).

Brush lamb and vegetables with reserved oil. Grill lamb loins and vegetables 2 to 3 minutes on each side. (Or heat reserved oil in large skillet; brown lamb about 5 minutes. Remove; keep warm. Add vegetables to skillet and sauté about 5 minutes or until tender.)

To serve, pour 1 tbsp garlic sauce onto one side of each of 4 plates. Slice lamb and place on top. Place vegetables beside lamb. Garnish with fresh thyme, if desired.

Makes 4 servings.

Per serving:

268 Calories
23 g protein
13 g fat
16 g carbohydrate
4 g fibre

Limelight Salad

This salad of mixed greens and fresh peppers moves into the 'limelight' with an easy-to-prepare dressing. Or, add seasonal fresh fruit for an interesting variation.

Chef:

Ralph Graham
Instructor
Culinary Arts Foundation
of Saskatchewan
Saskatoon,
Saskatchewan

	Dressing:	
2 tbsp	liquid honey	25 mL
2 tsp	grated gingerroot	10 mL
1 cup	light mayonnaise	250 mL
1 tsp	grated lime rind	5 mL
3 tbsp	fresh lime juice	50 mL

	Salad:	
1	head Bibb or Boston lettuce	1
1	head leaf lettuce	1
1	each medium sweet red, green and yellow pepper, cut into rings	1

Dietitian:

Rosanne E. Maluk, P.Dt.
Food Focus
Saskatoon Inc.
Saskatoon,
Saskatchewan

This salad is a treat for the eye as well as the palate. Use fresh ginger for that extra "zing."

Dressing: In small saucepan over medium heat, melt honey with gingerroot until bubbles form. (Or microwave at High for 25 seconds.) Stir into mayonnaise along with lime rind and juice, mixing well. Chill. (Dressing can be made up to 1 week ahead.)

Tear Bibb and leaf lettuce into bite-sized pieces; place in salad bowl. Top with sweet peppers; chill until serving time. Serve with dressing in pitcher for guests to serve themselves.

Makes 10 servings.

**Per serving:
(with 1 tbsp dressing)**

58 Calories
1 g protein
3 g fat
7 g carbohydrate
1 g fibre

Bulgur Salad

Bulgur is an ancient grain that's coming back into fashion. Commercial fat-free Italian salad dressing adds flavor without fat.

Chef:

Rainer Schindler, CCC
Spa Cuisine®
St. Clair College
Windsor, Ontario

Dietitian:

Monica Stanton, RD
Windsor Regional Hospital
Windsor, Ontario

This salad has it all: low calories, low fat, lots of vegetables — and color and flavor to spare.

1 cup	bulgur	250 mL
2 tbsp	finely chopped red or Spanish onion	25 mL
1	clove garlic, minced	1
1/2 cup	cooled cooked corn kernels	125 mL
1	tomato, seeded and diced	1
Half	small zucchini, thinly sliced	Half
1/4 cup	crumbled feta cheese	50 mL
1/4 cup	bottled fat-free Italian dressing	50 mL
pinch	crushed dried basil	pinch
	Salt and pepper	

Cover bulgur with 2 cups (500 mL) boiling water; let stand 30 minutes. Drain.

In bowl, combine bulgur, onion, garlic, corn, tomato and zucchini; stir in cheese, dressing and basil. Season with salt and pepper to taste. Cover and refrigerate at least 1 hour.

Makes 6 servings.

Per serving:

113 Calories
5 g protein
1 g fat
23 g carbohydrate
5 g fibre

Raita Cucumber Salad

Coriander and cumin are traditional spices in both Middle Eastern and Mexican cuisines, and give a whole new taste to cucumbers.

Chef:

Robert Neil
Cook Supervisor
Joyceville Correctional
Institute
Joyceville, Ontario

Dietitian:

Denise Hargrove, RD
Public Health Dietitian
Kingston, Frontenac and
Lennox and Addington
Health Unit
Kingston, Ontario

This flavorful and refreshing salad cools the palate and goes especially well with spicy ethnic dishes such as curries. And you can also boost your calcium intake at the same time.

2-1/2 cups	1% plain yogurt	625 mL
1 tbsp	chopped fresh parsley	15 mL
3/4 tsp	ground cumin	4 mL
1/2 tsp	ground coriander	2 mL
1/2 tsp	salt	2 mL
1/2 tsp	each grated lemon rind and orange rind	2 mL
1/4 tsp	hot pepper sauce	1 mL
Pinch	each paprika and pepper	Pinch
1	medium English cucumber, thinly sliced	1
1	large tomato, diced	1
1	medium onion, thinly sliced	1

In bowl, mix together yogurt, parsley, cumin, coriander, salt, lemon and orange rinds, hot pepper sauce, paprika and pepper.

Stir in cucumber, tomato and onion. Cover and chill at least 30 minutes before serving.

Makes 8 servings.

Per serving:

66 Calories
5 g protein
1 g fat
9 g carbohydrate
1 g fibre

Herb Polenta on Warm Braising Salad with Wild Mushrooms

Polenta — cornmeal and water — is bland by itself, but bursts with flavor in this salad, from a combination of basil, rosemary, thyme, garlic and pepper. If you want to use fresh herbs instead of dried, use three times the amount of dried the recipe calls for.

Chef:

Antony Nuth
Chef/Owner
Herbs Restaurant
Toronto, Ontario

Dietitian:

Lynda Chadwick, RD
National Medical
Manager
Nestlé Canada Inc.
Toronto, Ontario

This combination of polenta and warm salad is a great source of complex carbohydrates. Go easy on the oil when warming the salad.

1/1 cup	olive oil	50 mL
4 cups	sliced mushrooms (portobello, oyster, chanterelle or white)	1 L
4 cups	shredded salad greens (combination of kale, rapini, radicchio, Belgian endive)	1 L
2 tbsp	balsamic vinegar	25 mL
1/4 tsp	each salt and pepper	1 mL

Herb Polenta:

4 cups	chicken or vegetable broth	1 L
2	large cloves garlic, minced	2
1 tbsp	dried basil	15 mL
1-1/2 tsp	each crumbled dried rosemary and thyme	7 mL
1/4 tsp	each salt and pepper	1 mL
1 cup	cornmeal	250 mL

Herb Polenta: In large saucepan, bring broth to boil. Add garlic, basil, rosemary, thyme, salt and pepper; gradually add cornmeal, whisking constantly. Cook over low heat, stirring occasionally, for about 15 minutes or until thick and soft. Pour into 8- x 4-inch (1.5 L) loaf pan lined with plastic wrap. Cool. (Chill if prepared ahead of time.)

Slice polenta into 8 pieces. Coat with additional cornmeal. In large skillet sprayed with nonstick cooking spray, brown polenta on both sides. Remove from pan and keep warm.

Add 2 tbsp (25 mL) of the oil to skillet; sauté mushrooms 2 to 3 minutes. Add remaining oil, shredded braising salad greens, vinegar, salt and pepper; heat through.

Divide salad mixture among 8 plates; place polenta on top. Serve immediately.

Makes 8 servings.

Per serving:

160 Calories
5 g protein
8 g fat
17 g carbohydrate
2 g fibre

Heart to Heart Salad

Canned artichokes are available in most supermarkets and provide a convenient way to enjoy this vegetable. It will only take you minutes to make this salad, but let it marinate overnight before serving.

Chef:

Leo Pantel
Executive Chef
Saskatchewan Centre for
the Arts
Regina, Saskatchewan

3 tbsp	extra-virgin olive oil	50 mL
1 tbsp	lemon juice	15 mL
1 tbsp	finely diced red or green onion	15 mL
1/2 tsp	crushed dried thyme	2 mL
1	can (14 oz/398 mL) artichoke hearts, drained and quartered	1
1 tbsp	shredded Gruyère or Sbrinz cheese	15 mL
1 tbsp	finely chopped fresh parsley	15 mL

Dietitian:

Patti Neuman
Clinical Dietitian
Regina Health District
Regina, Saskatchewan

In a small bowl, mix together oil, lemon juice, onion and thyme. Add artichokes and lightly stir to coat well. Cover and chill at least 1 hour or overnight, stirring occasionally. Drain well.

Arrange artichokes on serving plate; sprinkle with cheese and parsley.

Makes 4 servings.

Blending your own salad dressing allows you to control the fat, and it is less expensive than store-bought dressings.

Per serving:

84 Calories
3 g protein
6 g fat
7 g carbohydrate
3 g fibre

Grilled Yellowfin Tuna with Julienne Vegetables

You may not be able to find yellowfin tuna, but any fresh tuna steak will work beautifully in this salad.

Chef:

Trent Breares, Sous Chef
Saskatchewan Centre for
the Arts
Regina, Saskatchewan

8 oz	yellowfin or other fresh tuna steak	250 g
2	medium carrots, cut in julienne strips	2
1	leek (white part only), cut in julienne strips	1
1	small red onion, cut in julienne strips	1
12	spears asparagus	12

Dressing:

1/4 cup	olive oil	50 mL
2 tbsp	Dijon mustard	25 mL
2 tbsp	lemon juice	25 mL
Pinch	pepper	Pinch

Dietitian:

Thomas Hamilton, P.Dt.
Diabetes Nutrition
Educator
Regina Health District
Regina, Saskatchewan

Tuna is a lean protein choice but go easy on the dressing. A little of this Dijon flavor packs lots of punch.

Dressing: Whisk together oil, mustard, lemon juice and pepper; chill.

Grill or broil tuna on greased grill for 3 to 5 minutes on each side or until fish flakes easily when tested with fork.

Meanwhile, steam or microwave carrots, leek, onion and asparagus just until tender.

To serve, divide vegetables among 4 plates. Cut tuna into 4 pieces; place on top of vegetables. Pour 1 tbsp dressing over each salad. Serve warm.

Makes 4 servings.

Per serving with 1 tbsp dressing:

193 Calories
16 g protein
10 g fat
11 g carbohydrate
2 g fibre

Vegetable Side Dishes

Stuffed Tomatoes or Zucchinis

Leek and Potato Pancakes

Mock Eels

Grilled Vegetable Souvlaki with Feta Tzatziki

Garlic Herb Potato Purée

Winter Bunch of Beans

Braised Red Cabbage with Apples

Golden Chanterelle Sauté

Vegetable Hodgepodge

Braised Curried Potatoes

Sweet Baked Tomatoes

Vegetable and Fennel Stew

Sunflower Seed and Orange Broccoli

Oven-Dried Tomatoes

Zucchini Spaghetti with Two Sauces

Stuffed Tomatoes or Zucchini

Chef:

Richard Franz,
Head Chef/Director of
Food and Beverages
Amberwood Village Golf
and Country Club
Ottawa, Ontario

Dietitian:

Susan Sutherland, RD
National Director of
Promotions
Fresh for Flavour
Foundation
Ottawa, Ontario

This is an easy way to reach for one of the five to 10 daily servings from the Vegetables and Fruit Group in "Canada's Food Guide to Healthy Eating."

You can prepare stuffed vegetables earlier in the day, then cover and chill until ready to heat and serve, but for best flavor and texture, don't make the day before.

6	small tomatoes or 2 large zucchini	6
	Provençale Stuffing:	
2	medium onions, finely chopped	2
2	cloves garlic, finely chopped	2
2 cups	packed fresh parsley, finely chopped	500 mL
1 tbsp	olive oil	15 mL
3	slices white bread, crusts removed	3
1/3 cup	freshly grated Parmesan cheese	75 mL
	Mushroom Stuffing:	
1	medium onion, finely chopped	1
1 tbsp	butter	15 mL
1/2 lb	mushrooms, chopped (about 15)	250 g
1/2 cup	beef broth	125 mL
1 tbsp	chopped fresh dill (or 1 tsp/5 mL dried dillweed)	15 mL
3	slices white bread, crusts removed	3
	Salt and pepper	

Stuffed Tomatoes Per serving:

112 Calories
5 g protein
4 g fat
14 g carbohydrate
3 g fibre

Stuffed Zucchinis Per serving:

62 Calories
2 g protein
2 g fat
9 g carbohydrate
1 g fibre

Halve tomatoes and hollow out using small spoon or melon baller. Slice each zucchini into six 1-inch (2.5 cm) pieces; hollow out, leaving bottom 1/4 inch (5 mm) thick. (If desired, before slicing zucchini, use vegetable peeler to cut lengthwise strips down zucchini to give striped effect.) Stuff with one of stuffing mixtures.

Provençale Stuffing: In skillet, sauté onions, garlic and parsley in olive oil about 3 minutes; remove from heat. Finely chop bread; add to onion mixture. Stir in cheese. Fill vegetables. Bake at 350°F (180°C) for 10 to 15 minutes or until heated through and lightly browned.

Mushroom Stuffing: In skillet, sauté onion in butter 2 minutes. Add mushrooms; cook about 2 minutes longer. Stir in beef broth and dill; bring to boil, stirring until slightly thickened. Remove from heat. Finely chop bread; stir into mushroom mixture. Season with salt and pepper to taste. Fill vegetables. Bake at 350°F (180°C) for 10 to 15 minutes or until heated through.

Makes 6 servings.

Leek and Potato Pancakes

The secret to making these delicious pancakes is cooking the potatoes the day before in their skins, then refrigerating overnight.

Chef:

*Richard Franz
Head Chef/Director of
Food and Beverages
Amberwood Village Golf
and Country Club
Ottawa, Ontario*

4	large baking potatoes, cooked and chilled	4
1 tbsp	butter	15 mL
3	bunch leeks (white part only), coarsely chopped	3
1/2 cup	water	125 mL
2	eggs, lightly beaten	2
1/2 tsp	salt	2 mL
1/4 tsp	white pepper	1 mL
Pinch	nutmeg	Pinch

Dietitian:

*Susan Sutherland, RD
National Director of
Promotions
Fresh for Flavour
Foundation
Ottawa, Ontario*

Baking these pancakes rather than the traditional frying method makes them light tasting and lower in fat.

Peel chilled potatoes; coarsely grate.

In skillet, melt butter over medium heat; cook leeks, stirring, for 3 minutes. Add water, and bring to boil; simmer 2 to 3 minutes. Drain.

In bowl, gently mix potatoes, leeks, eggs, salt, pepper and nutmeg. Spoon onto greased baking sheet, forming 16 mounds; flatten to 1/4-inch (5 mm) thickness. Bake at 375°F (190°C) for 10 to 15 minutes or until golden.

Makes 8 servings of 2 pancakes each.

Per serving:

124 Calories
4 g protein
3 g fat
22 g carbohydrate
2 g fibre

Mock Eels

Slices of Chinese mushrooms are coated with exotic seasoning and cornstarch then fried in oil until brown. The name comes from the shape of the fried mushrooms, which resemble eels.

Chef:

Jon Paudler
Chef/Instructor,
Culinary Arts
Northern Alberta
Institute of Technology
Edmonton, Alberta

Dietitian:

Leslie Maze, RD
Diabetes Outpatient
Clinic
Royal Alexandra
Hospital
Edmonton, Alberta

The secret to low-fat deep-frying is proper coating with cornstarch. If all of the mushrooms are coated, very little fat will penetrate the food.

4	green onions	4
10	large dried Chinese mushrooms	10
1/2 cup	water	125 mL
4 tsp	cornstarch	20 mL
1 tsp	granulated sugar	5 mL
1 tsp	rice vinegar	5 mL
3-1/2 tsp	tamari sauce or soy sauce	17 mL
1/4 tsp	sesame oil	1 mL
Pinch	five-spice powder	Pinch
	Vegetable oil for frying	
1	slice gingerroot	1
Half	head iceberg lettuce, shredded	Half

Cut green portion of onions lengthwise into slivers, without detaching from white part. Soak in bowl of water until slivers have curled. Soak mushrooms in medium bowl of water until soft, about 30 minutes.

Meanwhile, in small saucepan, combine water, 1 tsp (5 mL) of the cornstarch, sugar, vinegar, 1/2 tsp (2 mL) of the tamari sauce and sesame oil. Bring to boil and cook until thickened; set aside.

Drain and rinse mushrooms; squeeze out excess water. Discard stems; slice caps into strips. Toss with 3 tsp (15 mL) of the tamari sauce; sprinkle with five-spice powder and toss to coat. Roll mushrooms in remaining cornstarch.

In wok or frying pan, heat 1/4 inch (5 mm) oil to 350°F (180°C). Fry gingerroot until lightly browned; discard. In small batches, fry mushroom strips until crisp, gently stirring with fork to prevent sticking. Drain on paper towels.

Place bed of lettuce on 4 individual plates. Rewarm sauce, then toss mushroom strips in sauce. Place strips on lettuce; drizzle with sauce. Garnish with curled green onion.

Makes 4 servings.

Per serving:

79 Calories
2 g protein
3 g fat
12 g carbohydrate
2 g fibre

Grilled Vegetable Souvlaki with Feta Tzatziki

Souvlaki usually consists of cubes of lamb or pork that are grilled on skewers then served on a bun. For a light luncheon, serve our vegetable version with rice and pita bread. The Feta Tzatziki provides more than a hint of garlic!

Chef:

David McQuinn, CCC
Executive Chef
Coast Victoria
Harbourside Hotel/
Blue Crab Bar and Grill
Victoria,
British Columbia

Dietitian:

Helen Dubas, RDN
Manager,
Nutrition Services
Victoria General
Hospital
Victoria,
British Columbia

A delicious vegetarian version of a popular Greek dish, it's a tasty way to boost your fibre and also provides calcium. Invite a group of friends and enjoy any time of the year.

24	cherry tomatoes	24
24	mushrooms	24
1	each large sweet red and green pepper, cut in 1-inch (2.5 cm) squares	1
2	red onions, cut in wedges	2
1	can (14 oz/398 mL) artichoke hearts, drained and halved	1
	Marinade:	
1/2 cup	olive oil	125 mL
2 tbsp	lemon juice	25 mL
1 tbsp	minced garlic	15 mL
2 tsp	crushed dried oregano	10 mL
1 tsp	crushed dried mint	5 mL
1 tsp	pepper	5 mL
Pinch	red pepper flakes	Pinch
	Feta Tzatziki:	
1-1/2 cups	1% plain yogurt	375 mL
1/2 cup	grated English cucumber	125 mL
1/2 cup	crumbled feta cheese	125 mL
1	large clove garlic, minced	1
2 tbsp	lemon juice	25 mL

Dividing evenly and alternating vegetables, thread tomatoes, mushrooms, red and green peppers, onions and artichoke hearts onto 12 bamboo skewers.

Marinade: In large shallow nonmetallic dish, combine oil, lemon juice, garlic, oregano, mint, pepper and red pepper flakes; add skewers, turning to coat well. Chill for 3 to 6 hours, turning occasionally.

Feta Tzatziki: In serving bowl, combine yogurt, cucumber, feta, garlic and lemon juice; refrigerate.

Remove souvlaki from marinade. Grill over medium heat for 10 minutes. Or bake on greased baking sheet at 425°F (220°C) for about 15 minutes. Serve with Feta Tzatziki.

Makes 6 side-dish servings.

Per serving:

262 Calories
10 g protein
13 g fat
31 g carbohydrate
7 g fibre

Garlic Herb Potato Purée

Mashed potatoes are making a comeback! Eight cloves of garlic may seem overpowering, but when roasted, garlic assumes a more mellow and gentle flavor.

Chef:

Larry DeVries
Chef/Instructor
Crocus Plains Secondary
School
Brandon, Manitoba

8	cloves garlic	8
1/2 tsp	olive oil	2 mL
4	medium potatoes (russet, Yukon Gold)	4
1/2 cup	2% evaporated milk	125 mL
2 tsp	chopped fresh parsley	10 mL
1 tsp	chopped fresh chives (or green onions)	5 mL
1/4 tsp	crumbled dried tarragon	1 mL
1/2 tsp	salt	2 mL
1/4 tsp	white pepper	1 mL

Dietitians:

Jackie Kopilas, RD
Rachel Barkley, RD
Brandon and Westman
Area Dietitians
Heather Duncan,
P.H.Ec.
Manitoba Association of
Home Economists—
Southwest Branch
Brandon, Manitoba

In small ovenproof dish, toss garlic with olive oil; roast at 350°F (180°C) for 20 to 25 minutes or until lightly browned.

Peel potatoes; boil or microwave until tender. Mash potatoes with garlic.

Add milk, parsley, chives, tarragon, salt and pepper; mash until soft and creamy. (Add more milk if necessary to give desired consistency.)

Makes 6 servings.

Don't fall for the myth that potatoes are fattening; it is usually the topping, not the potato.

Per serving:

105 Calories
3 g protein
1 g fat
21 g carbohydrate
1 g fibre

Winter Bunch of Beans

This economical meatless recipe uses an assortment of dried beans with lots of local winter produce. Serve with a fresh salad and whole wheat bread for a complete meal.

Chef:

Janice Mitchell, CCC
Janice's Fine Country
Catering
London, Ontario

Dietitian:

Jane Henderson, RD
Consulting Dietitian
Kintore, Ontario

This hearty, low-fat dish is chock-full of protein, fibre and vitamins.

2 cups	assorted dried beans (romano, white, kidney, pinto)	500 mL
1	can (28 oz/796 mL) tomatoes	1
1	can (19 oz/540 mL) chick-peas, drained	1
2	medium carrots, sliced	2
1	medium onion, chopped	1
1	clove garlic, minced	1
1 cup	shredded cabbage	250 mL
1/2 cup	diced peeled turnip	125 mL
1 tbsp	chili powder	15 mL
1 tsp	Worcestershire sauce	5 mL
1/2 tsp	salt	2 mL
1/4 tsp	pepper	1 mL
	Chopped fresh parsley	

Cover beans with water and soak overnight; drain and rinse. In 4-quart (4 L) saucepan, cover beans with fresh water; bring to boil. Reduce heat and simmer, uncovered, for 40 to 50 minutes or until tender. Add tomatoes, chick-peas, carrots, onion, garlic, cabbage, turnip, chili powder, Worcestershire sauce, salt and pepper; bring to boil. Reduce heat and simmer, uncovered, for 30 to 40 minutes or until vegetables are tender. Garnish with parsley.

Makes 6 servings.

Per serving:

356 Calories
21 g protein
3 g fat
66 g carbohydrate
18 g fibre

Braised Red Cabbage with Apples

Long, slow cooking develops the flavors in this fabulous fall or winter dish. It will reheat well and may be stored for one week in the refrigerator.

Chef:

Alastair Gray
Executive Chef
The York Club
Toronto, Ontario

Dietitian:

Mary Margaret Laing, RD
M.M. Laing & Associates
Healthcare Marketing Services
Cambridge, Ontario

There is no microwave match for the flavor and aroma of this great dish, reminding us of traditional oven cooking: vegetables, fruit and herbs gently mingle, creating a taste to make your mouth water. Just combine and bake — easy, tasty and nutritious!

Per serving:

44 Calories
1 g protein
1 g fat
8 g carbohydrate
2 g fibre

1	small red cabbage (about 1-1/2 lb/750 g)	1
1/3 cup	red wine vinegar	75 mL
1 tbsp	granulated sugar	15 mL
1 tsp	salt	5 mL
1	slice bacon, chopped (or 1 tbsp/15 mL olive oil)	1
1/3 cup	chopped onion	75 mL
2	Granny Smith apples, peeled, cored and cut into eighths	2
1	whole clove	1
1	small onion	1
1	bay leaf	1
1/2 cup	boiling water	125 mL
2 tbsp	dry red wine (optional)	25 mL

Remove outer leaves of cabbage and discard. Cut cabbage into quarters; trim off excess white heart. Shred about 1/8 inch (3 mm) thick to make 6 cups (1.5 L). Place in bowl; toss with vinegar, sugar and salt.

In large skillet, brown bacon; remove bacon, reserving drippings in pan; set bacon aside. Add chopped onion; cook, stirring, for 2 minutes. Add apples; cook 5 minutes.

Push clove into onion; add to skillet along with cabbage mixture, bay leaf, boiling water and bacon. Mix well. Pour into 8-cup (2 L) casserole. Cover and bake at 325°F (160°C) for 2 hours, stirring occasionally. (If it becomes dry, add more water.) Remove onion and bay leaf. Stir in wine, if desired.

Makes 10 servings.

Golden Chanterelle Sauté

Chanterelle mushrooms and small button mushrooms combine in this aromatic 'stew' that can be served as either a side dish or on rice as a main dish.

Chef:

Hans Anderegg
Chef/Instructor
Culinary Institute of
Canada
Charlottetown,
Prince Edward Island

I tsp	olive oil	5 mL
I	medium onion, chopped	I
2	cloves garlic, minced	2
I-1/4 lb	chanterelle or portobello mushrooms, sliced	625 g
1/2 lb	small button mushrooms	250 g
3	sun-dried tomatoes, softened and chopped	3
3/4 cup	chicken broth	175 mL
1/2 cup	dry white wine	125 mL
2 tbsp	lemon juice	25 mL
I tbsp	sweet Hungarian paprika	15 mL
1/2 tsp	caraway seeds	2 mL
	Salt and pepper	
2 tbsp	chopped fresh parsley	25 mL

Dietitian:

Cheryl Turnbull-Bruce,
P.Dt.
Nutrition Consultant
Charlottetown,
Prince Edward Island

This sauté has a great mix of herbs and spices that results in spectacular flavor with little fat.

In large skillet, heat oil over medium heat; cook onion, stirring, for 2 minutes. Add garlic, chanterelle and button mushrooms and tomatoes; cook for 2 to 3 minutes.

Add chicken broth, wine, lemon juice, paprika and caraway seeds; bring to boil. Simmer over low heat about 15 minutes or until slightly thickened, stirring occasionally. Season with salt and pepper to taste. Sprinkle with parsley.

Makes 4 main-dish servings or 8 side-dish servings.

Tip: To soften sun-dried tomatoes, cover with boiling water and let stand 10 minutes. Drain well.

Per side-dish serving:

44 Calories
2 g protein
I g fat
6 g carbohydrate
2 g fibre

Vegetable Hodgepodge

Hodgepodge is served as a main dish in the Annapolis Valley when vegetables are fresh from the garden. Frozen peas may be substituted for the snow peas.

Chef:

Howard Selig
Chef/Owner
Finest Kind Food Co.
Middleton, Nova Scotia

12	small red-skinned potatoes (unpeeled)	12
16	baby carrots	16
1 cup	snow peas	250 mL
1 cup	yellow wax beans	250 mL
1 tbsp	all-purpose flour	15 mL
1 cup	2% milk or 2% evaporated milk	250 mL
1/2 tsp	salt	2 mL
1/4 tsp	pepper	1 mL
1 tsp	butter	5 mL

Dietitian:

Tricia Cochrane, P.Dt.
Dietitian
Soldiers Memorial
Hospital
Middleton, Nova Scotia

In skillet of small amount of boiling water, cook potatoes covered for 10 to 15 minutes or until almost tender. Add carrots; cook 5 minutes longer. Add snow peas and beans; cook 3 minutes longer or until all vegetables are tender. Drain.

Dissolve flour in milk; stir into vegetables until thickened. Add salt, pepper and butter.

Makes 4 servings.

Loaded with protein and fibre, this colorful mix is a "down East" tradition that takes advantage of fresh vegetables.

Per serving:

349 Calories
10 g protein
3 g fat
74 g carbohydrate
7 g fibre

Braised Curried Potatoes

Curry with potatoes? Absolutely, as this easy-to-make dish proves!

Chef:

*Jon Paudler
Chef/Instructor,
Culinary Arts
Northern Alberta
Institute of Technology
Edmonton, Alberta*

1	medium onion, chopped	1
2 tbsp	vegetable oil	25 mL
1 tbsp	curry powder	15 mL
1/2 tsp	granulated sugar	2 mL
3	medium potatoes, cut into wedges, slices or cubes	3
3/4 cup	water	175 mL
	Salt	

Dietitian:

*Leslie Maze, RD
Diabetes Outpatient
Clinic
Royal Alexandra
Hospital
Edmonton, Alberta*

In skillet or wok over medium heat, stir-fry onion in oil until tender. Add curry and sugar; stir-fry 1 minute, ensuring curry doesn't burn. Add potatoes; stir-fry until coated, about 2 minutes.

Add water and bring to boil; cover, reduce heat and simmer 8 to 10 minutes or until potatoes are tender. Uncover and simmer until liquid evaporates. Season with salt to taste.

Makes 4 servings.

This wonderful pungent side dish is even better when reheated the next day. Microwave, covered, at Medium until hot.

Per serving:

174 Calories
3 g protein
7 g fat
26 g carbohydrate
2 g fibre

Sweet Baked Tomatoes

The tomatoes serve as the holder for the fruit-and-nut filling— a tasty combination and a different way to serve tomatoes!

Chef:

Ralph Graham
Instructor
Culinary Arts Foundation
of Saskatchewan
Saskatoon, Saskatchewan

Dietitian:

Rosanne E. Maluk, P.Dt.
Food Focus
Saskatoon Inc.
Saskatoon, Saskatchewan

Tomatoes with a "twist"—this may be served at room temperature, or chilled for those hot summer days.

4	medium tomatoes	4
1/4 cup	sultana raisins	50 mL
1/4 cup	currants	50 mL
2 tbsp	liquid honey	25 mL
1 tbsp	lemon juice	15 mL
1/4 tsp	cinnamon	1 mL
1/4 tsp	ginger	1 mL
1/4 cup	chopped walnuts or pecans, lightly toasted	50 mL
	Salt	
1/2 cup	apple cider or juice	125 mL
	Grated orange rind or 4 mint leaves	

Slice tops off tomatoes; seed, scoop out pulp and reserve. Invert tomato shells on paper towels to drain, at least 15 minutes.

In bowl, coarsely mash tomato pulp; stir in raisins, currants, honey, lemon juice, cinnamon and ginger. Refrigerate 1 hour to allow flavors to blend. Stir in nuts.

Sprinkle inside of each tomato shell lightly with salt; evenly spoon in raisin mixture. Place in small baking dish or pie pan; drizzle cider over and around tomatoes. Bake at 325°F (160°C) for 15 to 20 minutes or just until soft.

With slotted spoon, transfer tomatoes to serving dish or small individual dishes, reserving juice. Cover tomatoes and juice; refrigerate at least 2 hours or until thoroughly chilled. At serving time, drizzle some juice over each tomato and garnish with orange rind or mint.

Makes 4 servings.

Per serving:

177 Calories
3 g protein
5 g fat
34 g carbohydrate
3 g fibre

Vegetable and Fennel Stew

Here's a one-pot recipe that's ready in less than 20 minutes and takes advantage of the taste and nutritional value of fall vegetables.

Chef:

Guy Blain
Chef/Owner
Restaurant L'Orée
du bois
Chelsea, Québec

Dietitian:

Debra Reid, Ph.D., RD
Ottawa–Carleton
Health Dept.
Ottawa, Ontario

To make this hearty stew the centerpiece of your meal, add other food groups, like hummus on whole grain bread.

I		large onion, quartered and thinly sliced	I
I tbsp		olive oil	15 mL
8		cloves garlic, chopped	8
2 cups		sliced small zucchini	500 mL
I cup		diced fresh fennel	250 mL
I		each medium sweet green and red pepper, cut in julienne strips	I
I		can (28 oz/796 mL) tomatoes, diced	I
I tsp		fennel seeds	5 mL
I tsp		salt	5 mL
1/4 tsp		pepper	I mL

In Dutch oven, sauté onion in oil until tender. Stir in garlic, zucchini, fennel, green and red peppers, tomatoes and fennel seeds; simmer, uncovered, until desired consistency and vegetables are tender, about 15 minutes. Season with salt and pepper.
    Makes 6 servings.

Tip: Substitute 3 medium seeded tomatoes for canned tomatoes, if desired. Add along with other vegetables; sauté 3 to 4 minutes, stirring constantly. Cover and simmer 10 minutes.

Per serving:

84 Calories
3 g protein
3 g fat
15 g carbohydrate
4 g fibre

Sunflower Seed and Orange Broccoli

Orange and lemon juice are combined with mustard, herbs and spices to give broccoli a new taste partner. Toasted sunflower seeds provide the finishing touch.

Chef:

Murray Henderson,
CFM,
Foodservice Director
ManuLife Financial
Waterloo, Ontario

1	bunch broccoli, cut into florettes	1
2 tbsp	orange juice	25 mL
2 tsp	lemon juice	10 mL
1 tbsp	vegetable oil	15 mL
1-1/2 tsp	granulated sugar	2 mL
1/2 tsp	crushed dried basil	2 mL
1/4 tsp	coarsely ground black pepper	1 mL
1/4 tsp	Dijon mustard	1 mL
2 tbsp	unsalted shelled sunflower seeds	25 mL

Dietitian:

Carole Doucet Love, RD
Public Health
Nutritionist
Waterloo Region
Community Health
Department
Waterloo, Ontario

This recipe is a delicious answer to dietitians' calls for all of us to eat more vegetables.

In saucepan of boiling water, blanch broccoli for 2 minutes or until tender-crisp. Drain and refresh in cold water; set aside.

In small bowl, combine orange and lemon juices, oil, sugar, basil, pepper and mustard; whisk until blended. In nonstick skillet lightly coated with vegetable oil spray, toast sunflower seeds over medium heat.

In skillet, drizzle broccoli with juice mixture; cover and heat 3 to 5 minutes or until heated through. Sprinkle with sunflower seeds.

Makes 6 servings.

Per serving:

57 Calories
2 g protein
4 g fat
4 g carbohydrate
2 g fibre

Oven-Dried Tomatoes

Consider these Oven-Dried Tomatoes somewhere in between fresh and sun-dried, with a flavor all their own.

Chef:

Wayne Fagan, Chef
Galt Country Club
Cambridge, Ontario

2 tbsp	dried basil	25 mL
2 tbsp	dried parsley	25 mL
	Salt and pepper	
12	plum tomatoes, halved	12

Mix together basil, parsley, and salt and pepper to taste: sprinkle on tomatoes. Place cut side up on wire rack over baking pan. Bake at 200°F (100°C) for 6 hours.

Makes 6 side-dish servings.

Variation: Slice tomatoes lengthwise into 1/4-inch (5 mm) thick slices. Prepare as above. Bake for 8 hours. Use in recipes calling for sun-dried tomatoes.

Tip: Dry tomatoes when they are in season for their greatest flavor.

Dietitian:

Mary Margaret Laing,
RD
President
M.M. Laing & Associates
Healthcare Marketing
Services
Cambridge, Ontario

A versatile tomato alternative: a great side dish arranged like a flower on lettuce, or a tasty, economical substitute for sun-dried tomatoes in your favorite recipe.

Per serving:

26 Calories
1 g protein
trace fat
6 g carbohydrate
2 g fibre

Zucchini Spaghetti with Two Sauces

If you've got a food processor, put it to work in this recipe! Thin slices of zucchini double for spaghetti and are topped with both white and tomato sauces.

Chef:

Hans Hartman, CCC
Instructor, Cook Training
Okanagan University
College
Kelowna,
British Columbia

Dietitian:

Donna Antonishak, RDN
Community Nutritionist
North Okanagan Health
Unit
Vernon, British Columbia

4	medium zucchini, trimmed	4
1 tbsp	butter	15 mL
	White Sauce:	
1 tbsp	butter	15 mL
1/2 cup	finely chopped carrots	125 mL
1/4 tsp	crushed dried thyme	1 mL
1	bay leaf	1
1/2 cup	dry white wine	125 mL
1 tbsp	all-purpose flour	15 mL
1-1/2 cups	2% milk	375 mL
1 tbsp	lemon juice	15 mL
1 tsp	chopped fresh chives or green onion	5 mL
1/4 tsp	each salt and pepper	1 mL
	Tomato Sauce:	
1	can (7-1/2 oz/213 mL) tomato sauce	1
1 tsp	dried basil	5 mL

Cut zucchini lengthwise into very thin slices; cut into thin spaghetti-like strands. Set aside.

White Sauce: In skillet, melt butter over medium heat; add carrots, thyme and bay leaf. Cover and cook for 3 to 5 minutes, stirring occasionally. Add wine; simmer, uncovered, until wine is reduced by half.

Dissolve flour in milk; stir into skillet and bring to boil. Simmer until slightly thickened. Remove bay leaf. Pour into food processor and blend until smooth. Add lemon juice, chives, salt and pepper; keep warm.

Tomato Sauce: In small saucepan, gently bring tomato sauce and basil to boil; keep warm.

In large skillet, melt butter over medium-high heat; sauté zucchini about 2 minutes or until slightly softened. Do not overcook. Drain off any liquid.

To serve, divide zucchini among 4 plates; swirl with fork. Top with white sauce; drizzle with tomato sauce.

Makes 4 servings.

Per serving:

161 Calories
5 g protein
8 g fat
18 g carbohydrate
4 g fibre

PASTA, GRAINS & LEGUMES

Farfalle with Snow Peas, Chèvre and Tomato Coulis

Zucchini, Tomato and Basil Fettuccine

Whole Wheat Spaghetti with Scallops

Garden Fresh Fettuccine

Smoked Salmon and Shiitake Mushrooms in Tomato Saffron Sauce with Pasta

Spaghetti with Zucchini Balls and Tomato Sauce

Ham and Mushroom Fettuccine

Linguine with Hazelnuts and Roasted Garlic

Fresh Beet Pasta with Goat Cheese

Broccoli, Yams and Mushrooms with Noodles

Pasta with Chicken and Apples

Cumin Shrimp Linguine

Pasta Shells Stuffed with Three Cheeses and Sun-dried Tomatoes

Roast Lamb Loin with Tomato Basil Linguine

Aphrodite's Pasta

The Goodness of Grain

Grains, fruits and vegetables are the foundation of all healthy diets world-wide. Almost every region and culture in the world has a staple grain that has featured prominently in its cuisine for centuries: wheat in the Mediterranean, corn in Latin America, rice and millet in Asia, and rye and buckwheat in Eastern Europe. Aside from their role in countless pastas, breads and other flour-based products, whole grains are ideal for breakfast, cereals, pilafs, salads, soups, casseroles, stuffings and desserts.

While evidence suggests that health-conscious Canadian consumers are eating more fruits and vegetables, our intake of grains is limited and falls short of current recommendations.

Why are grains so versatile and so highly regarded by nutrition professionals? The answer lies in the fact that grains are rich in nutrients—complex carbohydrates, B vitamins, iron and fibre. Whole grains are high in fibre and may help lower blood cholesterol and maintain bowel regularity. They also contain vitamin E and important trace minerals like copper and zinc. Even refined grains, which are often enriched to compensate for some of the vitamins and minerals that have been removed, are an economical source of long-lasting energy. All grains are naturally low in fat.

Carbohydrates can be simple or complex sugars or starches. For years, complex carbohydrates such as grains (wheat, oats, rice, wild rice, barley, buckwheat) and grain-based foods (breads, rolls, muffins, cereals and pastas) were considered the ugly ducklings of nutrition. Thought to be fattening with little nutritional value, these foods were often avoided in misguided efforts to control weight.

Today, dietitians are quick to point out that in order to meet current dietary recommendations, Canadians should be obtaining more calories from complex carbohydrates and fewer calories from fat and protein. In fact, the arc representing Grain Products in "Canada's Food Guide to Healthy Eating" is the largest arc of the rainbow and suggests that grain products should be the focus of daily nutrition. Because we need to choose 5 to 12 servings from this food group daily, the Food Guide challenges Canadians to start to look at meal planning in a new way. Rather than beginning with meat, why not consider your grains choice first? Make the rice, pasta, bread or cereal the centre of the meal, and then add meat or a meat alternative and vegetables to achieve a satisfying, budget-friendly balance.

The key to enjoying carbohydrates is to avoid the high-fat toppings, spreads and sauces. Bread can be brushed lightly with an unsaturated fat such as olive oil and garlic and grilled. Great breads like Icelandic Three-Grain Brown Bread and Herb Grain Bread need no accompaniment at all—they're tasty all by themselves. Pasta doesn't need a heavy cream sauce: it can be tomatoes, vegetables, seasonings, or small amounts of fish, meat, poultry or grated cheese. Chicken with Spinach Fettuccine is a great example. Recipes for cookies, muffins and loaves can be modified easily to accent the carbohydrates and lower the fat.

Not too long ago, it was difficult to find a good variety of whole grains in local stores. Today, most supermarkets carry a full range of products. Because of their oil content, whole grains are more susceptible to rancidity. It's a good idea to store whole grains packaged airtight in the refrigerator or freezer. Remember to rotate your grain supply, using the oldest ones first.

Ellen Vogel, RD
Winnipeg, Manitoba

Farfalle with Snow Peas, Chèvre and Tomato Coulis

Farfalle (bow tie pasta) and chèvre (goat cheese) can be found in most supermarkets and add a sophisticated note to this elegant recipe.

Chef:

Kenneth Peace, CCC
Chef de Cuisine
O'Keefe Centre for the
Performing Arts
Toronto, Ontario

Dietitian:

Maye Musk, RD
Maye Musk Nutrition
Consultants
Toronto, Ontario

When you're serving pasta, remember that whole wheat pasta and different vegetables, herbs and spices add both flavor and variety.

4 cups	farfalle (bow tie) pasta (about 1/2 lb/250 g)	1 L
1 tbsp	olive oil	15 mL
8 oz	snow peas	250 g
1 tbsp	crushed dried basil	15 mL
	Salt and pepper	
4 oz	chèvre, crumbled (or shredded mozzarella)	125 g

Tomato Coulis:		
1/2 cup	diced shallots	125 mL
1/4 cup	diced celery	50 mL
1	can (28 oz/796 mL) tomatoes	1
2	cloves garlic, minced	2
2 tbsp	chopped fresh parsley	25 mL
1 tbsp	crushed dried basil	15 mL
2 tsp	brown sugar	10 mL
1/4 tsp	each salt and pepper	1 mL

Tomato Coulis: In large skillet, combine shallots, celery and 1/4 cup (50 mL) water; cook over medium heat until soft. Add tomatoes, garlic, parsley, basil, sugar, salt and pepper; bring to boil. Reduce heat and simmer for 10 minutes, stirring occasionally. Purée in food processor or blender. Keep warm.

Cook pasta according to package directions; drain.

In large skillet, heat olive over medium heat; cook snow peas with basil, stirring, for 3 to 5 minutes or until tender. Stir in pasta. Season with salt and pepper to taste.

To serve, place tomato coulis in pasta bowl; top with pasta mixture. Sprinkle with chèvre.

Makes 4 servings.

Tip: Baked garlic may be tossed with pasta, if desired. Place 12 cloves garlic in foil with 1 tsp (5 mL) olive oil. Bake at 325°F (160°C) until soft, about 20 minutes.

Per serving:

432 Calories
17 g protein
11 g fat
67 g carbohydrate
7 g fibre

Zucchini, Tomato and Basil Fettuccine

Nothing could be easier than this quick recipe. Make it when tomatoes, zucchini and basil are in season for maximum flavor.

Chef:

Barb Armstrong
Chef/Instructor
Spectrum Community
School
Victoria,
British Columbia

6 oz	fettuccine pasta	175 g
2 tbsp	olive oil	25 mL
2	cloves garlic, minced	2
1	medium zucchini, diced	1
4	medium tomatoes, seeded and chopped	4
2 tsp	crushed dried basil	10 mL
1/4 tsp	granulated sugar	1 mL
1/4 tsp	each salt and pepper	1 mL
1/4 cup	chopped fresh parsley	50 mL
3 tbsp	grated Parmesan cheese	50 mL

Cook fettuccine according to package directions; drain.

Meanwhile, in skillet, heat oil over medium-high heat; sauté garlic and zucchini for 3 to 5 minutes until softened.

Stir in tomatoes, basil, sugar, salt and pepper; cook for 3 to 4 minutes.

Toss with cooked pasta, parsley and cheese.

Makes 4 servings.

Dietitian:

Marianna Fiocco, RDN
Consulting Dietitian
Westcoast Dietetics Ltd.
Vancouver,
British Columbia

The basil and parsley give this dish lots of flavor, so use the Parmesan cheese sparingly.

Per serving:

272 Calories
9 g protein
9 g fat
39 g carbohydrate
4 g fibre

Whole Wheat Spaghetti with Scallops

Whole wheat spaghetti, available both dry and fresh, is an interesting change and goes well with the flavors of the peppers and scallops.

Chef:

Ron Glover
Chef/Instructor
Southern Alberta
Institute of Technology
Edmonton, Alberta

Dietitian:

Mary Sue Waisman, RD
Nutrition Coordinator
Nutrition and Food
Services
Calgary Regional Health
Authority
Calgary, Alberta

12 oz	whole wheat spaghetti	375 g
2 tbsp	olive oil	25 mL
1	medium red onion, chopped	1
1	each medium red, green and yellow pepper, cut into thin strips	1
12	mushrooms, sliced	12
2	cloves garlic, minced	2
2 tsp	dried basil	10 mL
1/2 tsp	salt	2 mL
1/4 tsp	pepper	1 mL
Pinch	cayenne	Pinch
1-1/2 lb	scallops	625 g
3	medium tomatoes, seeded and chopped	3
	Chopped fresh parsley and basil	3

Cook spaghetti according to package directions; drain.

Meanwhile, in large skillet, heat oil over medium-high heat. Sauté onion, peppers and mushrooms for 5 to 8 minutes or until tender. Stir in garlic, basil, salt, pepper and cayenne. Add scallops and heat until white but tender, 3 to 5 minutes. Add tomatoes and heat through.

Toss with pasta and garnish with chopped parsley and basil.
Makes 6 servings.

Per serving:

382 Calories
27 g protein
7 g fat
58 g carbohydrate
10 g fibre

Grilled Vegetable Souvlaki with Feta Tzatziki (page 72)
Overleaf: Easy Risotto Provençale (page 106)
Overleaf: Broccoli, Yams and Mushrooms with Noodles (page 98)

Garden Fresh Fettuccine

Here's a simple recipe that takes advantage of seasonal vegetables in a colorful medley.

Chef:

Eric Fergie, Chef/Owner
Fettucini's Café
Vancouver,
British Columbia

4 cups	julienned vegetables (peppers, broccoli or cauliflower florettes, zucchini, red onion, carrots, celery, sliced mushrooms)	1 L
12 oz	fettuccine (or 3 cups/750 mL) penne pasta	375 g
	Grated Parmesan cheese	

Dietitian:

Jane Thornthwaite, RDN
Nutrition Consultant
Fresh Choice Restaurant
Program
Vancouver,
British Columbia

Sauce:

1 cup	vegetable stock or water	250 mL
1/4 cup	white wine	50 mL
1	clove garlic, minced	1
1 tbsp	chopped fresh parsley	15 mL
1 tbsp	dried basil	15 mL
2 tsp	lemon juice	10 mL
1 tsp	each crushed dried oregano, thyme and tarragon	5 mL
3/4 tsp	crumbled dried rosemary	5 mL

By selecting fresh herbs and vegetables, you won't even miss the fat in this delicious Italian favorite.

Sauce: In large skillet, combine stock, wine, garlic, parsley, basil, lemon juice, oregano, thyme, tarragon and rosemary; bring to boil.

Add firmer vegetables; cover and simmer for 5 minutes. Add softer vegetables; simmer for 5 more minutes.

Meanwhile, cook fettuccine according to package directions; drain. Toss with vegetables. Garnish with cheese.

Makes 4 main-course servings.

Tip: Fresh herbs may be used instead of dried, but use three times as much.

Sesame Steak (page 127) with
Garlic Herb Potato Purée (page 73) and
Stuffed Tomatoes (page 69)

Smoked Salmon and Shiitake Mushrooms in Tomato Saffron Sauce with Pasta

You can reduce the cost of this elegant recipe by using smoked salmon bits instead of the more expensive sliced salmon, and white or brown mushrooms rather than shiitake.

Chef:

Hans Hartmann, CCC
Instructor, Cook Training
Okanagan University
College
Kelowna,
British Columbia

Dietitian:

Donna Antonishak, RDN
Community Nutritionist
North Okanagan Health
Unit
Vernon, British Columbia

When served in this delicious lower fat sauce, salmon offers a high level of nutrition for few calories.

Per serving:

497 Calories
25 g protein
8 g fat
81 g carbohydrate
8 g fibre

1 tbsp	olive oil	15 mL
1	medium onion, diced	1
1	stalk celery, diced	1
1	medium carrot, diced	1
4	cloves garlic, minced	4
1	large shallot, diced	1
1	can (28 oz/796 mL) tomatoes	1
2 cups	vegetable stock (see recipe on next page)	500 mL
6 oz	shiitake mushrooms, stems discarded, coarsely sliced	175 g
2 tbsp	lemon juice	25 mL
1/4 tsp	ground saffron	1 mL
8 oz	smoked salmon, slivered	250 g
2 tbsp	chopped fresh Italian parsley	25 mL
1 tsp	grated lemon rind	5 mL
12 oz	tagliatelle (or fettuccine) pasta	375 g

In large skillet, heat oil over medium-high heat; cook onion, celery and carrot, stirring, for 2 minutes. Add garlic and shallot; cook 1 minute.

Purée tomatoes with juice; add to skillet along with vegetable stock, mushrooms, lemon juice and saffron. Bring to boil; reduce heat and simmer, uncovered, until reduced by half, about 25 minutes. Stir in salmon, parsley and lemon rind; heat through.

Meanwhile, cook pasta according to package directions. Drain and place on 4 serving plates. Top with sauce.

Makes 4 servings.

Vegetable Stock:

3 cups	cold water	750 mL
1	medium carrot, sliced	1
1	stalk celery, sliced	1
1	medium onion, chopped	1
1	leek (white part only), sliced	1
1	bay leaf	1
1 tsp	crumbled dried rosemary	5 mL
1/2 tsp	crushed dried thyme	2 mL

In saucepan, combine water, carrot, celery, onion, leek, bay leaf, rosemary and thyme; bring to boil. Reduce heat and simmer, uncovered, for 30 minutes until reduced to three-quarters of original volume. Strain.

Makes 2 cups (500 mL).

Spaghetti with Zucchini Balls and Tomato Sauce

You might consider this flavorful vegetarian recipe a falafel on pasta! It's a sure winner with kids and adults alike.

Chef:

Kim Densmore
Sous Chef
Vance Creek Hotel
Silver Star Mountain
Okanagan,
British Columbia

Dietitian:

Cathy Richards, RDN
Community Nutritionist
South Okanagan Health
Unit
Kelowna,
British Columbia

This recipe is a fun way to get the family to eat a vegetarian meal, to increase their intake of vegetables and to expand their spice repertoire.

1 tsp	olive oil	5 mL
1	medium onion, finely chopped	1
1	can (28 oz/796 mL) crushed tomatoes	1
3	cloves garlic, minced	3
1 tsp	crushed dried oregano	5 mL
1 tsp	ground cumin	5 mL
1	stick (5-inch/12 cm) cinnamon	1
1/4 tsp	granulated sugar	1 mL
1/4 tsp	each salt and pepper	1 mL
12 oz	spaghetti	375 g

Zucchini Balls:

3 cups	shredded zucchini (2 medium), drained	750 mL
1 cup	drained chick-peas	250 mL
1	slice whole wheat bread, crumbled	1
3/4 cup	quick-cooking rolled oats	175 mL
1/2 cup	cornmeal	125 mL
2	cloves garlic, minced	2
1 tsp	ground cumin	5 mL
1/2 tsp	each ground coriander and ginger	2 mL
1/2 tsp	each salt and pepper	2 mL
1/4 tsp	cardamom	1 mL
2	eggs, lightly beaten	2
	Grated Parmesan cheese (optional)	

In large skillet, heat oil over medium-high heat; sauté onion for 3 minutes. Add tomatoes, garlic, oregano, cumin, cinnamon, sugar, salt and pepper; bring to boil. Reduce heat and simmer, uncovered, for 30 minutes, stirring occasionally. Remove cinnamon stick.

Zucchini Balls: Squeeze out excess moisture from zucchini. Purée half of the chick-peas. Mix all ingredients together well.

In bowl, mix together zucchini, puréed and whole chick-peas, bread, rolled oats, cornmeal, garlic, cumin, coriander, ginger, salt, pepper, cardamom and eggs. Form into 1-inch (2.5 cm) balls; place on greased baking sheet. Bake at 400°F (200°C) for 10 to 15 minutes or until lightly browned.

Meanwhile, cook spaghetti according to package directions; drain and arrange on 4 plates. Spoon tomato sauce over spaghetti; top with zucchini balls. Serve with Parmesan cheese, if desired.

Makes 4 servings.

Per serving:

632 Calories
24 g protein
8 g fat
117 g carbohydrate
12 g fibre

Ham and Mushroom Fettuccine

Ingredients you're likely to have on hand can still star in recipes, as this quick and easy dish proves.

Chef:

Beth Van Arenthals
Food Service
Supervisor/Chef
Fiddick's Nursing and
Retirement Home
Petrolia, Ontario

12 oz	fettuccine pasta	375 g
1 tbsp	olive oil	15 mL
2 cups	sliced mushrooms	500 mL
1/2 cup	slivered sweet green pepper	125 mL
2 tbsp	white wine	25 mL
6 oz	lean ham, cut in thin strips	175 g
2 tbsp	all-purpose flour	25 mL
1-1/2 cups	2% milk	375 mL
1/2 tsp	dried basil	2 mL
1/4 tsp	each salt and white pepper	1 mL
1/2 cup	chopped green onions	125 mL

Dietitian:

Connie Mallette, RD
Nutrition Educator
Lambton County Health
Unit
Point Edward, Ontario

A lower fat version of a higher fat favorite.

Cook fettuccine according to package directions. Drain well.

Meanwhile, in large skillet, heat oil over medium-high heat; cook mushrooms and green pepper, stirring, for 3 minutes. Stir in wine; simmer for a few minutes until reduced. Stir in ham.

Dissolve flour in milk; stir into skillet along with basil, salt and pepper. Bring to boil, stirring constantly. Stir in green onions; cook 1 minute longer. Stir in fettuccine.

Makes 4 servings.

Tips: Instead of wine, you can use 2 tbsp (25 mL) water and 1/2 tsp (2 mL) lemon juice.
1% milk may be used instead but sauce will be thinner.

Per serving:

478 Calories
23 g protein
9 g fat
74 g carbohydrate
5 g fibre

Linguine with Hazelnuts and Roasted Garlic

A pasta without a sauce? Sure thing, and you won't miss it in this flavorful recipe seasoned with garlic and balsamic vinegar!

Chef:

Tim Wood
Chef/Instructor,
Culinary Arts
Northern Alberta
Institute of Technology
Edmonton, Alberta

Dietitian:

Leslie Maze, RD
Diabetes Outpatient
Clinic
Royal Alexandra
Hospital
Edmonton, Alberta

Definitely not a low-fat dish. Treat yourself to this delicacy when you've had a really good spell of low-fat eating.

2	bulbs garlic	2
3/4 cup	whole hazelnuts	175 mL
12 oz	linguine pasta	375 g
1/4 cup	olive oil	50 mL
1/4 cup	chopped fresh parsley	50 mL
2 tbsp	balsamic vinegar	25 mL
1/4 tsp	salt	1 mL
	Pepper	
1/3 cup	grated Parmesan cheese	75 mL

Slice 1/4 inch (5 mm) off top of garlic bulbs; wrap in foil. Bake at 350°F (180°C) for about 30 minutes or until very soft. Cool. Squeeze out garlic; mash with fork and set aside.

Spread hazelnuts on baking sheet. Toast at 350°F (180°C) for 10 to 15 minutes or until fragrant. Immediately roll nuts in kitchen towel against work surface to loosen skins. Remove skins with towel and fingers. Crush nuts in food processor.

Cook linguine according to package directions; drain.

In large bowl, combine garlic, oil, parsley, vinegar, salt, pepper to taste and three-quarters of the hazelnuts. Add linguine and toss to coat. Garnish with remaining nuts and cheese.

Makes 6 servings.

Per serving:

450 Calories
12 g protein
24 g fat
48 g carbohydrate
4 g fibre

Fresh Beet Pasta with Goat Cheese

Here's your chance to make your own pasta using a pasta machine. To roast garlic, wrap garlic bulbs in foil and bake at 350°F (180°C) about 30 minutes, until soft and fragrant.

Chef:

Mark Mogensen
Chef
HealthWinds
Therapeutic Spa
Toronto, Ontario

Dietitian:

Marsha Rosen, RD
Consulting Dietitian
HealthWinds
Therapeutic Spa
Toronto, Ontario

A creamy pasta dish that is high in flavor and low in fat.

3 cups	all-purpose flour	750 mL
1 tsp	salt	5 mL
1/2 cup	drained pickled beets	125 mL
1/2 cup	water	125 mL
2	egg whites	2

	Sauce:	
1	large (unpeeled) apple, diced	1
1-1/4 cups	apple juice	300 mL
1 tsp	crushed dried thyme	5 mL
1/4 tsp	nutmeg	1 mL
1 tbsp	roasted garlic	15 mL
2 cups	coarsely chopped Swiss chard, beet greens or spinach	500 mL
1 tbsp	goat cheese	15 mL

In food processor, pulse flour and salt to blend. Add beets, water and egg whites; process 30 seconds or until dough forms ball.

Set pasta machine rollers to widest setting. Divide dough into about 8 pieces. Working with one piece at a time, flatten slightly and lightly dust with flour; pass through machine. Fold in half; pass through machine again. Repeat rolling and folding 6 to 8 times.

Adjust rollers to next smallest setting; feed sheet, without folding, through machine. Continue to reduce thickness and roll sheet until pasta is desired thickness. Cut sheet in half for easier manageability; run through cutting rollers of pasta machine. Repeat with remaining dough.

Sauce: In large skillet or Dutch oven, sauté apple over high heat for 30 seconds. Pour in apple juice and bring to rapid boil. Add thyme and nutmeg; stir in garlic and Swiss chard. Cook until apple juice has reduced to about 2 tbsp (25 mL) and Swiss chard is tender.

Meanwhile, in saucepan of rapidly boiling water, cook pasta just until al dente, 3 to 5 minutes. Drain and toss with apple mixture and goat cheese.

Makes 4 servings.

Per serving:

453 Calories
13 g protein
2 g fat
94 g carbohydrate
5 g fibre

Broccoli, Yams and Mushrooms with Noodles

Here's a pasta with an oriental touch! You can use other vegetables (either fresh or frozen), such as sliced carrots, green beans, cauliflower or peas.

Chef:

Stephen Ashton
Head Chef/Instructor
Picasso Café
Vancouver,
British Columbia

Dietitian:

Leah Hawirko, RDN
Leah Hawirko Nutrition
Consulting and
The Vancouver Health
Department
Vancouver,
British Columbia

Packed with flavor, vitamins and minerals, this colorful one-pot meal includes dark green and orange vegetables that are recommended daily for optimum health.

2 cups	egg noodles or other pasta	500 mL
2	cloves garlic, sliced	2
1	yam (unpeeled), quartered and cut into 1/4-inch (5 mm) thick slices	1
1 cup	broccoli florettes	250 mL
1 cup	quartered mushrooms	250 mL
1 cup	shredded mozzarella cheese	250 mL
2 tbsp	light soy sauce	25 mL
1/4 tsp	crushed dried thyme	1 mL
1/4 tsp	pepper	1 mL

In large saucepan of boiling water, cook noodles and garlic for 4 minutes. Add yams; cook for 4 minutes. Add broccoli and mushrooms; cook for 2 minutes or until all vegetables are tender. Drain well.

In bowl, toss together noodle mixture, cheese, soy sauce, thyme and pepper until cheese melts.

Makes 4 servings.

Per serving:

207 Calories
10 g protein
8 g fat
24 g carbohydrate
2 g fibre

Pasta with Chicken and Apples

Chicken and apples are paired in many recipes, but you may not have thought of them as a topping for pasta.

Chef:

Howard Selig
Chef/Owner
Finest Kind Food Co.
Middleton, Nova Scotia

Dietitian:

Tricia Cochrane, P.Dt.
Soldiers Memorial
Hospital
Middleton, Nova Scotia

The inclusion of apple to this chicken dish adds a new flavor and flair.

12 oz	fettuccine or linguine pasta	375 g
1 tbsp	vegetable oil	15 mL
3/4 lb	boneless skinless chicken breasts, cut in thin strips	375 g
1	small onion, diced	1
1 cup	sliced mushrooms	250 mL
2 tbsp	all-purpose flour	25 mL
1-1/2 cups	chicken broth	375 mL
1	medium (unpeeled) apple, chopped	1
1/4 cup	apple juice	50 mL
1/2 tsp	crushed dried thyme	2 mL
1/4 tsp	pepper	1 mL
	Chopped fresh parsley (optional)	

Cook fettuccine according to package directions; drain well.

Meanwhile, in large skillet, heat oil over medium-high heat; brown chicken with onion, about 3 minutes. Add mushrooms; sauté 2 minutes.

Dissolve flour in chicken broth; add to skillet and cook, stirring, until bubbling and slightly thickened. Stir in apple, apple juice, thyme and pepper; heat through for 2 minutes. Serve over fettuccine. Garnish with parsley, if desired.

Makes 4 servings.

Per serving:

506 Calories
33 g protein
7 g fat
76 g carbohydrate
5 g fibre

Cumin Shrimp Linguine

This elegant recipe serves two and is ready in a matter of minutes.

Chef:

Eric Fergie, Chef/Owner
Fettucini's Café
Vancouver,
British Columbia

8 oz	linguine pasta	250 g
3/4 cup	vegetable or chicken broth	175 mL
1 tsp	ground cumin	5 mL
1/4 to 1/2 tsp	crushed red chilies	1 to 2 mL
1 cup	sliced mushrooms	250 mL
1/2 cup	sliced green onions	125 mL
1/2 lb	large shrimp, peeled and deveined	250 g
1 tbsp	cornstarch	15 mL
1 tbsp	cold water	15 mL

Dietitian:

Jane Thornthwaite, RDN
Nutrition Consultant
Fresh Choice Restaurant
Program
Vancouver,
British Columbia

This hot shrimp linguine dish is high in protein, low in fat, and has lots of fibre.

Cook linguine according to package directions; drain well.

Meanwhile, in skillet, bring broth, cumin and chilies to boil. Add mushrooms; simmer 3 minutes. Add green onion and shrimp; cook until shrimp turn pink. Combine cornstarch and water; stir into skillet until thickened. Divide linguine between 2 plates; top with shrimp sauce.

Makes 2 servings.

Per serving:

552 Calories
33 g protein
4 g fat
93 g carbohydrate
6 g fibre

Pasta Shells Stuffed with Three Cheeses and Sun-dried Tomatoes

In this make-ahead dish, jumbo pasta shells are stuffed with ricotta, Cheddar and Parmesan cheeses, sun-dried tomatoes and herbs, then baked in a creamy sauce.

Chef:

John Schroder
J.P. Brothers Food
Management Services
Ltd.
Toronto, Ontario

Dietitian:

Susie Langley, M.S., RD
Nutrition Consultant
Toronto, Ontario

With a modified béchamel sauce, lower fat cheeses and fresh herbs, this meatless dish allows you to add your own signature tomato sauce.

24	jumbo pasta shells	24
2	cloves garlic	2
1/4 cup	chopped onion	50 ml
1 tbsp	olive oil	15 mL
1	can (14 oz/398 mL) tomato sauce	1
2 cups	5% ricotta cheese (475 g)	500 mL
3/4 cup	shredded light medium Cheddar	175 mL
1/2 cup	grated Parmesan cheese	125 mL
1/4 cup	diced sun-dried tomatoes	50 mL
2 tbsp	chopped fresh basil (or 2 tsp/10 mL dried)	25 mL
3 tbsp	chopped fresh parsley	50 mL
1 tbsp	finely chopped green onions	15 mL
1 tsp	coarsely ground black pepper	5 mL
1	egg, lightly beaten	1
1-2/3 cups	2% milk	400 mL
5 tsp	cornstarch	25 mL
1/2 tsp	salt	2 mL

Cook pasta shells according to package directions; drain.

In saucepan, sauté garlic and onion in oil until tender. Add tomato sauce; simmer over low heat 8 to 10 minutes until reduced slightly. Pour into 13 x 9-inch (3.5 L) baking dish.

Combine ricotta, 1/2 cup (125 mL) of the Cheddar, 1/4 cup (50 mL) of the Parmesan, sun-dried tomatoes, basil, 2 tbsp (25 mL) of the parsley, onions, 1/2 tsp (2 mL) of the pepper and egg. Spoon or pipe into shells; arrange shells in single layer over tomato sauce.

In medium saucepan, heat 1-1/2 cups (375 mL) of the milk. Whisk cornstarch into remaining milk; whisk into hot milk and cook, stirring, until sauce thickens and boils. Stir in salt and remaining Parmesan, parsley and pepper; cool 5 minutes. Pour over prepared shells. Cover with foil and refrigerate for up to 8 hours.

Bake shells at 350°F (180°C) for 40 to 45 minutes or until heated through and bubbly. Remove foil and sprinkle with remaining Cheddar; bake 2 to 3 minutes or just until Cheddar melts.

Makes 8 servings.

Per serving:

309 Calories
19 g protein
11 g fat
32 g carbohydrate
2 g fibre

Roast Lamb Loin with Tomato Basil Linguine

Flavored pastas, such as tomato basil linguine, are becoming more popular all the time. In this recipe, the pasta makes a perfect backdrop for the lamb.

Chef:

Trent Breares, Sous Chef
Saskatchewan Centre for
the Arts
Regina, Saskatchewan

Dietitian:

Thomas Hamilton, P.Dt.
Diabetes Nutrition
Educator
Regina Health District
Regina, Saskatchewan

Lamb loin is a nice lean alternative to beef or pork in this colorful pasta dish.

4 tsp	olive oil	20 mL
I	medium onion, chopped	I
I	medium tomato, chopped	I
1/2 cup	chopped fresh parsley	125 mL
4 tsp	dried basil	20 mL
I cup	dry white wine	250 mL
1/4 tsp	each salt and pepper	I mL
12 oz	tomato basil linguine or plain linguine pasta	375 g
4	frozen lamb loins, thawed (3 oz/85 or 90 g each)	4
1/4 cup	Dijon mustard	50 mL
1/3 cup	(approx.) fine dried bread crumbs	75 mL
	Fresh basil	

In skillet, heat 3 tsp (15 mL) of the oil over medium heat; cook onion, tomato, parsley and basil for 3 to 5 minutes or until tender. Stir in wine, salt and pepper; bring to boil, reduce heat and simmer until slightly thickened. Keep warm.

Cook linguine according to package directions; drain well.

Meanwhile, coat each lamb loin with mustard; roll in bread crumbs to coat well. In skillet, heat remaining 1 tsp (5 mL) oil over medium-high heat; brown lamb on all sides, about 5 minutes. Slice thinly.

Toss linguine with sauce; divide among 4 plates. Top with lamb. Garnish with fresh basil.

Makes 4 servings.

Per serving:

562 Calories

31 g protein

13 g fat

76 g carbohydrate

5 g fibre

Aphrodite's Pasta

Aphrodite was the Greek goddess of love, and this recipe makes two main-course servings — perfect for a romantic dinner!

Chef:

Leo Pantel
Executive Chef
Saskatchewan Centre for
the Arts
Regina, Saskatchewan

1/2 cup	2% milk	125 mL
4 tsp	cornstarch	20 mL
1 tsp	each finely minced gingerroot and garlic	5 mL
1/2 cup	1% plain yogurt	125 mL
1	small zucchini, cut into strips	1
3 cups	cooked, drained pasta (bows, shells or fusilli)	750 mL
	Pepper	
2 tbsp	coarsely chopped fresh parsley	25 mL
1/2 cup	diced seeded tomatoes	125 mL

Dietitian:

Patty Neuman, P.Dt.
Clinical Dietitian
Regina Health District
Regina, Saskatchewan

This is a classic pasta cream sauce made lower in fat by replacing cream with 2% milk and light plain yogurt.

In medium saucepan, mix milk and cornstarch until smooth; add ginger and garlic; bring to boil, stirring constantly until thickened.

Stir in yogurt and zucchini; simmer 2 to 3 minutes. Stir in pasta; simmer 1 to 2 minutes or until hot. Season with pepper to taste. Garnish with parsley and tomatoes.

Makes 4 side-dish servings or 2 main-course servings.

Tip: Approximately 2 cups (500 mL) small shells yields 3 cups (750 mL) cooked.

Per side-dish serving:

242 Calories
9 g protein
2 g fat
46 g carbohydrate
3 g fibre

Chicken with Spinach Fettuccine

The green-colored spinach fettuccine is served as a ring with the zesty chicken mixture in the middle!

Chef:

Robert Neil
Cook Supervisor
Joyceville Correctional
Institute
Joyceville, Ontario

Dietitian:

Denise Hargrove, RD
Public Health Dietitian
Kingston, Frontenac and
Lennox and Addington
Health Unit
Kingston, Ontario

Try this lower fat "cream" sauce as an alternative to high-fat pasta sauces. The unusual presentation is eye-appealing and easy.

12 oz	spinach fettuccine pasta	375 g
1 cup	chicken broth	250 mL
2 tbsp	cornstarch	25 mL
1 cup	1% milk	250 mL
1 tsp	vegetable oil	5 mL
8 oz	diced chicken	250 g
1	medium onion, diced	1
2 cups	sliced mushrooms	500 mL
1	clove garlic, minced	1
1	medium tomato, chopped	1
2 tbsp	lemon juice	25 mL
1 tsp	each dried basil and thyme	5 mL
1/4 tsp	salt	1 mL
Pinch	pepper	Pinch

Cook pasta according to package directions; drain well. Meanwhile, in large saucepan, bring chicken broth to boil. Dissolve cornstarch in milk; stir into broth. Bring to boil; simmer over low heat until thickened. Stir pasta into sauce.

Meanwhile, in large skillet, heat oil over medium-high heat; brown chicken with onion until chicken is no longer pink. Add mushrooms, cook 2 minutes. Add garlic and tomatoes; heat through. Stir in lemon juice, basil, thyme, salt and pepper.

Arrange pasta in ring around edge of plates. Place chicken mixture in centre.

Makes 4 servings.

Tip: Instead of spinach fettuccine, you can use 3-1/2 cup (875 mL) vegetable-flavored noodles such as tomato noodles.

Per serving:

459 Calories
29 g protein
5 g fat
75 g carbohydrate
5 g fibre

Turmeric Spaetzle

Spaetzle (little sparrow in German) is a tiny, light dumpling made from a runny pasta dough. Our variation of an Austrian recipe is flavored with turmeric, garlic and mint.

Chef:

Alastair Gray
Executive Chef
The York Club
Toronto, Ontario

Dietitian:

Mary Margaret Laing,
RD
M.M. Laing & Associates
Healthcare Marketing
Services
Cambridge, Ontario

Spaetzle is an economical alternative to traditional pasta, and the flavor in this version makes it a wonderful meal accompaniment. Try storing between two damp towels in the fridge for up to several days, and use it only as you need it.

2	eggs	2
2/3 cup	2% milk	150 mL
1-1/2 cups	all-purpose flour	375 mL
1/2 tsp	turmeric	2 mL
	Salt	
Pinch	ground mace or nutmeg	Pinch
1/4 cup	olive oil	50 mL
2	cloves garlic, minced	2
2 tbsp	chopped fresh mint (optional)	25 mL
	Pepper	

In mixing bowl, beat together eggs and milk. Combine flour, turmeric, 1/4 tsp (1 mL) salt and mace; gradually add to bowl, beating constantly on low speed until smooth and thick.

Place colander over large pot of boiling salted water. With rubber spatula, press the batter, in small batches, through colander, scraping particles off underneath so particles form drops of dough in water. Boil for 5 minutes.

With slotted spoon, remove to large bowl of ice water. Drain and spread on wet tea towel on baking sheet. Cover with another towel. Refrigerate until serving time or for several days.

In large skillet, heat olive oil over medium heat; cook garlic and spaetzle, stirring, until hot. Add mint; season with salt and pepper to taste.

Makes 6 servings.

Tip: Transferring to ice water after cooking prevents spaetzle from sticking together.

Per serving:

234 Calories
6 g protein
12 g fat
26 g carbohydrate
1 g fibre

Easy Risotto Provençale

Risotto is made with arborio rice, an Italian short-grain rice that has a very creamy texture when cooked, but should be firm to the tooth—al dente—when done. This recipe eliminates having to gradually add liquid while stirring.

Chef:

Ronald Davis
Executive Chef
Sheraton Parkway North
Richmond Hill, Ontario

Dietitian:

Debra McNair, RD
Consulting Dietitian
Toronto, Ontario

This vegetable and rice combo is a fine example of Mediterranean eating. Try it with your favorite baked or grilled fish.

2 tbsp	olive oil	25 mL
I	medium onion, chopped	I
I-I/4 cups	arborio rice	300 mL
2-I/2 cups	water	625 mL
I tsp	salt	5 mL
	Sauce:	
I tbsp	olive oil	15 mL
2	medium shallots, diced (or white part of 4 green onions)	2
2	cloves garlic, minced	2
I/2 cup	white wine	125 mL
4	medium tomatoes, peeled and chopped	4
I cup	quartered mushrooms	250 mL
2/3 cup	diced sweet green, red or yellow pepper	150 mL
I/2 cup	diced zucchini	125 mL
I tbsp	dried basil	15 mL
I tsp	each crushed dried oregano and thyme	5 mL
Pinch	each salt and pepper	Pinch
I/4 cup	chopped fresh parsley	50 mL
	Grated Parmesan cheese	

In medium saucepan, heat oil over medium heat; cook onion, stirring, for 3 minutes. Add rice; cook, stirring, until golden, about 5 minutes. Add water and salt; bring to boil. Reduce heat and simmer 15 to 18 minutes or just until al dente.

Sauce: Meanwhile, in medium saucepan, heat oil over medium heat; cook shallots and garlic, stirring, for 2 to 3 minutes or until softened. Stir in wine and tomatoes; cook 5 minutes. Stir in mushrooms, sweet pepper, zucchini, basil, oregano and thyme; simmer for 10 to 15 minutes until thickened slightly. Add salt and pepper.

Spoon rice into shape of ring on large warmed serving plate; spoon sauce into middle. Garnish with parsley and grated Parmesan cheese, if desired.

Makes 4 main-course servings.

Per serving:

375 Calories
6 g protein
II g fat
62 g carbohydrate
4 g fibre

Tip: You can substitute nonalcoholic wine or beef broth if you prefer.

Radicchio and Arugula Risotto

Radicchio and arugula are normally used to add a distinctive note to salads, and in this case to a classically prepared risotto.

Chef:

Rocco Suriano
Chef/Owner
Coco Pazzo Italian Café
Lethbridge, Alberta

Dietitian:

Denise Aucoin, RD,
CNSD
Consulting Dietitian
AuCoin Nutrition
Consulting/Haig Clinic
Associate
Lethbridge, Alberta

The bitter-tasting radicchio and the tangy mustard-green arugula adds to the flavor of this classical Italian dish.

2 tsp	olive oil	10 mL
1	small onion, chopped	1
1-1/2 cups	arborio rice	375 mL
3-1/2 cups	shredded radicchio	875 mL
2 cups	shredded arugula	500 mL
3 cups	chicken broth	750 mL
2 tbsp	grated Parmesan cheese	25 mL
	Salt and pepper	

In large saucepan, heat oil over medium heat; cook onion, stirring, until tender. Stir in rice and cook briefly. Add radicchio and arugula; mix well.

Add 1 cup (250 mL) of the broth; cook, stirring constantly, until absorbed. Continue to add broth 1/2 cup (125 mL) at a time, cooking and stirring constantly until each addition is absorbed before adding next. Total cooking time is 15 to 20 minutes or just until rice is tender. Stir in cheese. Season with salt and pepper to taste. Serve immediately.

Makes 8 servings.

Per serving:

177 Calories
6 g protein
2 g fat
32 g carbohydrate
1 g fibre

Brunch Rice Bake

Serve with a green salad for a brunch or light meal, and if you're pressed for time, prepare in advance, refrigerate, then bake just before serving.

Chef:

Louis Rodriguez
Executive Chef
Norwood Hotel
Winnipeg, Manitoba

Dietitian:

Joan Rew, RD
Co-op Coordinator,
Community Cooking
Nutrition Instructor
Red River Community
College
Winnipeg, Manitoba

This great-tasting dish features all of the four food groups which, when served with salad, makes it a complete meal deal!

2 cups	1% plain yogurt	500 mL
1/2 cup	chopped sweet green pepper	125 mL
1/2 cup	diced cooked chicken	125 mL
1/2 cup	diced cooked ham	125 mL
3 tbsp	ketchup	50 mL
1/2 tsp	crushed dried oregano	2 mL
1/4 tsp	pepper	1 mL
2 cups	cooked rice	500 mL
1 cup	light ricotta cheese	250 mL
1 cup	bread crumbs	250 mL
1/2 cup	grated Parmesan cheese	125 mL
1 tbsp	butter or margarine, melted	15 mL

In a bowl, combine yogurt, green pepper, chicken, ham, ketchup, oregano and pepper; stir in rice. Spoon half of the mixture into greased 6-cup (1.5 L) baking dish. Spoon ricotta cheese evenly on top. Top with remaining rice mixture.

Combine bread crumbs, cheese and butter; sprinkle over casserole. Bake at 350°F (180°C) for 25 to 30 minutes or until bubbling and golden brown.

Makes 4 servings.

Per serving:

438 Calories
31 g protein
15 g fat
44 g carbohydrate
1 g fibre

First Nations Wild Rice

Wild rice has been harvested and used by Canada's native people for centuries. Today, to stretch the budget, it's also combined with white or brown rice in many recipes.

Chef:

Jo-Anne Chalmers
Food Services
Manager/Chef
Dakota Oyate Lodge
Brandon, Manitoba

2-1/2 cups	water	625 mL
1 cup	wild rice	250 mL
1/2 tsp	salt	2 mL
1/2 cup	diced back bacon	125 mL
1/2 cup	chopped onion	125 mL
1/2 cup	diced celery	125 mL
1/2 cup	thinly sliced mushrooms	125 mL
2 tbsp	chopped fresh parsley	25 mL
1/2 cup	chicken stock (optional)	125 mL

Dietitian:

Christina Scheuer, RD
Community Dietitian
Sioux Valley Dakota
Nation
Griswold, Manitoba

In saucepan, bring water to boil; rinse rice under running water in strainer then add to water, with salt. Reduce heat, cover and simmer 45 minutes or until rice is tender. Drain off excess liquid.

Meanwhile, in skillet, cook bacon over medium heat until cooked through. Add onion, celery and mushrooms; cook, stirring, until tender. Stir into cooked rice along with parsley. Moisten with chicken stock, if desired.

Makes 6 servings.

Canadian back bacon tastes great and is a lower fat alternative to side bacon. Serve with a piece of warm bannock (see pages 115 and 118) for a traditional Sioux Valley Dakota Nation favorite.

Per serving:

121 Calories
6 g protein
1 g fat
22 g carbohydrate
2 g fibre

Wild Rice and Apple Pancakes

Unlike traditional batter pancakes, these are a perfect side dish to meat or poultry. You can cook the wild rice the day before to speed up the preparation time. Serve with maple syrup.

Chef:

Tim Wood
Chef/Instructor
Culinary Arts
North Alberta Institute
of Technology
Edmonton, Alberta

Dietitian:

Leslie Maze, RD
Diabetes Outpatient
Clinic
Royal Alexandra
Hospital
Edmonton, Alberta

Hold the butter for these pancakes with panache! Wild rice and apple add all the taste they need, as well as a healthy dose of fibre.

1 cup	water	250 mL
	Salt	
1/3 cup	wild rice	75 mL
1 tbsp	butter or margarine	15 mL
4	green onions, chopped	4
3	medium Granny Smith apples, peeled and diced	3
1-1/4 cups	all-purpose flour	300 mL
1 cup	whole wheat flour	250 mL
3/4 cup	cornmeal	175 mL
2 tbsp	baking powder	25 mL
1-1/2 tsp	brown sugar	7 mL
1 tsp	cinnamon	5 mL
4	eggs	4
2-1/2 cups	2% milk	625 mL
2 tbsp	butter or margarine, melted	25 mL

In small saucepan, bring water and pinch of salt to boil. Rinse rice under running water in strainer; add to pan and bring to boil. Cover and reduce heat to simmer 45 minutes or until tender but not mushy. Drain off excess liquid. Cool.

In skillet; melt 1 tbsp (15 mL) butter over medium heat; cook green onions and apples for 3 minutes. Cool.

In large bowl, mix together all-purpose and whole wheat flours, cornmeal, baking powder, sugar, 1 tsp (5 mL) salt and cinnamon. In another bowl, lightly beat eggs; blend in milk and melted butter. Stir into dry ingredients just until blended. Fold in rice and apple mixtures.

In lightly greased skillet or on griddle and using 1/3 cup (75 mL) batter for each pancake, cook pancakes until browned and bubbles form on surface. Turn and brown other side.

Makes about 18 pancakes.

Tips: Pancake batter may be prepared ahead and chilled up to 24 hours, but do not add baking powder until the last minute. The temperature of the griddle is critical to pancake lightness — a water drop should dance across surface of griddle when heat is perfect.

Per 3 pancakes:

459 Calories
16 g protein
12 g fat
73 g carbohydrate
7 g fibre

Wild Rice and Kernel Corn

The surprise ingredient in this dish is sunflower seeds — which add an extra crunch to this tasty side dish.

	Chef:
Guy Blain	
Chef/Owner	
Restaurant L'Orée	
du bois	
Chelsea, Québec	

2-1/4 cups	water	550 mL
	Salt	
3/4 cup	wild rice	175 mL
1 tbsp	butter	15 mL
1	large onion, chopped	1
1/2 cup	diced celery	125 mL
1 cup	chopped mushrooms	250 mL
1 tbsp	chopped garlic	15 mL
1-3/4 cups	frozen corn kernels, thawed	425 mL
1/4 cup	shelled sunflower seeds	50 mL
	Pepper	

Dietitian:

Debra Reid, Ph.D., RD
Ottawa–Carleton
Health Dept.
Ottawa, Ontario

An elegant and colorful way to showcase grains and vegetables.

In saucepan, bring water and 1/2 tsp (2 mL) salt to boil. Rinse rice under running water in strainer; add to pan and bring to boil. Cover and simmer over low heat 45 minutes or until tender but not mushy. Drain off excess liquid.

In large skillet, melt butter over medium heat; cook onion and celery, stirring, for 2 minutes. Add mushrooms and garlic; cook 2 to 3 minutes. Add rice, corn, sunflower seeds, and 1/4 tsp (1 mL) each salt and pepper; heat through.

Makes 8 servings.

Per serving:
131 Calories
5 g protein
4 g fat
22 g carbohydrate
3 g fibre

Cassoulet

Cassoulet is a country casserole that's made with beans and a variety of meats and poultry, then traditionally slow-cooked for days. It still takes about four hours of cooking in the oven, but the result is worth it.

Chef:

Alain Mercier, CCC
Independent Chef
Canadian Forces,
BFC Valcartier
Courcelette, Québec

Dietitian:

Fabiola Masri, P.Dt.
Présidente
Santé à la Carte
Québec City, Québec

This traditional French Canadian fare is packed with protein and fibre. Choose light accompaniments: Cassoulet has all the calories you need for a meal.

1 lb	dried white navy beans (about 2-1/2 cups/625 mL)	500 g
2 tbsp	olive oil	25 mL
8 oz	boneless skinless chicken or pheasant breast, cut into large pieces	250 g
8 oz	well-trimmed pork loin, cut into large pieces	250 g
4 oz	well-trimmed boneless lamb, cut into large pieces	125 g
4 oz	chicken livers	125 g
1	large onion, sliced	1
2	cloves garlic, minced	2
1	can (5-1/2 oz/156 mL) tomato paste	1
1/2 cup	maple syrup	125 mL
1/2 cup	dry white wine	125 mL
1 tbsp	dry mustard	15 mL
1 tsp	dried thyme	5 mL
1 tsp	salt	5 mL
1/2 tsp	pepper	2 mL
1	bay leaf	1

In 4-quart (4 L) saucepan, cover beans with cold water; soak for 8 hours or overnight. Drain and cover with fresh water; bring to boil. Simmer 30 minutes. Drain, reserving cooking water.

In large ovenproof saucepan or Dutch oven, heat oil over medium heat; brown chicken, pork, lamb and chicken livers all over. Remove and set aside. Place half of the beans, half of the onion and half of the garlic in bottom of pan; layer meats on top. Add remaining beans, onion and garlic.

Mix together tomato paste, maple syrup, wine, mustard, thyme, salt and pepper; pour over beans. Cover beans with reserved cooking water; nestle bay leaf in beans.

Cover and bake at 275°F (140°C) for 2 hours; uncover, stir and increase temperature to 325°F (160°C). Cook, uncovered, about 2 hours or until thickened and beans are tender. Discard bay leaf.

Makes 6 servings.

Tip: Quick-Soak Method for Beans: Cover beans with water and bring to boil for 2 minutes. Remove from heat and let stand 1 hour. Drain and proceed as directed above.

Per serving:

557 Calories
42 g protein
12 g fat
72 g carbohydrate
15 g fibre

Bread

Banana Apple Orange Oatmeal Raisin Muffins

Oatmeal Bannock

Icelandic Three-Grain Brown Bread

Herb Grain Bread

First Nations Ovenbannock

Fruit Malt Bread

Zucchini Nut Loaf

Mixed Herb Baguette

Banana Apple Orange Oatmeal Raisin Muffins

These muffins are chock-full of fruit and are best eaten warm from the oven. If you have to store them, do so in the freezer and thaw as required.

Chef:

Don Costello
Cook
Oak Bay Beach Hotel
Victoria,
British Columbia

Dietitian:

Lisa Diamond, RDN
Manager of Nutrition
and Food Services
Vancouver Island
Housing Association
for the
Physically Disabled
Victoria,
British Columbia

The fruit makes these muffins moist so you won't need to add butter.

2-1/2 cups	all-purpose flour	625 mL
1-1/2 cups	quick-cooking rolled oats	375 mL
1 cup	wheat germ	250 mL
3/4 cup	granulated sugar	175 mL
2 tbsp	baking powder	25 mL
1/2 tsp	salt	2 mL
1 cup	raisins	250 mL
1	medium (unpeeled) apple, chopped	1
1/3 cup	sunflower seeds	75 mL
2	eggs	2
1 cup	mashed ripe bananas	250 mL
3/4 cup	skim milk	175 mL
2 tbsp	grated orange rind	25 mL
1/2 cup	orange juice	125 mL
1/3 cup	vegetable oil	75 mL

In large bowl, combine flour, oats, wheat germ, sugar, baking powder and salt; stir in raisins, apple and sunflower seeds.

In another bowl, whisk eggs lightly; blend in bananas, milk, orange rind and juice and oil. Pour into dry ingredients, stirring just until moistened.

Spoon about 1/3 cup (75 mL) batter into each greased or paper-lined muffin cup. Bake at 400°F (200°C) for about 20 minutes or until firm to the touch. Cool in pans 5 minutes. Remove from tins and cool on rack. Store in airtight container in freezer.

Makes 20 large muffins.

Per muffin

230 Calories
6 g protein
7 g fat
39 g carbohydrate
3 g fibre

Oatmeal Bannock

Bannock is a bread that has been relied on for sustenance and enjoyment by Canada's native people. It's so tasty, quick and easy to make, it may soon become part of your cooking repertoire!

Chef:

Peter Graham, CCC
1st Chef
Whitehorse General
Hospital
Whitehorse
Yukon Territory

1 cup	whole wheat flour	250 mL
1/2 cup	quick-cooking rolled oats	125 mL
1 tbsp	baking powder	15 mL
1 tsp	granulated sugar	5 mL
1/2 tsp	salt	2 mL
1/3 cup	soft margarine	75 mL
1/3 cup	1% milk	75 mL

In medium bowl, combine flour, oats, baking powder, sugar and salt. With 2 knives or fork cut in margarine until crumbs are size of peas. Make well in middle; pour in milk and mix quickly just until dry ingredients are moistened.

Turn dough onto lightly floured board; knead 3 to 5 times. Pat out dough to about 3/4-inch (2 cm) thickness. Cut into 9 rounds with 2-inch (5 cm) cutter. Bake on ungreased baking sheet at 425°F (220°C) for 12 to 15 minutes or until lightly browned.

Makes 9 biscuits.

Dietitian:

Sharlene Clarke, RDN
Outpatient Dietitian
Whitehorse General
Hospital
Whitehorse
Yukon Territory

Bannock is traditionally fried. This healthier alternative is baked and uses whole wheat flour and oatmeal for added fibre.

Per biscuit:

129 Calories
3 g protein
7 g fat
14 g carbohydrate
2 g fibre

Icelandic Three-Grain Brown Bread

This is a hearty bread that's ideal for serving with lunch, dinner or as a snack.

Chef:

Gary Heaney
E.C. Drury School
for Deaf
Milton, Ontario

Dietitian:

Vicki Poirier, RD
Halton Healthy
Lifestyles Coalition
Oakville, Ontario

Think bread-making is too time-consuming? Try this easy-to-make bread. Your children will love it too!

1/2 cup	butter or margarine, softened	125 mL
1/2 cup	packed brown sugar	125 mL
2	large eggs	2
2 cups	whole wheat flour	500 mL
2 cups	all-purpose flour	500 mL
1 cup	dark rye flour	250 mL
1 cup	quick-cooking rolled oats	250 mL
2 tsp	baking soda	10 mL
1 tsp	salt	5 mL
2-1/2 cups	buttermilk	625 mL

In large bowl, cream butter and brown sugar until light; beat in eggs. Combine whole wheat, all-purpose and dark rye flours, oats, baking soda and salt. Add to creamed mixture alternately with buttermilk, making three additions of dry and two of buttermilk. Divide between two greased 9- X 5-inch (2 L) loaf pans.

Bake at 350°F (180°C) for 55 to 60 minutes or until wooden skewer inserted in centre comes out clean. Cool in pans 10 minutes, then remove from pans and cool on rack. Store in airtight container.

Makes 2 loaves.

Tip: If out of buttermilk, substitute 2 cups (500 mL) 2% milk with 2 tbsp (25 mL) fresh lemon juice or vinegar.

Per slice (1/12 loaf):

170 Calories
5 g protein
5 g fat
27 g carbohydrate
2 g fibre

Herb Grain Bread

This round loaf is made with cereal, oat or wheat bran and whole wheat cereal biscuit as well as two kinds of flour.

Chef:

Janice Mitchell, CCC
Janice's Fine Country
Catering
London, Ontario

Dietitian:

Jane Henderson, RD
Consulting Dietitian
Kintore, Ontario

A variety of grains adds fibre to this flavorful bread.

1 tsp	granulated sugar	5 mL
1/2 cup	warm water (105°-115°F/40°-46°C)	125 mL
1	pkg (8 g) active dry yeast (or 1 tbsp/15 mL)	1
3/4 cup	water	175 mL
1/2 cup	2% milk	125 mL
1/3 cup	packed brown sugar	75 mL
1/4 cup	olive oil	50 mL
1/4 cup	7-grain cereal	50 mL
1/4 cup	oat bran or wheat bran	50 mL
1/4 cup	crushed whole wheat cereal biscuit	50 mL
1 tsp	salt	5 mL
1 tsp	dried sage	5 mL
1/2 tsp	crushed dried thyme	2 mL
1/2 tsp	celery seed	2 mL
1 cup	whole wheat flour	250 mL
4 to 5 cups	all-purpose flour	1 to 1.25 L
1	egg	1

In large bowl, dissolve sugar in warm water. Sprinkle in yeast and let stand 10 minutes or until foamy; stir well.

Heat water and milk to 105°-115°F (40°-46°C); add to yeast mixture along with brown sugar, olive oil, 7-grain cereal, oat bran, cereal biscuit, salt, sage, thyme and celery seed. Add whole wheat flour and 2 cups (500 mL) of the all-purpose flour; blend well. Beat in egg. Add enough of the remaining flour to make soft dough.

Turn out onto floured board; knead until smooth and elastic, about 5 minutes. Place in greased bowl, turning to grease all over. Cover, and let rise in warm place until doubled in size, 30 to 45 minutes.

Punch dough down and cut in half; form each into round loaf. Place on greased baking sheet. Cover and let rise in warm place until doubled in size, about 30 minutes.

Bake at 375°F (190°C) for 35 to 40 minutes until golden brown and loaves sound hollow when tapped on bottom. Remove from baking sheet; let cool on rack.

Makes 2 loaves.

Tip: For a finishing touch, brush with milk and sprinkle with sesame seeds before baking. For Italian flavoring, use 1 tsp (5 mL) each dried basil and oregano instead of the seasonings indicated.

Per slice (1/12 loaf):

151 Calories
4 g protein
3 g fat
27 g carbohydrate
2 g fibre

First Nations Ovenbannock

Bannock, originally from Scotland, has become a staple on the menus of Canada's native people. It may be eaten with hot soup, stew, fresh vegetables, wild game and, even, seasonal fruit.

Chef:

Jo-Anne Chalmers
Food Services Manager/
Chef
Dakota Oyate Lodge
Brandon, Manitoba

Dietitian:

Christina Scheuer, RD
Community Dietitian
Sioux Valley Dakota
Nation
Griswold, Manitoba

Oven bread is a traditional favorite in the Dakota Nation. Low in fat and high in complex carbohydrate, its versatility is legend. Increase the fibre by using whole wheat flour or rolled oats.

2-1/2 cups	all-purpose flour	625 mL
2-1/2 tsp	baking powder	12 mL
1/2 tsp	salt	2 mL
1 cup	skim milk, at room temperature	250 mL

In medium bowl, combine flour, baking powder and salt. With fork, stir in milk until evenly blended. Knead 10 to 12 times.

Turn out onto lightly floured board; roll or pat into circle about 1-1/2 inches (4 cm) thick. Bake on greased baking sheet at 400°F (200°C) for 20 to 25 minutes or until golden. Serve warm.

Makes 6 servings.

Variations:

Whole Wheat Bannock: Use 1-1/2 cups (375 mL) all-purpose flour and 1 cup (250 mL) whole wheat flour.

Oat Bannock: Use 1 cup (250 mL) all-purpose flour and 1 cup (250 mL) quick-cooking rolled oats. Stir in 1/4 cup (50 mL) raisins.

Per serving:

206 Calories
7 g protein
1 g fat
42 g carbohydrate
2 g fibre

Fruit Malt Bread

The flavor is reminiscent of hot cross buns and this wonderful aromatic bread is perfect for breakfast, as a snack or for dessert.

Chef:

Margaret Carson
Chef/Instructor/Owner
Bonne Cuisine School of
Cooking
Halifax, Nova Scotia

Dietitian:

Pam Lynch, P.Dt.
Consultant Dietitian-
Nutritionist
Nutrition and
Counselling Services and
Associates
Halifax, Nova Scotia

I tsp	granulated sugar	5 mL
1-1/4 cups	warm water (105°-115°F/40°-46°C)	300 mL
I	pkg (8 g) active dry yeast (or 1 tbsp/15 mL)	I
1-1/2 cups	all-purpose flour	375 mL
I tbsp	brown sugar	15 mL
I tsp	salt	5 mL
1/2 tsp	each cinnamon, nutmeg and ginger	2 mL
1/4 tsp	ground cloves	I mL
I tbsp	vegetable oil	15 mL
I tbsp	barley malt extract or molasses	15 mL
1-1/2 cups	chopped dried fruit (raisins, currants, apricots and pitted prunes)	375 mL
1-1/2 to 2 cups	whole wheat flour	375 to 500 mL
	Milk	

In small bowl, dissolve sugar in 1/4 cup (50 mL) of the warm water. Sprinkle in yeast and let stand 10 minutes or until foamy; stir.

Combine all-purpose flour, sugar, salt, cinnamon, nutmeg, ginger and cloves. In large mixer bowl, combine yeast mixture, remaining 1 cup (250 mL) warm water, vegetable oil and barley malt extract. With electric mixer, gradually beat in flour mixture; beat until smooth, about 2 minutes. Stir in dried fruit. Gradually stir in enough whole wheat flour to make moderately stiff dough.

Turn out onto lightly floured board; knead until smooth and elastic, about 7 minutes. Place in bowl sprayed with vegetable-oil spray, turning to grease all over. Cover and let rise in warm place until doubled in size, about 1-1/2 to 2 hours.

Punch dough down and cut in half; shape each into ball. Place side by side in greased 8- x 4-inch (1.5 L) loaf pan. Cover and let rise until doubled in size, 1 to 1-1/2 hours.

Bake at 400°F (200°C) for 30 to 35 minutes or until loaf sounds hollow when tapped on bottom. (If tops are getting too dark, cover loosely with foil.) Brush with milk; remove from pan and cool on rack.

Makes 1 loaf.

Per slice (1/10 loaf):

228 Calories
6 g protein
2 g fat
49 g carbohydrate
5 g fibre

Zucchini Nut Loaf

Here's another idea for using zucchini when it's in season. Serve this easy-to-make, quick loaf as a snack or dessert.

Chef:

Dean Mitchell, CCC
Executive Chef
Canyon Meadows Golf
and Country Club
Calgary, Alberta

Dietitian:

Suzanne Journault-
Hemstock, RD
Food Production
Dietitian
Nutrition and Food
Services,
Foothills Hospital
Calgary, Alberta

If you want to reduce the fat, substitute 1/2 cup (125 mL) chopped fruit or raisins for the nuts.

1-1/2 cups	all-purpose flour	375 mL
1 tsp	cinnamon	5 mL
1/2 tsp	baking soda	2 mL
1/2 tsp	each salt and nutmeg	2 mL
1/4 tsp	baking powder	1 mL
1	egg	1
3/4 cup	granulated sugar	175 mL
1/3 cup	vegetable oil	75 mL
2 tbsp	2% milk	25 mL
1 cup	shredded (unpeeled) zucchini	250 mL
1/2 cup	chopped walnuts or pecans	125 mL
1/2 tsp	grated lemon rind (optional)	2 mL

In large bowl, combine flour, cinnamon, baking soda, salt, nutmeg and baking powder.

In medium bowl, beat egg; whisk in sugar, oil and milk. Stir in zucchini, nuts, and lemon rind, if desired; stir zucchini mixture into dry ingredients.

Pour batter into greased 8- x 4-inch (1.5 L) loaf pan. Bake at 350°F (180°C) for 50 minutes or until toothpick inserted in centre comes out clean. Cool 10 minutes in pan. Turn out onto rack to cool completely.

Makes 1 loaf.

Per slice (1/10 loaf):

242 Calories
4 g protein
12 g fat
31 g carbohydrate
1 g fibre

Mixed Herb Baguette

Baguettes are long thin loaves that are baked on a cookie sheet. You can change the flavor of this recipe by combining different herbs you have on hand.

Chef:

Peter Ochitwa
Executive Chef/Owner
Mad Apples Restaurant
Toronto, Ontario

Dietitian:

Susie Langley, M.S., RD
Nutrition Consultant
Toronto, Ontario

Making bread can be fun and easy! Use your own mixture of fresh or dried herbs for a special taste and aroma treat!

2 tsp	granulated sugar	10 mL
1-1/3 cups	warm water (105°-115°F/40°-46°C)	325 mL
1	pkg (8 g) active dry yeast (or 1 tbsp/15 mL)	1
2-1/2 to 3 cups	all-purpose flour	625 to 750 mL
1/4 cup	mixed chopped fresh herbs	50 mL
2 tsp	butter, melted	10 mL
1 tsp	salt	5 mL
	Cornmeal	
1	egg	1
2 tbsp	milk	25 mL

In large bowl, dissolve sugar in warm water. Sprinkle in yeast and let stand 10 minutes or until foamy; stir well. Stir in 2 cups (500 mL) of the flour, herbs, butter and salt. Add enough of the remaining flour to make a soft dough.

Turn out on floured board; knead for a few minutes or until smooth and elastic. Place in greased bowl, turning to grease all over. Cover and let rise in warm place until doubled in size, 45 to 60 minutes.

Punch dough down and cut in half; roll each into long thin cigar-shaped stick (about 15 inches/38 cm long). Place on corn-meal-dusted greased baking sheet; score top 3 times on the diagonal. Cover and let rise in warm place until doubled in size, 30 to 45 minutes.

Bake at 350°F (180°C) for 30 minutes. Combine egg and milk; brush over loaves. Bake 10 to 15 minutes longer or until loaves sound hollow when tapped on bottom. Cool on racks.

Makes 2 loaves.

Tip: Instead of fresh herbs, you can substitute a mixture of 1 tsp (5 mL) each dried oregano, thyme, rosemary, sage and tarragon.

Per slice (1/20 loaf):

37 Calories
1 g protein
trace fat
7 g carbohydrate
trace fibre

Meat
(Beef, Pork, Lamb, Game)

Simple Steak Dinner for Two

Sesame Steak

Beef and Bean Threads

Beef Tenderloin with Blue Cheese Herb Crust

Beef Tenderloin with Mixed Peppercorns

Poached Beef Tenderloin Ali Baba

Beef Fajitas

Beef with Peppers and Tomatoes

Beef Stroganoff

Spiced Veal Stir-Fry

Braised Roasted Veal

Smoked Pork Loin with Braised Red Cabbage

Orange Ginger Pork and Vegetables

Tamarind-Glazed Pork Loin

Escallop of Pork with Leeks on a Bed of Noodles

Quebec Pork Chops Stuffed with New Brunswick Crab

Lamb Loin with Carrot Thyme Sauce,
Sweet Potatoes and Apple Mango Relish

Lamb Brochette with Couscous and
Mixed Vegetables

Tomato-Braised Rabbit

Moose or Elk Stew

Gypsy Pie

Roast Buffalo Striploin

Prime Time: Meat, Poultry, Fish & Seafood

Cod cheeks; steamed clams straight from the beach; Pacific salmon barbecued in the sunset; sizzling pork satays and beef kabobs; hamburgers right off the grill; coq au vin with crispy baguette; Peking duck with Mandarin pancake; Thanksgiving turkey with all the trimmings. These and many other meat, poultry and seafood dishes have played a major role in meeting both the nutritional needs and the ethnic preferences of our multicultural society. And today, poultry, meat and seafood continue to make a significant contribution to our protein and iron needs and provide many lower fat options to choose from.

Most poultry, including chicken and turkey, is considered a lower fat meat choice when the skin is removed. But you also need to pay attention to the way you prepare it—deep-frying, sauces and the like can add a lot of fat to an otherwise lean choice. Some higher fat poultry choices, such as goose and duck, are rich in taste and are generally served as special or festive fare. Eaten on an occasional basis, they can fit into a healthy eating pattern.

Beef, veal, pork and other "red meats" continue to be popular choices. Although meat can be a primary source of fat, it is also a nutrient-dense food, rich in protein, B-vitamins, iron and zinc. Purchase the leaner cuts more often, trim any visible fat off the meat, and bake, barbecue, broil or microwave if possible. You can also enhance the flavor with herbs and spices, marinades and natural juices, rather than rich gravies and sauces.

Remember that the serving size of meat is important: one serving is 30 to 45 grams (2 to 3 ounces) of meat. Adults need only two servings from this food group daily. The days of eating huge portions of meat are thankfully behind us, saving more than just money.

It's recommended that we choose leaner cuts of meat more often, but some may seem to be more expensive. The good news—since we need smaller portions, you can buy less for a meal! Use the cost per serving as a guide rather than the cost per kilogram. For instance, a boneless cut of meat is generally more expensive but will yield more servings so may be more economical. You can stretch the amount of meat you use by adding rice, pasta and vegetables, while cooking meat at lower temperatures helps reduce shrinkage. And you can marinate or tenderize less expensive, tougher cuts for maximum tenderness.

There's a great variety of seafood available in the Canadian marketplace, and the Canadian fishing industry is working hard to acquaint us with many of the traditionally underused fish, such as shark, squid and octopus. Fish is extremely versatile to prepare—you can broil it, steam it, bake it, poach it, stir-fry it, microwave it, and even eat it raw in sushi. When you don't add sauces or fat for cooking, fish is generally low in calories, and even a serving of so-called "fatty fish," such as salmon or mackerel, is well within the range of acceptable fat content.

What could be more tempting than an appealing meal with lots of nutritional variety, color and eye appeal, and the succulent aromas of poultry, meat and seafood. Eat and enjoy!

Elizabeth Shears, P.Dt.
Halifax, Nova Scotia

Simple Steak Dinner for Two

Sometimes it's not just coming up with a recipe that's a challenge, it's deciding what to serve with it. You won't have to worry with this delicious, complete meal recipe.

Chef:

*Chris Klugman
Executive Chef
Wayne Gretzky's
Restaurant
Toronto, Ontario*

Dietitian:

*Susie Langley, M.S., RD
Nutrition Consultant
Toronto, Ontario*

This lower fat dinner for two can be made in less than 30 minutes. Pan-broiling without any fat makes this lean red meat and seasonal fresh vegetable combo a treat. The spinach salad with honey yogurt dressing completes the meal.

Per serving:

358 Calories

32 g protein

12 g fat

33 g carbohydrate

9 g fibre

8 oz	striploin steak	250 g
	Pepper	
1	small onion, sliced	1
1 cup	quartered mushrooms	250 mL
1/4 cup	water, red wine or beef broth	50 mL
	Spinach Salad:	
2 tbsp	1% plain yogurt	25 mL
2 tbsp	light mayonnaise	25 mL
2 tsp	cider vinegar	10 mL
1 tsp	liquid honey	5 mL
	Salt and pepper	
Half	bunch spinach,	Half
5	small white turnips, peeled (or red-skinned potatoes)	5

Spinach Salad: Combine yogurt, mayonnaise, vinegar and honey; season with salt and pepper to taste. Break spinach into bite-sized pieces. Set aside.

In saucepan of boiling water, cook or steam turnips until tender. (Or microwave in small covered bowl with few tablespoons water.) Slice into wedges.

Meanwhile, trim all visible fat from steak; cut into 2 pieces. Season with pepper to taste. In nonstick skillet sprayed with vegetable oil cooking spray, brown steak over high heat on both sides. Reduce heat to medium. Add onion and mushrooms; cook, stirring, until steak is done as desired, 3 to 5 minutes for medium. Remove steak from pan.

Stir water into vegetables; cook over high heat until 2 tbsp (25 mL) liquid remains.

To serve, toss spinach with dressing. Place on dinner plates along with steak and turnips. Top with vegetable sauce.

Makes 2 servings.

Sesame Steak

Flank steak has become somewhat trendy of late and for good reason. In this marinated recipe, it's both tender and packed with flavor. Serve with stir-fried vegetables or salad and garlic bread.

Chef:

Janice Mitchell, CCC
Junice's Fine Country
Catering
London, Ontario

Dietitian:

Jane Henderson, RD
Consulting Dietitian
Kintore, Ontario

The marinade of sesame seeds, ginger, onion, garlic and honey adds a wonderful flavor to this lean cut of beef.

1/4 cup	light soy sauce	50 mL
1	clove garlic, minced	1
1	small onion, finely chopped	1
1 tbsp	liquid honey	15 mL
1 tbsp	sesame seeds	15 mL
1 tsp	grated gingerroot	5 mL
1 tsp	pepper	5 mL
1 lb	flank steak	500 g

In shallow nonaluminum pan, mix together soy sauce, garlic, onion, honey, sesame seeds, ginger and pepper. Add steak, turning to coat. Cover and marinate in refrigerator at least 4 to 6 hours or preferably overnight.

Place steak on greased grill or under broiler; cook 4 to 5 minutes per side for medium-rare. Slice across the grain to serve.

Makes 4 servings.

Per serving:

200 Calories
26 g protein
9 g fat
2 g carbohydrate
trace fibre

Beef and Bean Threads

Strips of marinated beef are combined with rice vermicelli noodles (bean threads) in this quick stir-fry recipe.

Chef:

Jon Paudler
Chef/Instructor,
Culinary Arts
Northern Alberta
Institute of Technology
Edmonton, Alberta

Dietitian:

Leslie Maze, RD
Diabetes Outpatient
Clinic
Royal Alexandra
Hospital
Edmonton, Alberta

A variation on a popular dish, this meal can be prepared in less than half an hour. Because of the marinade and thin slicing, you can use a more economical cut of meat.

**Per serving
(4-serving size):**

273 Calories
16 g protein
10 g fat
29 g carbohydrate
2 g fibre

1/2 lb	lean boneless beef (round, sirloin or flank)	250 g
1/4 lb	rice vermicelli	125 g
2	slices gingerroot	2
3 tsp	vegetable oil	15 mL
1	clove garlic, chopped	1
1 tbsp	tamari or soy sauce	15 mL
2	green onions, cut into 1-inch (2.5 cm) pieces	2
2	stalks celery, cut in julienne strips	2
1	medium carrot, cut in julienne strips	1
1	medium sweet green pepper, cut in julienne strips	1

Marinade:

1 tbsp	vegetable oil	15 mL
2 tsp	tamari sauce or soy sauce	10 mL
1 tsp	cornstarch	5 mL
1 tsp	dry sherry	5 mL
Pinch	granulated sugar	Pinch

Marinade: in medium bowl, whisk together oil, tamari sauce, cornstarch, sherry and sugar. Cut beef across the grain into strips; toss with marinade. Let marinate 15 minutes.

Meanwhile, cover rice vermicelli with boiling water; let stand 15 minutes. Drain well.

In wok or skillet over high heat, stir-fry gingerroot in 1 tsp (5 mL) of the oil until lightly browned; discard ginger. Add garlic and beef; stir-fry 2 minutes or until beef is desired degree of doneness. Remove from wok and keep warm.

Add remaining 2 tsp (10 mL) oil; stir-fry rice vermicelli for 1 minute. Stir in tamari sauce. Remove from wok and keep warm.

Add onions, celery, carrot and green pepper to work; stir-fry until tender-crisp. Return beef and noodles to wok; stir-fry for 1 minute.

Makes 2 main-course servings or 4 servings in multi-course meal.

Beef Tenderloin with Blue Cheese Herb Crust

Beef tenderloin is both lean and tender with no waste. Serve with Garlic Herb Potato Purée (see page 73), if desired.

Chef:

Larry DeVries
Chef/Instructor
Crocus Plains Secondary
School
Brandon, Manitoba

1/3 cup	crumbled blue cheese	75 mL
1/4 cup	fresh white bread crumbs	50 mL
2 tbsp	chopped fresh parsley	25 mL
2 tbsp	chopped fresh chives (or green onions)	25 mL
1	clove garlic	1
4	beef tenderloin medallions (3 oz/90 g each)	4

Sauce:

1 cup	beef broth	250 mL
1 tbsp	cornstarch	15 mL
1/4 tsp	crushed dried thyme	1 mL

Dietitians:

Jackie Kopilas, RD
Rachel Barkley, RD
Brandon and Westman
Area Dietitians
Heather Duncan,
P.H.Ec.
Manitoba Association of
Home Economists–
Southwest Branch
Brandon, Manitoba

Sauce: In small saucepan, bring broth, cornstarch and thyme to boil, stirring; simmer 1 minute. Keep warm.

In food processor, process cheese, crumbs, parsley, chives and garlic until in fine crumbs.

In nonstick skillet, brown medallions quickly on each side. Remove from skillet and place on baking sheet. Pack cheese mixture evenly on top of each. Bake at 350°F (180°C) for about 20 minutes for medium doneness or as desired.

Spoon sauce onto plates and top with beef.

Makes 4 servings.

Stronger flavored foods such as garlic and blue cheese help to compensate for a lower fat preparation. The blue cheese adds a nice tang to the meat.

Per serving:

171 Calories
19 g protein
8 g fat
4 g carbohydrate
trace fibre

Beef Tenderloin with Mixed Peppercorns

Pepper comes in several colors. This quick and easy recipe uses green and red peppercorns as well as black.

Chef:

Edouard Colonerus
Master Chef
The Canadian National
Culinary Team
Brampton, Ontario

4	beef tenderloin steaks (about 4 oz/125 g each)	4
	Salt	
1 to 2 tbsp	crushed black, green and red peppercorns	15 to 25 mL
1 tbsp	vegetable oil	15 mL
1	envelope (34 g) demi-glace roast gravy mix	1
2 tbsp	10% cream	25 mL
1 tbsp	gin	15 mL

Dietitian:

Kerry Wright, RD
Food and Nutrition
Specialist
Beef Information Centre
Mississauga, Ontario

The fat in this recipe has been reduced with the use of a nonstick pan. This cooking method allows for traditional deglazing to create a flavorful sauce.

Season steaks lightly with salt. Place peppercorns on plate; press steaks into peppercorns to coat both sides.

In nonstick skillet, heat oil over medium heat; cook steaks until done as desired, about 5 minutes on each side for rare. Remove from pan and keep warm.

Remove any fat from pan. In same pan, prepare roast gravy mix according to package directions. Bring to boil, reduce heat and simmer until reduced slightly. Stir in cream and gin; simmer gently 2 minutes. Serve with steak.

Makes 4 servings.

Per serving:

231 Calories
23 g protein
12 g fat
6 g carbohydrate
1 g fibre

Poached Beef Tenderloin Ali Baba

Beef tenderloin is more likely to be grilled than poached, but in this recipe it's cooked in a tomato/beef consommé. Serve with Dauphine potatoes and green beans.

Chef:

*Yannick Vincent, Chef
Restaurant "L'Eau Vive"
Gatineau, Québec*

1	can (10 oz/284 mL) beef consommé	1
1-1/2 lb	beef tenderloin	750 g
1	can (5-1/2 oz/156 mL) tomato paste	1
1 tbsp	butter, melted	15 mL
1 tbsp	all-purpose flour	15 mL
2 tbsp	Madeira	25 mL
1/4 tsp	pepper	1 mL
	Watercress	

Dietitian:

*Debra Reid, Ph.D., RD
Ottawa–Carleton
Health Dept.
Ottawa, Ontario*

This lean meat recipe is moist, tender and flavorful. Balance your meal with lots of vegetables and tasty grain products.

In covered skillet, bring consommé and 1 soup can of water to boil. Add beef; cover and simmer for 25 to 30 minutes or until desired doneness. Remove beef and keep warm.

Reserve 1 cup (250 mL) cooking liquid in skillet; stir in tomato paste. Combine butter and flour; stir into skillet and cook, stirring, until thickened and bubbly. Add Madeira and pepper; heat through.

To serve, slice beef. Serve sauce on the side. Garnish with watercress.

Makes 8 servings.

Per serving:

158 Calories
18 g protein
7 g fat
6 g carbohydrate
1 g fibre

Beef Fajitas

Fajitas made their mark at restaurants and caught on, in part, because they are as fun to put together as to eat. Our version is assembled then baked. Serve with fresh salad greens for a complete meal.

Chef:

Robert Neil
Cook Supervisor
Joyceville Correctional
Institute
Joyceville, Ontario

1 tbsp	vegetable oil	15 mL
1	each medium sweet green and red pepper, cut in thin strips	1
2	medium onions, thinly sliced	2
1 lb	beef steak (round, flank or sirloin), trimmed and thinly sliced across the grain	500 g
2	medium tomatoes, diced	2
2	cloves garlic, minced	2
2 tsp	chili powder	10 mL
1 tsp	hot pepper sauce	5 mL
1/2 tsp	each pepper, dry mustard and ginger	2 mL
10	8-inch (20 cm) soft flour tortillas	10
2/3 cup	shredded light Cheddar-style cheese	150 mL

Dietitian:

Denise Hargrove, RD
Public Health Dietitian
Kingston, Frontenac and
Lennox and Addington
Health Unit
Kingston, Ontario

Combining lean beef with lots of vegetables and a bit of cheese in a tortilla provides maximum flavor and all four food groups. Olé!

In large nonstick skillet, heat oil over medium-high heat; cook green and red peppers and onions, stirring, for 4 to 5 minutes. Remove from pan.

Add beef to pan; brown 2 minutes. Stir in tomatoes, garlic, chili powder, hot pepper sauce, pepper, mustard and ginger; heat through. Return vegetables to skillet; heat through.

Divide mixture among tortillas; sprinkle mixture with 1 tbsp (15 mL) cheese and roll up. Place in greased 13 x 9-inch (3.5 L) baking dish. Bake at 350°F (180°C) for about 10 minutes to heat through.

Makes 5 servings.

Per fajita:

256 Calories
17 g protein
8 g fat
30 g carbohydrate
2 g fibre

Beef with Peppers and Tomatoes

Finding recipes the whole family will like and can be made in less than 20 minutes is still a challenge. This one fits the bill on both counts! Serve with rice.

Chef:

William King, Chef
Deer Lake Motel
Deer Lake,
Newfoundland

Dietitian:

Rosemary Duffenais,
R.Dt.
Sir Thomas Roddick
Hospital
Stephenville,
Newfoundland

1 lb	flank steak	500 g
1/4 cup	soy sauce	50 mL
1 tbsp	water	15 mL
2 tsp	cornstarch	10 mL
1 tsp	dry sherry	5 mL
1	clove garlic, minced	1
1 tbsp	vegetable oil	15 mL
2-1/2 cups	cubed sweet green pepper	625 mL
2	large tomatoes, cut in wedges	2
1/4 tsp	pepper	1 mL

Trim steak and thinly slice across the grain; cut into bite-sized pieces. In medium bowl, combine soy sauce, water, cornstarch, sherry and garlic. Stir in steak and let stand 10 minutes.

In nonstick skillet, heat oil over medium heat; cook green peppers, stirring, until almost tender. Add beef; cook to desired doneness, about 2 minutes. Stir in tomatoes and pepper; cook just until heated through.

Makes 6 servings.

Per serving:

174 Calories
18 g protein
8 g fat
7 g carbohydrate
2 g fibre

Beef Stroganoff

This classic stroganoff uses sauce made from scratch, but to save time, you can use a pre-packaged brown sauce or thick demi-glace mix—just add a little red wine and thyme for extra flavor. Serve with egg noodles and garnish with chopped fresh parsley.

Chef:

James Kennedy
Food and Service
Resource Group Ltd.
Vancouver,
British Columbia

2 cups	sliced mushrooms	500 mL
3/4 cup	diced onion	175 mL
1 cup	Brown Sauce (recipe follows)	250 mL
1/3 cup	1% plain yogurt	75 mL
1-1/2 tsp	Dijon mustard	7 mL
1 lb	boneless trimmed sirloin steak, cut in thin strips	500 g
1/4 cup	diced seeded tomato	50 mL

Spray medium skillet with nonstick cooking spray; heat over medium heat. Cook mushrooms and onion, stirring, 2 to 3 minutes or until onion is softened. Whisk together brown sauce, yogurt and mustard; mix into mushroom mixture and heat over low heat. Set aside.

Spray large skillet with nonstick cooking spray; heat over high heat. Add beef; cook, stirring, until browned. Stir in sauce and tomatoes; heat through.

Makes 4 servings.

Dietitian:

Pat Scarlett, RDN
National Nutrition
Manager
Beef Information Centre
Vancouver,
British Columbia

This recipe is a lower fat alternative to those that use sauces or gravies made with roux.

Brown Sauce:

1/4 cup	each diced onion, leek and celery	50 mL
2 tbsp	diced carrot	25 mL
2 tbsp	tomato paste	25 mL
1/2 cup	red wine	125 mL
4 cups	strong beef broth	1 L
1	clove garlic, chopped	1
1 tsp	dried thyme	5 mL
1	bay leaf	1
1/4 cup	arrowroot (or 3 tbsp/45 mL cornstarch)	50 mL
1/4 cup	water	50 mL

Spray medium skillet with nonstick cooking spray; heat over medium-high heat. Cook onion, leek, celery and carrot, stirring, until well browned. Mix in tomato paste. Add half the wine; cook, stirring, until evaporated. Repeat with remaining wine.

Add beef stock, garlic, thyme and bay leaf; bring to boil. Reduce heat and simmer until reduced by half. Strain, discarding vegetables and returning liquid to skillet. Mix arrowroot and water until smooth; stir into hot liquid and cook, stirring constantly, until thickened. Makes about 2 cups (500 mL).

Per serving:

208 Calories
28 g protein
5 g fat
10 g carbohydrate
1 g fibre

Spiced Veal Stir-Fry

This great stir-fry recipe uses veal seasoned with ginger, garlic, red pepper flakes — and cinnamon! Serve over rice.

Chef:

Tyrone Miller, CCC
Chef
Kitchener-Waterloo
Hospital
Kitchener, Ontario

Dietitian:

Karen Jackson, RD
Patient Food Service
Manager,
The Mississauga
Hospital
Mississauga, Ontario

Instead of sautéing them, try blanching the vegetables to just "al dente." This enhances the nutritional value.

I tsp	ginger	5 mL
1/2 tsp	garlic powder	2 mL
1/4 tsp	red pepper flakes	I mL
Pinch	cinnamon	Pinch
Pinch	each allspice and ground cloves	Pinch
1-1/4 lb	veal scaloppine, cut into thin strips	625 g
I cup	chicken broth	250 mL
1/4 cup	dry white wine (optional)	50 mL
3 tbsp	soy sauce	50 mL
2 tbsp	cornstarch	25 mL
2 tbsp	vegetable oil	25 mL
I	medium onion, chopped	I
2 cups	mushrooms, quartered	500 mL
3	medium carrots, sliced	3
3	stalks celery, diagonally sliced	3
I	medium sweet green pepper, chopped	I

Combine ginger, garlic powder, red pepper flakes, cinnamon, allspice and cloves. Transfer one-third of the spice mixture to bowl; add veal and toss to coat. Chill for 1 to 2 hours.

Combine remaining spice mixture, chicken broth, wine, soy sauce and cornstarch; set sauce aside.

In large skillet, heat 1 tbsp (15 mL) of the oil over medium-high heat; sauté onion, mushrooms, carrots, celery and green pepper for 5 minutes or until tender. Remove from pan.

Add remaining oil to skillet; brown veal about 2 minutes. Add sauce mixture and bring to boil, stirring until thickened. Return vegetables to skillet and heat through.

Makes 6 servings.

Per serving:

200 Calories
23 g protein
7 g fat
12 g carbohydrate
2 g fibre

Braised Roasted Veal

This marvelously moist dish (which you can make the day before) is excellent served on a cold buffet with salads and bread.

Chef:

Ronald Davis
Executive Chef
Sheraton Parkway North
Richmond Hill, Ontario

2 lb	veal leg (top portion)	1 kg
1/2 tsp	each crumbled dried rosemary and thyme	2 mL
Pinch	dried tarragon	Pinch
1	stalk celery, chopped	1
1	medium onion, chopped	1
1	medium carrot, diced	1
1/3 cup	water	75 mL
1/4 cup	white vinegar	50 mL
1/4 cup	white wine	50 mL
1 tsp	grated lemon rind	5 mL
1 tbsp	lemon juice	15 mL

Dietitian:

Debra McNair, RD
Consulting Dietitian
Toronto, Ontario

Using vegetables, herbs and lemon is a great example of how to increase taste without increasing the fat content.

Place veal in roasting pan; sprinkle with rosemary, thyme and tarragon. Place celery, onion and carrot around veal. Roast at 475°F (240°C) for 10 minutes.

Reduce temperature to 375°F (190°C). Add water, vinegar, wine, lemon rind and juice. Cover and roast for 1 hour. Remove from pan and cool. Then chill. Slice to serve.

Makes 8 servings.

Per serving:

144 Calories
25 g protein
4 g fat
0 g carbohydrate
0 g fibre

Smoked Pork Loin with Braised Red Cabbage

Smoked pork loin is often available through butchers or you can substitute thickly sliced pea meal bacon. The smoky flavor goes well with the cabbage and raisins. Serve with egg noodles if desired.

Chef:

John Scott
Executive Chef
D'Arcy Ranch Golf Club
Okotoks, Alberta

Dietitian:

Suzanne Journault-
Hemstock, RD
Food Production
Dietitian
Nutrition and Food
Services,
Foothills Hospital
Calgary, Alberta

**Slower, low-heat cooking is the secret to preserving the flavor in the cabbage and raisins.
Trim pork well to economize on fat.**

12 oz	shredded red cabbage (about 3 cups/750 mL)	375 g
1/4 cup	red wine vinegar	50 mL
1/3 cup	water	75 mL
1/4 cup	granulated sugar	50 mL
1/4 cup	raisins	50 mL
1 tbsp	butter	15 mL
1 lb	boneless smoked pork loin	500 g
1/4 cup	consommé or beef broth	50 mL
3 tbsp	grainy mustard	50 mL
1	green onion, chopped	1
1/2 cup	light sour cream	125 mL

In medium saucepan, combine cabbage, vinegar, water, sugar and raisins. Cover and cook over medium-low heat, stirring frequently, until tender, 20 to 30 minutes, adding more water if necessary. Stir in butter.

Trim fat from top of pork loin; cut into 1/2-inch (2 cm) thick slices. Broil 2 to 3 minutes on each side; set aside.

In small saucepan, bring consommé, mustard and onion to boil; reduce heat and stir in sour cream. Simmer 2 to 3 minutes or until hot.

Spoon cabbage onto large platter or serving plates; arrange pork on top, overlapping slightly. Drizzle sauce over pork.

Makes 4 servings.

Per serving:

341 Calories
28 g protein
13 g fat
30 g carbohydrate
2 g fibre

Orange Ginger Pork and Vegetables

Ginger has been called the spice of the 1990s and grated ginger-root brings out the best of both the pork and vegetables in this skillet stir-fry. Serve over rice or pasta.

Chef:

David Powell
Executive Chef
Ramada Hotel
Downtown
Saskatoon,
Saskatchewan

Dietitian:

Rosanne E. Maluk, P.Dt.
Food Focus Saskatoon
Inc.
Saskatoon,
Saskatchewan

Taste and more taste—this dish is full of surprises! You may want to adjust the amount of red pepper flakes to suit your audience.

2 tbsp	vegetable oil	25 mL
1	medium onion, sliced	1
2	medium carrots, sliced	2
1	each medium sweet green and red pepper, cut into thin strips	1
1 cup	sliced celery	250 mL
1 lb	boneless well-trimmed pork loin, cut into thin strips	500 g
1	clove garlic, minced	1
2 tsp	grated gingerroot	10 mL
1/4 tsp	red pepper flakes	1 mL
2 cups	shredded bok choy	500 mL
1/2 cup	orange juice	125 mL
	Salt	

In large skillet, heat 1 tbsp (15 mL) of the oil over medium-high heat; sauté onion, carrots, green and red peppers and celery for about 5 minutes or until tender. Remove from pan.

Add remaining oil to skillet. Brown pork with garlic, ginger-root and red pepper flakes until pork is no longer pink.

Return vegetables to skillet; add bok choy. Add orange juice; heat through, 2 to 3 minutes. Season with salt to taste.

Makes 4 servings.

Per serving:

291 Calories
26 g protein
14 g fat
16 g carbohydrate
4 g fibre

Tamarind-Glazed Pork Loin

You'll find tamarind paste in the specialty section of many supermarkets, and it adds a slightly bitter note to the glaze in this recipe. Serve with an apricot or mango chutney.

Chef:

David Nicolson
Executive Chef
Gourmet Goodies
Catering
Edmonton, Alberta

2 lb	boneless pork loin	1 kg
1/2 cup	sun-dried tomatoes, softened	125 mL
1/2 cup	chopped fresh basil (or 2 tbsp/25 ml dried)	125 mL
	Salt and pepper	
1/2 cup	water	125 mL

	Glaze:	
1/4 cup	red wine vinegar	50 mL
1/4 cup	chicken broth	50 mL
1/4 cup	packed brown sugar	50 mL
1 tbsp	tamarind paste (or concentrate)	15 mL

Dietitian:

Leslie Maze, RD
Diabetes Outpatient
Clinic
Royal Alexandra
Hospital
Edmonton, Alberta

**Tamarind—
the bittersweet fruit
of the evergreen—
is used extensively in
Southwestern and
Mexican cooking.**

Glaze: In small saucepan, combine vinegar, broth, sugar and tamarind paste; bring to boil over medium heat, stirring occasionally. Reduce heat to simmer 10 to 15 minutes or until slightly thickened. Transfer to small bowl; cool.

Slice pork in half lengthwise, but not completely through to other side; open and lay flat like book. Place sun-dried tomatoes and basil evenly on one side; sprinkle with salt and pepper to taste. Fold roast back to original shape; tie with butcher twine.

Bake on rack in roasting pan at 425°F (220°C) for 20 minutes. Reduce temperature to 375°F (190°C). Add water to pan. Brush roast with glaze. Bake for 45 to 60 minutes, basting with glaze every 15 minutes, until no longer pink.

Makes 8 servings.

Tip: To soften sun-dried tomatoes, cover with boiling water and let stand 10 minutes. Drain.

Per serving:

163 Calories
18 g protein
7 g fat
7 g carbohydrate
1 g fibre

Escallop of Pork with Leeks on a Bed of Noodles

Pork tenderloin is one of the leanest cuts and is also extremely tender. Here its delicate flavor is enhanced with the yogurt-honey-lemon sauce.

Chef:

Anton Koch, CCC
Chef/Owner
Rotisserie St. Moritz
Dorval, Québec

Dietitian:

Kim Arrey, P.Dt.
Consulting Dietitian
Montréal, Québec

If cholesterol is a concern, use yolk-free egg noodles in this classy pork dish—cuts down on fat, too.

3/4 lb	pork tenderloin	375 g
	Pepper	
	Strips of rind from 1 lemon	
2 tbsp	vegetable oil	25 mL
3	leeks (white part only), cut into julienne strips	3
1/2 cup	dry white wine	125 mL
2/3 cup	1% plain yogurt	150 mL
2 tbsp	liquid honey	25 mL
1 tsp	lemon juice	5 mL
1/4 tsp	salt	1 mL
1 tsp	cornstarch	5 mL
1 tbsp	cold water	15 mL
1 tsp	green peppercorns	5 mL

	Noodles:	
3 cups	egg noodles	750 mL
1 tbsp	butter	15 mL
Pinch	each salt and nutmeg	Pinch

Slice pork diagonally into 8 pieces. Place between plastic wrap and pound with meat mallet to 1/4-inch (5 mm) thickness. Sprinkle with pepper to taste. Cover lemon rind with boiling water; drain and set aside for garnish.

In large skillet, heat 1 tbsp (15 mL) of the oil over medium-high heat; brown pork on both sides until no longer pink. Remove from pan and keep warm.

Add remaining oil to skillet; cook leeks, stirring, for 5 minutes. Add wine; simmer until reduced by half. Over low heat, stir in yogurt, honey, lemon juice and salt. Dissolve cornstarch in water; add to skillet and stir until thickened. Stir in peppercorns.

Noodles: Meanwhile, cook noodles according to package directions; drain and add butter, salt and nutmeg. Divide noodles among 4 plates. Top each with 2 pork escallops; spoon sauce over. Garnish with lemon rind.

Makes 4 servings.

Per serving:

389 Calories
25 g protein
14 g fat
40 g carbohydrate
3 g fibre

Quebec Pork Chops Stuffed with New Brunswick Crab

Two fabulous Canadian foods are combined in this hearty recipe—perfect for a dinner party for eight. Serve with fiddle-heads, rice, lemon wedges and crab claws (if available).

Chef:

Nanak Chand Vig
Executive Chef
Hôtel Manoir Victoria
Québec City, Québec

Dietitian:

Fabiola Masri, P.Dt.
Présidente
Santé à la Carte
Québec City, Québec

You'll find the preparation well worth it for this spectacular — but rich — dish.

8	butterfly pork chops (about 2 lb/1 kg), trimmed	8
1/3 cup	all-purpose flour	75 mL
1/2 tsp	salt	2 mL
1/4 tsp	pepper	1 mL
2	eggs, lightly beaten	2
1 cup	fine dry bread crumbs	250 mL
2 tbsp	butter	25 mL
2 tbsp	vegetable oil	25 mL
	Crab Filling:	
3	cloves garlic	3
1	sprig fresh parsley	1
1/4 lb	boneless pork (shoulder, leg or chop), trimmed	125 g
1/3 cup	whipping cream	75 mL
1	egg	1
1/4 tsp	salt	1 mL
Pinch	each pepper and crushed dried thyme	Pinch
Pinch	each ground coriander, marjoram and savory	Pinch
1/2 cup	fresh or frozen cooked flaked crabmeat (about 150 g)	125 mL

Crab Filling: In food processor, mince garlic and parsley. Add pork and mince. With machine running, add whipping cream, egg, salt, pepper, thyme, coriander, marjoram and savory. Transfer to bowl; stir in crabmeat. Refrigerate.

Pound pork chops with mallet until at least double original size. Divide filling into 8 portions: spoon onto 1 side of each chop. Fold other side over; press edges to seal.

Combine flour, salt and pepper; dredge chops in mixture. Dip into beaten eggs and then into bread crumbs. In skillet, heat butter and oil over low heat; cook chops until browned, turning once. Place in single layer on large baking sheet. Bake at 350°F (180°C) for 20 minutes or until cooked through.

Makes 8 servings.

Per serving:

394 Calories
36 g protein
20 g fat
15 g carbohydrate
trace fibre

Lamb Loin with Carrot Thyme Sauce, Sweet Potatoes and Apple Mango Relish

Here's a recipe that's ideal for a special occasion when you need to pull out all the stops and impress. Serve with green beans.

Chef:

John Cordeaux
Chef Executif des
Cuisines
Hôtel le Reine Elizabeth
Montréal, Québec

Dietitian:

Kim Arrey, P.Dt.
Consulting Dietitian
Montréal, Québec

Sweet potatoes are an excellent source of beta-carotene. Keep portion size in mind—a 1/4 lb (125 g) portion of lamb provides adequate protein at a meal.

1	pkg (500 g) frozen boneless lamb loins, thawed (8 loins)	1

Sweet Potato Purée

1	large sweet potato, peeled and cut into 1-inch (2.5 cm) pieces	1
1	clove garlic, minced	1
2 tbsp	butter or margarine	25 mL
1/4 tsp	salt	1 mL

Carrot Thyme Sauce:

1 tbsp	vegetable oil	15 mL
2	shallots, chopped	2
1-1/2 cups	chicken broth	375 mL
1/2 cup	dry red wine	125 mL
1/4 tsp	crushed dried thyme	1 mL
3	medium carrots, diced	3

Apple Mango Relish:

1	small apple, peeled and diced	1
1/2 cup	diced peeled mango	125 mL
2 tbsp	lemon juice	25 mL
1 tbsp	liquid honey	15 mL
1/2 tsp	chopped fresh mint	2 mL

Per serving:

401 Calories
30 g protein
18 g fat
30 g carbohydrate
4 g fibre

Sweet Potato Purée: In saucepan of boiling water, simmer potato, covered, about 25 minutes or until tender; drain. Purée in food processor or blender; blend in garlic, butter and salt. Keep warm.

Carrot Thyme Sauce: Meanwhile, in saucepan, heat oil over medium heat; cook shallots until softened. Stir in broth, wine, thyme and carrots; bring to boil. Reduce heat to simmer, uncovered, for 30 minutes. Purée in blender or food processor until smooth.

Apple Mango Relish: Meanwhile, in small bowl, combine apple, mango, lemon juice, honey and mint; cover and chill.

Coat lamb loins generously with pepper. Bake on rack on baking sheet at 450°F (230°C) for 8 to 10 minutes. Slice and arrange 2 loins on each plate. Using piping bag, pipe sweet potato purée into rosette in centre of lamb. Spoon sauce on lamb and add relish. Garnish with thyme.

Makes 4 servings.

Lamb Brochette with Couscous and Mixed Vegetables

Lamb is eaten all over the world, and this Middle-Eastern-inspired dish truly does it justice.

Chef:

André Charlebois
Executive Chef
Holiday Inn Crowne
Plaza
Hull, Québec

Dietitian:

Renée C. Crompton, RD
Regional Municipality of
Ottawa–Carleton
Health Dept.
Ottawa, Ontario

You will be transported to a far-away land by the flavors and textures of lamb, couscous and chick-peas.

6	frozen lamb loins, thawed (3 oz/85 or 90 g each)	6
1	medium Spanish onion, cut into 1-inch (2.5 cm) cubes	1
1 cup	dry red wine	250 mL
1/4 cup	finely chopped onion	50 mL
2 tbsp	olive oil	25 mL
1	bay leaf	1
8	black peppercorns	8
1/4 tsp	ground cumin	1 mL
1/2 cup	beef broth	125 mL
1 tbsp	cornstarch	15 mL
2 tbsp	cold water	25 mL

Couscous:

1 cup	couscous	250 mL
1-1/2 cups	boiling water	375 mL
1 tsp	olive oil	5 mL
1/2 tsp	salt	2 mL
1/4 tsp	pepper	1 mL

Vegetables:

1 tbsp	olive oil	15 mL
2	stalks celery, diced	2
1	each small sweet green and red pepper, diced	1
1	small zucchini, chopped	1
1/2 cup	drained canned chick-peas	125 mL
1/4 cup	chopped onion	50 mL

Cut lamb into 1-inch (2.5 cm) cubes. Alternately thread lamb and onion cubes onto 8-inch (20 cm) skewers. In 12- x 9-inch (3.5 L) glass dish, combine wine, onion, oil, bay leaf, peppercorns and cumin; add skewers and marinate for 6 to 12 hours in refrigerator, basting occasionally.

Remove brochettes. Strain marinade into saucepan and bring to boil; cook until reduced by half. Add beef broth; bring to boil. Dissolve cornstarch in cold water; stir into saucepan until thickened and bubbling. Keep warm.

Couscous: In 8-inch (2 L) square pan, pour boiling water over couscous; cover and let stand 10 minutes. Stir in oil, salt and pepper.

Broil or grill lamb skewers for 3 to 4 minutes on each side or to desired doneness.

Vegetables: Meanwhile, in skillet, heat oil over medium heat; cook celery, green and red pepper, zucchini, chick-peas and onion until tender, about 5 minutes.

To serve, place brochette on couscous on each plate. Arrange vegetables to one side and sauce on other side.

Makes 6 servings.

Tomato-Braised Rabbit

If you haven't eaten rabbit before, you may be surprised to discover its mild taste is very similar to chicken and adapts well to different seasonings. Serve over pasta and garnish with low-fat sour cream.

Chef:

Julius Pokomandy, CCC
Chef/Instructor
South Delta Secondary
School
Delta, British Columbia

2-1/2 lb	fresh rabbit	1.2 kg
1 tbsp	olive oil	15 mL
2	medium onions, chopped	2
1	medium sweet green pepper, chopped	1
1	can (19 oz/540 mL) tomatoes	1
1/2 cup	chicken broth	125 mL
1 tsp	paprika	5 mL
1/4 tsp	each salt and pepper	1 mL
2 tbsp	cornstarch	25 mL
2 tbsp	water	25 mL

Dietitian:

Leah Hawirko, RDN
Leah Hawirko Nutrition
Consulting and
The Vancouver Health
Department
Vancouver,
British Columbia

Cut rabbit into serving-size pieces. In large skillet, heat oil over medium-high heat; brown rabbit with onions and green pepper.

Add tomatoes, broth, paprika, salt and pepper; bring to boil. Cover and simmer for 25 to 30 minutes or until rabbit is tender. Dissolve cornstarch in 2 tbsp (25 mL) water; stir into skillet until bubbling and thickened.

Makes 6 servings.

An underutilized meat, rabbit is a good source of iron. Garnish sparingly: this flavorful dish doesn't need many additions.

Per serving:

267 Calories
31 g protein
11 g fat
11 g carbohydrate
2 g fibre

Moose or Elk Stew

You may have difficulty finding moose, but elk, which is available through some specialty butchers and at game farms, is a good substitute.

Chef:

Peter Graham, CCC
1st Chef
Whitehorse General
Hospital
Whitehorse,
Yukon Territory

Dietitian:

Sharlene Clarke, RDN
Outpatient Dietitian
Whitehorse General
Hospital
Whitehorse,
Yukon Territory

Moose or elk meat is very lean and when stewed or boiled, it's tender and tasty. A great lower fat source of protein!

1-1/2 lb	cubed boneless moose, elk or stewing beef	750 g
4 cups	game or beef broth	1 L
1/2 cup	dry red wine	125 mL
1 tsp	minced garlic	5 mL
1 cup	each cubed peeled turnip and potato	250 mL
1 cup	each thickly sliced carrots and celery	250 mL
1 cup	coarsely chopped onions	250 mL
1/2 cup	sliced leeks	125 mL
1	can (19 oz/540 mL) tomatoes	1
1 tsp	Worcestershire sauce	5 mL
	Salt and pepper	
1/4 cup	all-purpose flour	50 mL
1/3 cup	water	75 mL

In large skillet, bring moose, broth, red wine and garlic to boil; reduce heat, cover and simmer for 45 minutes.

Add turnip, potato, carrots, celery, onions and leeks; cook 10 to 15 minutes or until vegetables are just tender. Stir in tomatoes, breaking up with spoon; add Worcestershire sauce. Simmer 5 to 10 minutes or until meat is tender. Season with salt and pepper to taste.

Mix flour and water to form smooth paste; stir into stew and bring to boil, stirring until thickened.

Makes 4 servings.

Per serving:

330 Calories
45 g protein
2 g fat
30 g carbohydrate
5 g fibre

Gypsy Pie

This is one of the most flavorful meat-and-vegetable pies you're likely to eat! The three meats — smoked sausage, venison and rabbit — impart a rich taste without being overpowering.

Chef:

Brian Holden
Head Chef
Elora Mill Restaurant
& Inn
Elora, Ontario

Dietitian:

Jane Curry, RD
Community Dietitian
Woolwich Community
Health Centre
St. Jacobs, Ontario

This succulent entrée with a distinctive Canadian flavor is quite rich: be sure to choose lighter accompaniments.

8 oz	smoked sausage	250 g
1 lb	stewing venison cubes	500 g
1 lb	boneless rabbit cubes (see Tip)	500 g
1-1/2 cups	game or beef broth (see Tip)	375 mL
1/2 tsp	dried thyme	2 mL
2	medium potatoes, peeled and cubed	2
1	large carrot, thickly sliced	1
Half	medium leek, sliced	Half
1/4 tsp	each salt and pepper	1 mL
1/4 cup	all-purpose flour	50 mL
1/3 cup	water	75 mL
3 tbsp	Drambuie or Scotch (optional)	50 mL
	Pastry for 9-inch (23 cm) single crust pie	

Remove casing from sausage and thinly slice. In large nonstick saucepan, cook sausage over medium heat, stirring, for 3 to 4 minutes. Stir in venison and rabbit; cook, stirring, 5 minutes.

Add broth and thyme; bring to boil. Cover and reduce heat to simmer 15 to 20 minutes. Add potatoes and carrots; cover and simmer 10 minutes. Add leek; cover and simmer 5 to 10 minutes or until meat and vegetables are tender. Add salt and pepper.

Mix flour with water to form smooth paste; stir into stew and bring to boil, stirring until thickened. Add Drambuie, if desired. Spoon into 9-inch (23 cm) pie plate. Roll out pastry and place on top, sealing at edge. Cut slits in pastry top. Bake at 400°F (200°C) for 25 to 30 minutes or until pastry is golden and filling is bubbling.

Makes 8 servings.

Tips: Substitute turkey or chicken if rabbit is not available. Rabbit simmered in broth or water is much easier to bone than when raw. Use the simmered liquid for broth in recipe and add cooked rabbit meat with potatoes.

Per serving:

395 Calories
32 g protein
19 g fat
23 g carbohydrate
2 g fibre

Roast Buffalo Striploin

Buffalo is now being raised on farms and is available at meat shops that specialize in game, so you can enjoy its beef-like flavor year round. Serve with garlic-seasoned wild rice, steamed spinach and carrot-green bean medley.

Chef:

Trent Breares
Sous Chef
Saskatchewan Centre for
the Arts
Regina, Saskatchewan

12 oz	buffalo striploin roast	375 g
3/4 cup	dry red wine	175 mL
1/2 cup	red currant jelly	125 mL
1 tsp	dried basil	5 mL
1 tbsp	chopped fresh parsley	15 mL
	Fresh basil or parsley leaves	

Dietitian:

Thomas Hamilton, P.Dt.
Diabetes Nutrition
Educator
Regina Health District
Regina, Saskatchewan

In small shallow roasting pan, roast buffalo at 325°F (160°C) for 45 minutes or until meat thermometer reads 135°F (55°C). Remove from oven and place on warm plate; cover and let stand for about 20 minutes.

Add red wine, currant jelly and basil to roasting pan; bring to boil over medium-high heat. Reduce heat and simmer 15 minutes to thicken, stirring occasionally. Stir in parsley.

Thinly slice buffalo and arrange on plates. Drizzle sauce over slices. Garnish with basil.

Makes 4 servings.

Flavorful wild rice complements the unique taste of this leaner meat entrée.

Tip: Substitute eye of round for striploin and cut in half horizontally to approximately 2-inch (5 cm) thickness. Marinate in red wine for 4 to 6 hours, covered, in refrigerator. Roast in 275°F (140°C) oven approximately 1 hour or until meat thermometer reaches 135°F (55°C). Finish as directed.

Per serving:

210 Calories
19 g protein
2 g fat
27 g carbohydrate
trace fibre

POULTRY

Roasted Pepper-Stuffed Chicken and Cantaloupe

Breast of Chicken Mary Ellen

Tarragon Chicken Stew

Grilled Mexican Chicken Stir-Fry

Saskatoon Berry Chicken

Cottage Cheese Pastry Pouches with Chicken

Poached Chicken with Shrimp Stuffing in
Yogurt Lime Sauce

Grilled Chicken Breast with Mediterranean
Dried Fruit Salsa

Honey Dijon Glazed Chicken

Yogurt-Marinated Chicken

Middle Eastern Pita Pockets with Grilled Chicken

Chicken Curry Casimir

Almond Chicken Dinner

Supreme of Chicken with Sun-dried Tomatoes

Spiced Chicken with Peach Chutney

Grilled Chicken and Peaches with Leeks and
Red Cabbage

Commonwealth Games Chicken

Cajun-Style Turkey Cutlet with Citrus

Skewered Turkey Escallops with
Herbed Fall Slaw and Maple Leeks

Roasted Quail with Bulgur Stuffing and Orange Sauce

Breast of Pheasant St. Andrews

Roasted Pepper-Stuffed Chicken and Cantaloupe

Peppers, roasted in the oven, add both flavor and color to this chicken dish.

Chef:

Vern Dean, Chef
Inlet Bistro/
Blue Horizon Hotel
Vancouver,
British Columbia

Half	each large sweet red and green pepper, seeded	Half
4	boneless skinless chicken breasts (4 oz/125 g each)	4
	Salt and pepper	
2 cups	water	500 mL
1	stalk celery, cut in 1/2-inch (1 cm) pieces	1
1	small onion, sliced	1
1	bay leaf	1
Quarter	large cantaloupe, peeled	Quarter
2 tsp	lemon juice	10 mL
	Chopped fresh parsley	

Dietitian:

Jane Thornthwaite, RDN
Nutrition Consultant
Fresh Choice Restaurant
Program
Vancouver,
British Columbia

The peppers and cantaloupe boost the vitamin C and beta-carotene content of this low-fat chicken dish.

Place peppers, cut side down, on baking sheet; broil about 10 minutes or until skin has blackened. Place in plastic bag; cool 10 minutes. Peel off charred skins; cut each into 4 long strips.

Place chicken between plastic wrap; flatten with mallet. Sprinkle with salt and pepper to taste. Place 1 green and 1 red pepper strip on each chicken breast; roll up tightly and secure with toothpick.

In skillet, bring water, celery, onion, bay leaf and 1/4 tsp (1 mL) each salt and pepper to boil; add chicken rolls. Cover and simmer 10 to 15 minutes or until chicken is no longer pink. Remove from liquid; drain.

In food processor or blender, purée cantaloupe with lemon juice. Heat gently in small saucepan. Divide among 4 plates. Slice each chicken breast into 3 diagonal pieces. Place on cantaloupe purée. Sprinkle with parsley.

Makes 4 servings.

Per serving:

169 Calories
28 g protein
2 g fat
10 g carbohydrate
1 g fibre

Breast of Chicken Mary Ellen

Stuffed chicken breasts are easier to make than you may think and always provide an element of surprise at serving time. Serve with couscous or rice and steamed snow peas with red pepper strips.

Chef:

Robert Warren, CCC
Executive Chef
Ronville Catering &
Muskoka Flag Inn
Huntsville, Ontario

4	boneless skinless chicken beasts (4 oz/125 g each)	4
4 tsp	pesto sauce	20 mL
2 oz	Brie cheese, rind removed and diced (1/2 cup/125 mL)	50 g
3/4 cup	chicken broth	175 mL
1/4 cup	white wine	50 mL
2 tbsp	lemon juice	25 mL
1/2 cup	2% evaporated milk	125 mL

Dietitian:

Mary Ellen Deane, RD
Public Health Dietitian
Muskoka-Parry Sound
Health Unit
Bracebridge, Ontario

Boneless skinless chicken breasts are lean, tender and the original convenience food! Evaporated 2% milk is a wonderful substitute for cream in this rich-tasting, velvety sauce.

Per serving:

234 Calories
33 g protein
8 g fat
5 g carbohydrate
trace fibre

With meat mallet, pound chicken between plastic wrap to 1/4-inch (5 mm) thickness. Spread 1 tsp (5 mL) pesto over each breast; place Brie cheese in middle. Fold up sides and ends, over-lapping to cover cheese completely; secure with toothpick if nec-essary. Place, seam side down, in 4-cup (1 L) covered casserole.

In saucepan, bring chicken broth, wine and lemon juice just to boil; pour over chicken. Cover and bake at 350°F (180°C) for 15 to 20 minutes or until no longer pink.

Reduce temperature to 200°F (100°C). Drain liquid from breasts into rinsed saucepan; return covered breasts to oven to keep warm.

Boil liquid until reduced by one-half. Stir in evaporated milk; simmer until hot.

Slice chicken breasts and fan on warmed plates; drizzle with sauce.

Makes 4 servings.

Tip: Prepared pesto sauce can be found in supermarkets near fresh pasta or from the deli.

Tarragon Chicken Stew

Chicken stew has never gone out of style, and this quick 1990s version is flavored with tarragon and lemon.

Chef:

William King, Chef
Deer Lake Motel
Deer Lake,
Newfoundland

Dietitian:

Rosemary Duffenais,
R.Dt.
Sir Thomas Roddick
Hospital
Stephenville,
Newfoundland

4	chicken breasts (about 7 oz/200 g each)	4
1 tbsp	butter	15 mL
1/4 cup	all-purpose flour	50 mL
2 cups	chicken broth	500 mL
1 cup	dry white wine	250 mL
2 tsp	crushed dried tarragon	10 mL
1 tsp	grated lemon rind	5 mL
1/2 tsp	sugar	2 mL
1/4 tsp	each salt and pepper	1 mL
4	medium carrots, cut into 1-inch (2.5 cm) pieces	4
2	large potatoes, peeled and cut into 1-inch (2.5 cm) pieces	2
2	cloves garlic	2
1/2 lb	mushrooms, sliced	250 g
1/2 cup	frozen peas	125 mL

Remove skin from chicken and trim any fat. In large skillet, melt butter over medium-high heat; brown chicken for 3 minutes each side. Remove from pan.

Dissolve flour in chicken broth; add to skillet along with wine, tarragon, lemon rind, sugar, salt and pepper. Cook, stirring, until boiling.

Return chicken to pan along with carrots, potatoes and garlic; cover and simmer for 25 to 30 minutes or until vegetables are tender.

Remove chicken from skillet; debone and cut into bite-sized pieces. Remove garlic and mash with fork. Add mushrooms and increase heat until sauce boils gently. Return chicken and garlic to pan; add peas and heat through.

Makes 4 servings.

Per serving:

374 Calories
38 g protein
6 g fat
40 g carbohydrate
6 g fibre

Lamb Brochette with Couscous and Mixed Vegetables (page 144)
Overleaf: Orange Ginger Pork and Vegetables (page 138)
Overleaf: Poached Fish Jardinière (page 197)

Grilled Mexican Chicken Stir-Fry

Combine Mexican and Chinese cuisines with the barbecue and you've got this great recipe! Serve over rice.

Chef:

Donald Pattie, CCC
Executive Chef
Niakwa Country Club
Winnipeg, Manitoba

4	boneless skinless chicken breasts (3 oz/90 g each)	4
I	lime	I
I tsp	soy sauce	5 mL
4	stalks celery	4
I	each medium sweet red and green pepper	I
I	large onion	I
I	medium carrot	I
I-1/2 tsp	each ground cumin and chili powder	7 mL
I tsp	lemon pepper	5 mL
1/2 cup	chicken broth	125 mL

Dietitian:

Joan Rew, RD
Co-op Coordinator,
Community Cooking
Nutrition Instructor
Red River Community
College
Winnipeg, Manitoba

Quick, easy and light— what more could you ask for?

Using meat mallet, pound chicken between plastic wrap to 3/8-inch (9 mm) thickness. Place chicken in glass dish; squeeze lime juice over all. Coat with soy sauce. Set aside.

Cut celery on angle 1/8-inch (3 mm) thick and 2 inches (5 cm) long. Cut red and green peppers and onion into long thin strips. Using peeler, peel carrot into long thin strips. Combine vegetables with cumin, chili powder and lemon pepper. Set aside.

Broil or barbecue chicken until no longer pink, 4 to 5 minutes on each side.

Meanwhile, in large nonstick skillet sprayed with nonstick cooking spray, cook vegetables, stirring, until hot. Stir in chicken broth; cook until vegetables are tender, about 8 minutes. Serve over chicken.

Makes 4 servings.

Per serving:

152 Calories
22 g protein
2 g fat
13 g carbohydrate
3 g fibre

Grilled Chicken and Peaches with Leeks and Red Cabbage (page 170)

Saskatoon Berry Chicken

Saskatoon berries grow wild in Saskatchewan and parts of the other Prairie provinces. If you don't have access to Saskatoon berries, use blueberries instead. Serve over rice and garnish with mint sprigs, if desired.

Chef:

David Powell
Executive Chef
Ramada Hotel
Downtown
Saskatoon,
Saskatchewan

1 cup	Saskatoon berries (or blueberries)	250 mL
1 cup	strong chicken broth	250 mL
2 tbsp	granulated sugar	25 mL
1/2 tsp	crushed dried mint	2 mL
1/4 tsp	each nutmeg and cinnamon	1 mL
1 tbsp	vegetable oil	15 mL
6	boneless skinless chicken breasts (about 1-1/2 lb/750 g)	6
2 tbsp	cornstarch	25 mL
2 tbsp	water	25 mL

Dietitian:

Rosanne E. Maluk, P.Dt.
Food Focus Saskatoon
Inc.
Saskatoon,
Saskatchewan

In food processor or blender, purée berries; add broth, sugar, mint, nutmeg and cinnamon, blending well.

In skillet, heat oil over medium-high heat; brown chicken on both sides. Drain off fat. Stir in berry sauce. Cover and simmer 10 to 15 minutes or until chicken is no longer pink inside. Dissolve cornstarch in 2 tbsp (25 mL) water; stir into skillet until bubbling and thickened.

Makes 6 servings.

This low-fat sauce gives the chicken a unique flavor and is sure to have your guests asking for seconds as well as the recipe!

Per serving:

187 Calories
28 g protein
3 g fat
10 g carbohydrate
1 g fibre

Cottage Cheese Pastry Pouches with Chicken

Cottage cheese pastry is thicker and firmer than traditional flaky pastry, is easy to work with, and has added flavor.

Chef:

Tyrone Miller, CCC
Chef
Kitchener-Waterloo
Hospital,
Kitchener, Ontario

Dietitian:

Karen Jackson, RD
Patient Food Services
Manager
The Mississauga
Hospital
Mississauga, Ontario

Use this lower fat pastry option with similar dishes. Its lighter ingredients make it a great choice for all kinds of "pockets".

2 tbsp	vegetable oil	25 mL
1	medium onion, chopped	1
1	clove garlic, minced	1
1 cup	sliced carrot	250 mL
1/2 cup	diced celery	125 mL
1 lb	boneless skinless chicken breasts, cut into thin strips	500 g
3 tbsp	all-purpose flour	50 mL
1 cup	chicken broth	250 mL
1/2 tsp	crushed dried thyme	2 mL
1/4 tsp	crushed dried rosemary	1 mL
1/4 tsp	each salt and pepper	1 mL
1	medium potato, peeled, cooked and diced	1

Cottage Cheese Pastry:

2/3 cup	2% creamed cottage cheese	150 mL
3 tbsp	vegetable oil	50 mL
2	egg whites	2
2-3/4 cups	all-purpose flour	675 mL
2 tsp	baking powder	10 mL
1/2 tsp	salt	2 mL
1	egg, lightly beaten	1

In large skillet, heat 1 tbsp (15 mL) of the oil over medium heat; cook onion, garlic, carrots and celery for 5 minutes. Remove from pan.

Add remaining oil to skillet; brown chicken until no longer pink inside. Stir in flour. Add chicken broth, thyme, rosemary, salt and pepper; bring to boil. Add cooked vegetables and potato; heat through. Cool slightly.

Cottage Cheese Pastry: In blender or food processor, process cottage cheese until smooth; blend in oil and egg whites. In bowl, combine flour, baking powder and salt; stir in cheese mixture until dough forms, adding a little cold water, if necessary. Form into ball; wrap in plastic wrap. Store in refrigerator at least 1 hour.

Per serving:

371 Calories
23 g protein
11 g fat
43 g carbohydrate
2 g fibre

On floured board, form dough into 8-inch (20 cm) oblong tube and cut into 8 pieces. Roll each piece to 7-inch (18 cm) circle; top with about 1/2 cup (125 mL) chicken mixture. Brush edges with egg; fold pastry over filling to form half-moon shape. Crimp edges. Brush with egg and cut slits to vent. Bake on baking sheet at 375°F (190°C) for 15 to 20 minutes or until lightly browned.

Makes 8 servings.

Poached Chicken with Shrimp Stuffing in Yogurt Lime Sauce

Coriander, ginger and lime give this chicken recipe a touch of the orient. Serve with mixed vegetables and a wild rice and mushroom pilaf garnished with strips of red and green peppers.

Chef:

Ron Glover
Chef/Instructor
Southern Alberta
Institute of Technology
Calgary, Alberta

Dietitian:

Mary Sue Waisman, RD
Nutrition Coordinator
Nutrition and Food
Services
Calgary Regional Health
Authority
Calgary, Alberta

The fat is greatly reduced in this tangy entrée by poaching the chicken and using low-fat yogurt in the sauce.

Per serving with sauce:

210 Calories
35 g protein
4 g fat
7 g carbohydrate
1 g fibre

25	medium raw shrimp, peeled and deveined	25
1/2 cup	firm tofu	125 mL
1/4 cup	chopped onion	50 mL
2	cloves garlic, minced	2
1 tbsp	grated gingerroot	15 mL
1 tbsp	lime juice	15 mL
1 tbsp	chopped fresh coriander	15 mL
2 tsp	soy sauce	10 mL
1/4 tsp	each salt and white pepper	1 mL
6	boneless skinless chicken breasts (about 1-1/2 lb/750 g)	6
1	egg white, lightly beaten	1
	Grated lime rind	

	Yogurt Lime Sauce:	
1 cup	strong chicken broth	250 mL
1 tbsp	chopped shallots	15 mL
2 tbsp	cornstarch	25 mL
2 tbsp	lime juice	25 mL
1 tbsp	Dijon mustard	15 mL
1/4 cup	1% plain yogurt	50 mL

In food processor, chop shrimp very fine. Add tofu, onion, garlic, gingerroot, lime juice, coriander, soy sauce, salt and pepper; process to form paste.

With meat mallet, pound chicken between plastic wrap to flatten. Divide shrimp mixture among breasts. Brush edges with egg white; fold chicken around filling to seal. Wrap individually in plastic wrap; place in 9-inch (2.5 L) square baking pan. Place in roasting pan (or broiler pan). Add boiling water to reach three-quarters up sides of square pan. Cover and bake at 350°F (180°C) for 25 to 30 minutes or until firm and moist.

Yogurt Lime Sauce: In saucepan, bring broth and shallots to boil. Combine cornstarch, lime juice and mustard; stir into broth until boiling and thickened. Over low heat, add yogurt and heat through. Serve with chicken. Garnish with lime rind.

Makes 6 servings.

Grilled Chicken Breast with Mediterranean Dried Fruit Salsa

Say 'salsa' and you probably think of tomatoes, onions and peppers. But this salsa adds dried fruit—raisins, apricots and pears. You can poach the chicken instead of grilling, and serve it hot or cold.

Chef:

Samuel Glass, CWC
Executive Chef
Caterers York
Toronto, Ontario

Dietitian:

Rosie Schwartz, RD
Consulting Dietitian
Nutrition Guidance
Services Inc.
Toronto, Ontario

Salsas are a super way to boost fruit and vegetable consumption while adding taste to lower fat cooking.

6	boneless skinless chicken breasts (3 oz/90 g each)	6
	Dried Fruit Salsa:	
1	medium sweet red pepper, diced	1
1/3 cup	raisins or diced pitted prunes	75 mL
1/3 cup	each diced dried apricots and pears	75 mL
1/4 cup	diced red onion	50 mL
1/4 cup	coarsely chopped fresh coriander	50 mL
1/3 cup	lime juice	75 mL
1 tbsp	olive oil	15 mL
1/4 tsp	each salt and pepper	1 mL

Dried Fruit Salsa: In a glass bowl, combine red pepper, raisins, apricot, pears, onion, coriander, lime juice, oil, salt and pepper. Cover and chill at least 1 hour.

Grill or broil chicken for 4 to 5 minutes on each side until no longer pink inside. Serve topped with salsa.

Makes 6 servings.

Per serving:

195 Calories
20 g protein
4 g fat
22 g carbohydrate
3 g fibre

Honey Dijon Glazed Chicken

You'd never guess by the taste just how quick and simple this recipe is to make!

Chef:

Alastair Gray
Executive Chef
The York Club
Toronto, Ontario

2 tbsp	all-purpose flour	25 mL
1/4 tsp	each salt and pepper	1 mL
4	boneless skinless chicken breasts (3 oz/90 g each)	4
2 tbsp	liquid honey	25 mL
2 tbsp	Dijon mustard	25 mL
1 tbsp	olive oil	15 mL

Dietitian:

Mary Margaret Laing,
RD
M.M. Laing & Associates
Healthcare Marketing
Services
Cambridge, Ontario

On piece of waxed paper, combine flour, salt and pepper; coat chicken with mixture. In small dish, combine honey and mustard; set aside.

In skillet, heat oil over medium-high heat; quickly brown chicken on both sides. Place on greased baking sheet; spread with honey mixture. Bake at 350°F (180°C) for 10 to 15 minutes or until chicken is no longer pink inside.

Makes 4 servings.

Add flavor without adding fat — honey and mustard are superb ingredient combinations. For a fast, easy dinner on the run, this chicken dish has it all: easy, fast, nutritious and great, zippy taste!

Per serving:

177 Calories
21 g protein
5 g fat
12 g carbohydrate
trace fibre

Yogurt-Marinated Chicken

Most marinated recipes call for vinegar, lemon juice or wine, but this Indian-style recipe uses yogurt instead. Serve with rice pilaf and salad.

Chef:

Nanak Chand Vig
Executive Chef
Hôtel Manoir Victoria
Québec City, Québec

Dietitian:

Fabiola Masri, P.Dt.
Présidente
Santé à la Carte
Québec City, Québec

Yogurt is an excellent marinade for meat. It enhances the taste and tenderizes the texture without adding a lot of fat.

1-1/4 cups	1% plain yogurt	300 mL
3	cloves garlic, minced	3
1 tbsp	minced gingerroot (or 2 tsp/10 ml ground ginger)	15 mL
1 tbsp	lemon juice	15 mL
1 tbsp	vegetable oil	15 mL
2 tsp	paprika	10 mL
1 tsp	chili powder	5 mL
1 tsp	crumbled dried rosemary	5 mL
1 tsp	pepper	5 mL
1/2 tsp	turmeric	2 mL
8	boneless skinless chicken breasts (about 1-1/2 lb/750 g)	8

In large bowl, combine yogurt, garlic, gingerroot, lemon juice, oil, paprika, chili powder, rosemary, pepper and turmeric; whisk until smooth. Add chicken, tuning to coat all over. Cover and refrigerate to marinate for at least 12 or up to 24 hours.

Place chicken in single layer in baking pan, reserving marinade. Bake at 350°F (180°C) for 20 to 25 minutes, or until no longer pink inside; spooning additional marinade over chicken half-way through baking.

Makes 8 servings.

Tip: Instead of only chicken breasts, you can substitute one 3 lb (1.5 kg) chicken, cut into 8 pieces; bake for 45 to 60 minutes.

Per serving:

129 Calories
21 g protein
3 g fat
3 g carbohydrate
trace fibre

Middle Eastern Pita Pockets with Grilled Chicken

Here's a perfect recipe for a family lunch or dinner, and everyone can put their own pita together. Leftover hummus is also an excellent appetizer, served with crackers and raw vegetables.

Chef:

James McLean
Sous Chef
Benjamin's Restaurant
St. Jacobs, Ontario

Dietitian:

Jane Curry, RD
Community Dietitian
Woolwich Community
Health Centre
St. Jacobs, Ontario

This meal provides a variety of grains, protein sources and vegetables. Team it with milk and you have the four food groups covered!

Per serving:

554 Calories
41 g protein
13 g fat
69 g carbohydrate
12 g fibre

6	boneless skinless chicken breasts	6
1 tbsp	olive oil	15 mL
	Salt and pepper	
Half	English cucumber, diced	Half
2	medium tomatoes, seeded and diced	2
Half	box (145 g) alfalfa sprouts	Half
6	whole wheat pitas, halved	6

	Tabbouleh:	
3/4 cup	bulgur	175 mL
1-1/2 cups	boiling water	375 mL
3	medium tomatoes, seeded and diced	3
2 cups	chopped fresh parsley	500 mL
1/4 cup	lemon juice	50 mL
2 tbsp	chopped fresh mint	25 mL
1/2 tsp	salt	2 mL
1/4 tsp	pepper	1 mL

	Hummus:	
1	clove garlic	1
1	can (19 oz/540 mL) chick-peas, drained	1
3 tbsp	sesame oil	50 mL
2 tbsp	lemon juice	25 mL
1/2 tsp	salt	2 mL
1/4 tsp	pepper	1 mL

Tabbouleh: Cover bulgur with boiling water and let stand 30 minutes; drain. Stir in tomatoes, parsley, lemon juice, mint, salt and pepper.

Hummus: In food processor, mince garlic; add chick-peas and process until puréed. Add oil, lemon juice, salt and pepper; process until blended.

Brush chicken with oil; grill or broil until no longer pink inside. Season with salt and pepper to taste. Slice into thin strips.

Place chicken, cucumber, tomatoes, sprouts, hummus and tabbouleh in separate bowls. Serve warm pita halves in basket for guests to fill.

Makes 6 servings.

Chicken Curry Casimir

You can make this quick curry in minutes. The fruit adds a soothing note to the spices as well as great color and texture.

Chef:

Anton Koch, CCC
Chef/Owner
Rotisserie St. Moritz
Dorval, Québec

Dietitian:

Kim Arrey, P.Dt.
Consulting Dietitian
Montréal, Québec

Using 1% plain yogurt makes a creamy sauce with lower fat.

3/4 cup	long grain rice	175 mL
1 tbsp	olive oil	15 mL
3/4 lb	boneless skinless chicken breasts, cut into thin strips	375 g
2	medium oranges, peeled and cubed	2
1	medium (unpeeled) apple, cubed	1
3/4 cup	red seedless grapes	175 mL
1	can (8 oz/227 mL) pineapple chunks, drained	1
1 tbsp	curry powder	15 mL
1 tsp	ground cumin	5 mL
1/2 tsp	salt	2 mL
1/4 tsp	pepper	1 mL
1 cup	1% plain yogurt	250 mL
2 tbsp	sliced almonds, toasted	25 mL

Cook rice according to package directions.

Meanwhile, in large skillet, heat oil over medium-high heat; brown chicken on all sides until no longer pink inside, about 3 minutes. Reduce heat; stir in oranges, apple, grapes and pineapple and heat gently for 3 minutes. Sprinkle with curry powder, cumin, salt and pepper; mix well. Stir in yogurt and heat through.

Divide rice among 4 plates. Top with chicken curry; sprinkle with almonds.

Makes 4 servings.

Tip: To toast almonds, bake on baking sheet at 350°F (180°C) for 3 to 5 minutes or until fragrant.

Per serving:

414 Calories
27 g protein
8 g fat
59 g carbohydrate
4 g fibre

Almond Chicken Dinner

This is perfect for a family meal or a brunch with a green salad. You can make this casserole ahead, refrigerate and bake before serving, allowing a slightly longer baking time.

Chef:

Don Costello
Cook
Oak Bay Beach Hotel
Victoria,
British Columbia

Dietitian:

Lisa Diamond, RDN
Manager of Nutrition
and Food Services
Vancouver Island
Housing Association
for the
Physically Disabled
Victoria, British
Columbia

If you want to reduce the fat in this chicken dish, omit the almonds and increase the cornflake crumbs by half.

1 tsp	vegetable oil	5 mL
1	large onion, chopped	1
1	medium carrot, grated	1
1-1/2 cups	sliced mushrooms	375 mL
1 cup	chopped celery	250 mL
1/2 cup	chopped sweet red or green pepper	125 mL
2 tbsp	all-purpose flour	25 mL
1-1/2 cups	1% milk	375 mL
2	cloves garlic, minced	2
1/2 tsp	each crushed dried thyme and basil	2 mL
1/4 tsp	crushed dried rosemary	1 mL
1/4 tsp	salt	1 mL
1/2 cup	light sour cream	125 mL
2 tbsp	lemon juice	25 mL
1 tsp	Worcestershire sauce	5 mL
3 cups	cubed cooked chicken	750 mL
2 cups	cooked rice	500 mL
1	can (10 oz/284 mL) sliced water chestnuts, drained	1

Topping:		
1 cup	cornflakes, coarsely crushed	250 mL
1/2 cup	slivered almonds	125 mL

In large skillet, heat oil over medium-high heat; cook onion, carrot, mushrooms, celery and green pepper, stirring, for 5 minutes. Dissolve flour in milk; stir into skillet along with garlic, thyme, basil, rosemary and salt. Cook, stirring, until thickened and bubbling. Remove from heat.

Stir in sour cream, lemon juice and Worcestershire sauce. Add chicken, rice and water chestnuts; mix well. Pour into greased shallow 3-quart (3 L) casserole.

Topping: Mix cornflakes with almonds; sprinkle over casserole. Bake at 350°F (180°C) for 35 to 40 minutes or until heated through.

Makes 6 servings.

Per serving:

393 Calories
30 g protein
13 g fat
41 g carbohydrate
4 g fibre

Supreme of Chicken with Sun-dried Tomatoes

Sun-dried tomatoes are available in packages in many produce shops and Italian delis. If possible, choose tomatoes that are not packed in oil.

Chefs:

Takashi Ito, CCC, and
Scott Brown
Executive Sous Chef
Palliser Hotel
Calgary, Alberta

Dietitian:

Mary Sue Waisman, RD
Nutrition Coordinator
Nutrition and Food
Services
Calgary Regional Health
Authority
Calgary, Alberta

This recipe has a definite Italian flair. Try it with whole wheat pasta.

4	boneless skinless chicken breasts (4 oz/125 g each)	4
4	large basil leaves (or 1 tsp/5 mL dried)	4
4	sun-dried tomatoes, softened	4
2 oz	fontina or mozzarella cheese cut in 4 long strips	60 g
1 cup	chicken broth	250 mL

Sauce:

8	sun-dried tomatoes, softened	8
1 tbsp	chopped fresh basil (or 1 tsp/5 mL dried)	15 mL

Cut slit in underside of thickest part of chicken breast. Insert 1 basil leaf (or sprinkle with dried basil), 1 sun-dried tomato and 1 strip of cheese into each breast; seal with toothpick.

In skillet, bring chicken broth to boil; add chicken and bring to boil. Cover and reduce heat to simmer for 10 to 15 minutes or until chicken is no longer pink inside. Remove chicken from pan and keep warm.

Sauce: Add sun-dried tomatoes and dried basil, if using, to stock in skillet; bring to boil and cook until reduced to1/2 cup (125 mL). In food processor or blender, purée until smooth. Add fresh basil, if using. Serve over chicken.

Makes 4 servings.

Tip: To soften sun-dried tomatoes, cover with boiling water and let stand 10 minutes; drain.

Per serving:
206 Calories
32 g protein
6 g fat
4 g carbohydrate
1 g fibre

Spiced Chicken with Peach Chutney

You can make the Peach Chutney in advance and chill — but be warned, it may not last long once you discover its great zippy taste!

Chef:

*Chris Klugman
Executive Chef
Wayne Gretzky's
Restaurant
Toronto, Ontario*

4 tsp	dried oregano leaves	20 mL
I tbsp	minced garlic	15 mL
I tbsp	vegetable oil	15 mL
3/4 tsp	fennel seeds	4 mL
3/4 tsp	cinnamon	4 mL
3/4 tsp	chopped green chilies	4 mL
4	chicken breasts (about 6 oz/175 g each)	4
	Peach Chutney:	
I lb	peaches, peeled and thinly sliced (4 medium)	500 g
1/2 cup	packed brown sugar	125 mL
1/2 cup	finely chopped red onion	125 mL
1/3 cup	cider vinegar	75 mL
1/4 cup	lemon juice	50 mL
I	clove garlic, minced	I
I tsp	chopped gingerroot	5 mL
I tsp	chopped green chilies	5 mL

Dietitian:

*Susie Langley, M.S., RD
Nutrition Consultant
Toronto, Ontario*

Adding a spice rub both on and under the skin before barbecuing ensures moist and tasty chicken...and if desired, the skin can be removed before serving. Serve with fresh sprig of smoldering rosemary to tantalize the senses.

Peach Chutney: In saucepan, combine peaches, sugar, onion, vinegar, lemon juice, garlic, gingerroot and chilies; bring to boil. Reduce heat and simmer 5 minutes. With slotted spoon, remove peaches and set aside. Simmer liquid until reduced to thick syrup. Return peaches to saucepan and return to boil. Remove from heat. Cool. (Chill if prepared ahead.)

In small food processor, combine oregano, garlic, oil, fennel seeds, cinnamon and chilies; process until smooth. Lift up skin from chicken but do not remove. Spread spice mixture on chicken and replace skin over top. Let stand 30 minutes.

Barbecue on greased grill until no longer pink inside, about 30 minutes. Or bake on greased baking sheet at 400°F (200°C) for about 35 minutes. Remove skin before serving with Peach Chutney.

Makes 4 servings.

Per serving:

341 Calories
26 g protein
8 g fat
42 g carbohydrate
2 g fibre

Tip: Use 1/4 cup (50 mL) chopped fresh oregano instead of dried, if desired.

Grilled Chicken and Peaches with Leeks and Red Cabbage

Grilled chicken can be served so many ways. In this recipe, the presentation on the plate adds eye-appeal to complement the tarragon-flavored chicken and vegetables.

Chef:

Kenneth Peace, CCC
Chef de Cuisine
O'Keefe Centre for the
Performing Arts
Toronto, Ontario

1/4 cup	vegetable oil	50 mL
1/4 cup	orange juice	50 mL
1 tbsp	crushed dried tarragon	15 mL
1 tbsp	cracked black pepper	15 mL
4	boneless skinless chicken breasts (about 1 lb/500 g)	4
1	can (14 oz/398 mL) peach halves, drained	1
3	leeks (white part only), cut in julienne strips	3
1-1/2 cups	shredded red cabbage	375 mL
1-1/2 cups	chicken broth	375 mL
1 tbsp	crushed dried tarragon	15 mL

Dietitian:

Maye Musk, RD
Maye Musk Nutrition
Consultants
Toronto, Ontario

Impress your friends on a special occasion with this colorful entrée. You don't have to be a skilled cook — just follow the easy instructions.

In small saucepan, combine oil, orange juice, tarragon and pepper; bring to boil. Cool. Pour three-quarters over chicken in shallow dish. Cover and refrigerate at least 2 hours or up to 8 hours. About 30 minutes before cooking, stir peaches into remaining marinade and let stand at room temperature.

In skillet, combine leeks, cabbage, chicken broth and tarragon; bring to boil. Simmer over medium heat about 15 minutes or until vegetables are tender and most liquid has evaporated.

Meanwhile, grill chicken over medium-high heat or broil 5 to 7 minutes on each side or until no longer pink inside, brushing occasionally with marinade. Grill peaches 1 minute on each side. To serve, place vegetables on centre of plate; top with chicken and peach half.

Makes 4 servings.

Tip: Instead of canned peaches, you can use 3 large fresh peaches, peeled, pitted and quartered.

Per serving:

222 Calories
30 g protein
4 g fat
17 g carbohydrate
2 g fibre

Commonwealth Games Chicken

Inspired by the Commonwealth Games in Victoria, this delightful chicken recipe combines a variety of flavors for international appeal.

Chef:

Barb Armstrong
Chef/Instructor
Spectrum Community
School
Victoria,
British Columbia

Dietitian:

Marianna Fiocco, RDN
Consulting Dietitian
Westcoast Dietetics Ltd.
Vancouver,
British Columbia

4	boneless skinless chicken breasts (about 1 lb/500 g)	4
2 tsp	grated lemon or lime rind	10 mL
1/3 cup	lemon or lime juice	75 mL
2 tbsp	chopped fresh basil (or 2 tsp/10 mL dried)	25 mL
4 tsp	Dijon mustard	20 mL
2 tsp	chopped fresh thyme (or 1/4 tsp/1 mL dried)	5 mL
	Pepper	

Curry Sauce:		
1/4 cup	light mayonnaise	50 mL
1/4 cup	2% plain yogurt	50 mL
1 tsp	grated lime rind	5 mL
1 tbsp	lime juice	15 mL
1/2 tsp	curry powder	2 mL

Place chicken in single layer in glass dish. Combine lemon rind and juice, basil, mustard, thyme, and pepper to taste; pour over chicken. Cover and refrigerate for 3 to 12 hours, turning chicken occasionally. Grill chicken 6 to 8 minutes on each side or until no longer pink inside.

Curry Sauce: In bowl, combine mayonnaise, yogurt, lime rind and juice and curry powder. Serve with chicken.
      Makes 4 servings.

Per serving with curry sauce:

186 Calories
28 g protein
6 g fat
3 g carbohydrate
trace fibre

Cajun-Style Turkey Cutlet with Citrus

Turkey cutlets are available fresh and frozen in most supermarkets and are a convenient way of enjoying turkey — without the leftovers! Serve with a mixture of steamed wild and long grain rice, acorn squash wedges and a green vegetable.

Chef:

Dean Mitchell, CCC
Executive Chef
Canyon Meadows Golf
and Country Club
Calgary, Alberta

2 tbsp	paprika	25 mL
1 tbsp	ground sage	15 mL
1 tsp	pepper	5 mL
1/2 tsp	each salt, garlic powder and cayenne	2 mL
6	turkey cutlets (3 oz/90 g each)	6
1 tbsp	vegetable oil	15 mL
1	large orange, peeled and sectioned	1
1	medium grapefruit, peeled and sectioned	1

Mix together paprika, sage, pepper, salt, garlic powder and cayenne; place on wax paper. With meat mallet, pound turkey between two pieces of plastic wrap to 3/8-inch (9 mm) thickness. Coat cutlets well with seasoning mixture.

In large skillet, heat oil over high heat; quickly brown turkey on both sides. Reduce heat and add orange and grapefruit; cook until turkey is tender, 3 to 5 minutes.

Makes 6 servings.

Dietitian:

Suzanne Journault-
Hemstock, RD
Food Production
Dietitian
Nutrition and Food
Services
Foothills Hospital
Calgary, Alberta

This cutlet recipe substitutes breadcrumbs with Cajun spices. Using less oil in a nonstick skillet is a good way to further reduce fat.

Per serving:

153 Calories
21 g protein
4 g fat
8 g carbohydrate
2 g fibre

Skewered Turkey Escallops with Herbed Fall Slaw and Maple Leeks

This beautiful dish pairs pecan-coated skewers of turkey with a colorful fruit slaw and crisp leeks. Serve as luncheon dish.

Chef:

John Higgins
Executive Chef
King Edward Hotel
Toronto, Ontario

Dietitian:

Susan Iantorno, M.H.Sc.,
RD
Food and Nutrition
Communications
Specialist
NutriQuest
Etobicoke, Ontario

This simple turkey dish with fall slaw and maple-herbed leeks offers an unusual combination of fruit and vegetables.

I cup	julienned leeks (white part only)	250 mL
I tbsp	maple syrup	15 mL
I-1/2 tsp	rice wine or cider vinegar	7 mL
4	thin turkey cutlets (2 to 3 oz/60 to 90 g)	4
2 tbsp	all-purpose flour	25 mL
I	egg, beaten	I
I/3 cup	fine dry bread crumbs	75 mL
2 tbsp	finely chopped pecans	25 mL
2 tbsp	olive oil	25 mL
I/4 cup	coarsely chopped toasted hazelnuts or pecans	50 mL

Slaw:

I cup	thinly sliced cabbage	250 mL
I	carrot, grated (1/2 cup/125 mL)	I
I/2 cup	finely diced red onion	125 mL
I/2 cup	finely chopped dried apricots	125 mL
I/2 cup	light sour cream	125 mL
2	small zucchini (or I yellow and I green), finely chopped	2
I/3 cup	coarsely chopped cranberries	75 mL
I	red apple, seeded and diced	I
I/4 cup	apple juice	50 mL
I/4 tsp	dried herbs de Provence (or mixture of thyme, tarragon and marjoram)	2 mL

Slaw: In large bowl, mix together cabbage, carrot, onion, apricots, sour cream, zucchini, cranberries, apple, apple juice and herbs; chill.

Mix leeks with maple syrup and vinegar; set aside.

Dip turkey cutlets in flour, then in egg, and finally in bread crumbs mixed with pecans. Weave cutlets onto 8-inch (20 cm) skewers. In 12-inch (30 cm) nonstick skillet, heat oil over medium heat; brown turkey skewers on each side, 3 to 5 minutes.

Spoon slaw onto salad plates; top with turkey skewers. Garnish with leeks and hazelnuts.

Makes 4 servings.

Per serving:

437 Calories
25 g protein
19 g fat
45 g carbohydrate
6 g fibre

Roasted Quail with Bulgur Stuffing and Orange Sauce

Quail is a delicacy and it's not difficult to make at home. The stuffing and sauce can be made in advance, then simply stuff and wrap the quail just before baking.

Chefs:

*Blair Woodruff and
Kurt Zwingli
Instructors, Professional
Cook Program
University College of the
Cariboo
Kamloops,
British Columbia*

Dietitian:

*Cathy Thibault, RDN
Co-Manager, Food and
Nutrition Services
Royal Inland Hospital
Kamloops,
British Columbia*

Alternative meats and grains are highlighted in this recipe, giving an interesting twist to your diet while providing a healthy variety. The bulgur stuffing can also be used as a separate stuffing recipe for poultry dishes.

4	partially deboned quail (breast bones removed)	4
	Salt and pepper	
4	thin slices prosciutto	4

	Stuffing:	
I	small onion, finely chopped	I
I	stalk celery, finely diced	I
I	clove garlic, minced	I
I tsp	extra virgin olive oil	5 mL
1/2 cup	bulgur	125 mL
I cup	chicken broth	250 mL
I tsp	crushed dried rosemary	5 mL
I	bay leaf	I
I tsp	chopped fresh parsley	5 mL
Pinch	each salt and pepper	Pinch

	Sauce:	
1/2 cup	blood orange juice or fresh orange juice	125 mL
1/2 cup	orange juice	125 mL
1/3 cup	chicken broth	75 mL
I tsp	crushed dried rosemary	5 mL
2 tsp	cornstarch	10 mL
I tbsp	water	15 mL
	Salt and pepper	

Per serving:

316 Calories
28 g protein
12 g fat
24 g carbohydrate
4 g fibre

Stuffing: In saucepan, sauté onion, celery and garlic in oil 2 to 3 minutes. Stir in bulgur; cook 2 to 3 minutes, stirring constantly. Stir in broth, rosemary and bay leaf; bring to boil. Cover and simmer 5 minutes or until liquid is absorbed. Remove bay leaf; stir in parsley, salt and pepper.

Sauce: In medium saucepan, combine orange juices and broth; bring to boil and simmer until reduced to I cup (250 mL). Add rosemary; simmer 5 minutes. Blend cornstarch and water; stir into sauce and simmer 2 to 3 minutes or until thickened and glossy. Season with salt and pepper to taste.

Season inside of quail lightly with salt and pepper. Fill quail with bulgur mixture and reassemble into original shape, overlapping seam to prevent loss of stuffing. Wrap each in prosciutto slice; place on ungreased baking sheet. Bake at 375°F (190°C) for 20 to 25 minutes.

Pour sauce onto 4 serving plates. Cut quail in half to expose stuffing; place over sauce.

Makes 4 servings.

Breast of Pheasant St. Andrews

Pheasant makes a delicious alternative to turkey and is available in specialty meat shops. Be sure to follow the recommended cooking times so the pheasant does not overcook and dry out. Garnish with fresh cranberries, if desired.

Chef:

Thomas Pitt, CCC
Chef de Cuisine
Larters at St. Andrews
Golf and Country Club
Winnipeg, Manitoba

4	slices white bread, crusts removed	4
4	skinned pheasant breasts	4
3 tbsp	butter or margarine, melted	50 mL
1/2 cup	jellied cranberry sauce	125 mL
1/4 cup	chicken broth	50 mL
1 tbsp	butter	15 mL
1-1/2 tsp	cornstarch	7 mL
2 tbsp	gin	25 mL

Dietitian:

Joan Rew, RD
Co-op Coordinator,
Community Cooking
Nutrition Instructor
Red River Community
College
Winnipeg, Manitoba

Balance this succulent, rich poultry dish with wild rice and baked squash.

In food processor or blender, process bread into crumbs. Dip breasts in melted butter, then in crumbs. Transfer remaining melted butter to skillet; brown pheasant on both sides. Place on baking sheet. Bake at 300°F (150°C) for 15 to 25 minutes or until barely pink inside. (Do not overcook.)

Meanwhile, in saucepan, combine cranberry sauce, broth and butter; bring to boil, whisking to eliminate any lumps. Whisk cornstarch into gin; add to cranberry mixture and cook, stirring, until sauce thickens and boils. Spoon onto plate; arrange fanned slices of pheasant over.

Makes 4 servings.

Per serving:

472 Calories
46 g protein
18 g fat
26 g carbohydrate
1 g fibre

Fish and Seafood

Lemon Shrimp and Spinach Crepes

Swordfish Steaks with Warm Basil Gazpacho

Rosemary Smoked Halibut with
Balsamic Vinaigrette

Sole and Shrimp Paupiettes

Cedar-Baked Salmon

Lobster à la Jardinière

Grilled Halibut or Swordfish

Acadian Smothered Salmon with Spinach

Pan-Seared Mahi Mahi with Fresh Papaya
Mint Relish

Atlantic Salmon Medallions with Two Purées

The Narrows Crab Cakes

Paella Valencia

Fish Cakes with Cranberry Chutney

Shrimp Over Zucchini Ribbons with
Buttermilk Sauce

South Side Halibut

Grilled Salmon with Warm Cranberry and
Caper Vinaigrette

Seafood Pot-au-Feu

Poached Fish Jardinière

Lemon Shrimp and Spinach Crepes

Crepes are not difficult to make, and in this recipe you don't even need to worry about flipping them over. If you prefer, you can prepare the crepes in advance then reheat before filling.

Chef:

Conrad Courchesne,
Executive Chef
Sawridge Hotel
Fort McMurray, Alberta

Dietitian:

Kathleen Oro, RD
Oro Consulting Services
Fort McMurray, Alberta

The combination of nutrient-rich spinach with a delicate low-fat crepe, seafood and delicious seasonings makes this recipe a hit with even the most spinach-shy person.

2 tbsp	soft margarine	25 mL
1	clove garlic, minced	1
2	green onions, sliced	2
2 cups	packed sliced trimmed spinach	500 mL
1-1/2 cups	sliced mushrooms	375 mL
1 tbsp	grated lemon rind	15 mL
1/4 cup	all-purpose flour	50 mL
1 cup	skim milk	250 mL
1/3 cup	water	75 mL
1 lb	cooked peeled deveined shrimp	500 g
1/3 cup	chopped fresh coriander or parsley	75 mL
1 tbsp	lemon juice	15 mL
	Lemon pepper	

Crepes:		
2	egg whites	2
6 tbsp	all-purpose flour	90 mL
1/3 cup	skim milk	75 mL

Crepes: In small bowl, beat egg whites with flour; gradually beat in milk. Lightly spray 6- to 7-inch (15 to 18 cm) crepe or omelette pan with nonstick cooking spray; heat over medium-low heat. Pour about 3 tbsp (50 mL) batter into pan, swirling quickly to cover bottom. Cook until bottom is lightly browned; flip crepe onto baking sheet. (Or flip onto wire rack to cool, if not using immediately; rewarm before using.) Repeat with remaining batter to make 6 crepes. Cover with foil and keep warm.

In large saucepan, melt margarine over medium heat; cook garlic, onions, spinach, mushrooms and lemon rind until spinach has wilted. Stir in flour. Gradually add milk and water; cook, stirring, until thickened. Stir in shrimp, coriander and lemon juice; heat through.

Place crepes on serving plates. Spoon 2 large spoonfuls filling onto each crepe, reserving some for garnish. Fold sides over filling. Serve remaining filling as sauce on top. Sprinkle with lemon pepper to taste.

Makes 6 servings.

Per serving:

227 Calories
26 g protein
6 g fat
16 g carbohydrate
2 g fibre

Swordfish Steaks with Warm Basil Gazpacho

Both swordfish and shark are available in season at many seafood counters or fish shops. Gazpacho is a cold Spanish soup made with cucumber, onion and tomatoes, and in this recipe, it's given a twist as a warm topping for the fish. Serve over steamed rice.

Chef:

*Ronald Davis
Executive Chef
Sheraton Parkway North,
Richmond Hill Ontario*

Dietitian:

*Debra McNair, RD
Consulting Dietitian
Toronto, Ontario*

2 tbsp	olive oil	25 mL
2	cloves garlic, minced	2
4	swordfish or shark steaks (4 oz/125 g each)	4
1	small onion, chopped	1
3	tomatoes, peeled and chopped (about 2 cups/500 mL)	3
1 cup	chopped seeded peeled cucumber	250 mL
2	green onions, sliced	2
2 tbsp	lemon juice	25 mL
2 tsp	dried basil (or 2 tbsp/25 mL chopped fresh)	10 mL
1/2 tsp	ground cumin	2 mL
Pinch	each dried thyme and pepper	Pinch

In large skillet, heat oil over medium-high heat; cook garlic, stirring, for few seconds. Add fish; lightly brown on both sides. Add onion; cook 1 to 2 minutes.

Add tomatoes, cucumber, green onions, lemon juice, basil, cumin, thyme and pepper. Reduce heat and simmer until fish flakes, easily when tested with fork, about 5 minutes.

Makes 4 servings.

Tip: Substitute drained canned tomatoes if ripe fresh tomatoes are not available.

Per serving:

219 Calories
22 g protein
11 g fat
8 g carbohydrate
2 g fibre

Rosemary Smoked Halibut with Balsamic Vinaigrette

You actually set the rosemary briefly aflame in this easy-to-make recipe, and it gives the fish a wonderful herb flavor and aroma.

Chef:

Pamela Good
Chef de Partie, Pastry
Prince Edward Hotel
Charlottetown,
Prince Edward Island

Dietitian:

Carrie Roach, P.Dt.
Community Nutritionist
Health and Community
Services
Charlottetown,
Prince Edward Island

The flavor added by the smoked rosemary means you need less vinaigrette: you control the fat by controlling how much you use.

Per serving:

208 Calories
24 g protein
12 g fat
1 g carbohydrate
trace fibre

2 or 3	sprigs fresh rosemary	2 or 3
1-1/2 lb	halibut fillets	750 g
	Balsamic Vinaigrette:	
1/4 cup	olive oil	50 mL
2 tbsp	balsamic vinegar	25 mL
1/4 tsp	coarsely crushed black pepper	1 mL
1/8 tsp	salt	0.5 mL
1/2 cup	diced seeded tomato	125 mL
1 tsp	finely chopped shallot	5 mL

In baking dish, place rosemary beside halibut; light rosemary with match (rosemary may not remain lit). Cover tightly with foil. Bake at 425°F (220°C) for 8 to 12 minutes or until fish flakes easily when tested with fork.

Balsamic Vinaigrette: Meanwhile, in small bowl, whisk together oil, balsamic vinegar, pepper, and salt; stir in tomato and shallot. Serve with halibut.

Makes 6 servings.

Sole and Shrimp Paupiettes

This is a deliciously lower fat variation of the traditional veal or beef paupiette fried or braised in wine. Accompany with fresh vegetables.

Chef:

David Nicolson
Executive Chef
Gourmet Goodies
Catering
Edmonton, Alberta

1	medium orange	1
1	lemon	1
4	sole fillets (about 8 oz/250 g total)	4
	Salt and pepper	
8	large shrimp, peeled and deveined	8
1/2 cup	dry white wine	125 mL
1 cup	hot cooked rice	250 mL
2 tbsp	chopped fresh dill	25 mL
1 tbsp	butter	15 mL

Dietitian:

Leslie Maze, RD
Diabetes Outpatient
Clinic
Royal Alexandra
Hospital
Edmonton, Alberta

Lemon and orange create a bittersweet but lively flavor subtly accented with fresh dill.

With sharp knife, peel orange and lemon, removing all pith. Cut into segments between the membranes, discarding any seeds. Coarsely chop and set aside.

Season sole fillets with salt and pepper to taste. Place 2 shrimp on each fillet with tails on either side; roll up to form paupiette. Secure with toothpick.

In saucepan of wine, poach paupiettes over low heat 5 to 7 minutes or just until fish flakes easily when tested with fork. With slotted spoon, place paupiettes on bed of rice on individual plates. Remove picks. Keep warm.

Bring wine to rapid boil and boil until reduced to 1/4 cup (50 mL). Whisk in dill and butter; stir in orange and lemon and heat through. Spoon over fish.

Makes 2 servings.

Per serving:

375 Calories
36 g protein
8 g fat
32 g carbohydrate
2 g fibre

Cedar-Baked Salmon

Cedar shingles and shims, available at lumberyards, impart a special flavor to salmon when baking. You'll need to soak two untreated cedar shingles or one package cedar shims in water at least two hours, or preferably overnight.

Chef:

Judson Simpson, CCC
Executive Chef
House of Commons
Ottawa, Ontario

Dietitian:

Violaine Sauvé, RD
General Manager
Food Services Branch
House of Commons
Ottawa, Ontario

1-1/2 lb	Atlantic salmon fillets	750 g
	Grated rind and juice of 1 lime	
1-1/2 cups	diagonally sliced asparagus	375 mL
1/4 cup	julienned leek	50 mL
1	thin slices red onion	1
1/4 cup	diagonally sliced celery	50 mL
1/2 cup	thickly sliced shiitake mushrooms	125 mL
2	medium tomatoes, seeded and cut into strips	2
8	fresh basil leaves, slivered	8
1	bag (10 oz/284 g) spinach, trimmed	1
	Salt and pepper	

Place soaked shingles or shims on baking sheet; lightly brush with oil. Remove skin and any bones from salmon; cut in 6 serving-size pieces and place on cedar. Sprinkle with lime rind and juice. Bake at 425°F (220°C) for 10 to 15 minutes or until fish flakes easily when tested with fork.

Meanwhile, in steamer basket, combine asparagus, leek, onion and celery; steam until partially cooked. Add mushrooms, tomatoes, basil and spinach; steam just until tender-crisp and spinach has wilted. Place on 6 individual plates; season with salt and pepper to taste. Top each with salmon.

Makes 6 servings.

Per serving:

181 Calories
23 g protein
7 g fat
7 g carbohydrate
3 g fibre

Lobster à la Jardinière

This dish is as pretty as a picture: slices of succulent lobster meat surrounded with colorful vegetable bundles.

Chef:

Serge Desjardins, Chef
Instructor
New Brunswick
Community College
Edmundston,
New Brunswick

Dietitian:

Sylvie Morency, P.Dt.
Consulting Dietitian
Edmundston,
New Brunswick

This recipe is a good source of carbohydrate and a much lighter version of the traditional recipe.

2	live lobsters (about 1 lb/500 g each)	2
2 cups	cooked rice	500 mL
1-1/2 tsp	butter, melted	7 mL
2 tsp	chopped fresh dill	10 mL
	Salt and pepper	
10	asparagus tips, about 2 inches (5 cm) long	10
1	medium carrot, peeled and cut in julienne strips	1
1	leek, cut in julienne strips	1
1	sweet yellow pepper, cut in julienne strips	1
1	green onion	1
	Lemon wedges	

Bring large saucepan of lightly salted water to full boil. Grasp each lobster by body and plunge, head first, into water. Reduce heat and simmer for 12 minutes. With tongs, remove lobsters and let cool. Return water to boil.

Combine rice and melted butter; spread over 2 dinner plates. Sprinkle with dill, and salt and pepper to taste. Set aside.

One vegetable at a time, add asparagus, carrot, leek and yellow pepper to boiling water; cook just until tender-crisp. Refresh in cold water. Cut green onion lengthwise into eight 1/8-inch (3 mm) thick strips; blanch in boiling water just until pliable, about 10 seconds. Prepare two bundles of each vegetable and tie with green onion strips.

Twist tail from lobster. Cut underside with kitchen shears or sharp knife; carefully remove tail meat in one piece. Cut tail fin and one joint off tail shell; rinse and set aside. Remove meat from claws in one piece, using crackers or hammer to open shell. Carefully rinse tail and claw meat. Remove head of lobster by cutting along indented line behind head with sharp knife. Discard contents and rinse shell.

Reassemble each lobster by placing head on one side of rice-covered plate. Cut tail meat into 1/4-inch (5 mm) thick slices; arrange in overlapping row across plate starting at head. Finish with tail shell. Place claw meat on each side of body. Arrange vegetable bundles attractively on rice. Cover with plastic wrap and refrigerate until required.

At serving time, microwave each covered plate at Medium just until heated through, about 5 minutes. Garnish with lemon wedges.

Makes 2 servings.

Per serving:

412 Calories
31 g protein
5 g fat
61 g carbohydrate
5 g fibre

Grilled Halibut or Swordfish

You can marinate fish to add flavor but, since you don't need to worry about tenderizing, the marinating time is short, as in this easy recipe.

Chef:

Kris Bauchman
School District #72
Carihi Secondary School
Campbell River,
British Columbia

1-1/2 lb	halibut or swordfish steaks	750 g
1/3 cup	minced onion	75 mL
2 tbsp	white wine vinegar	25 mL
1 tbsp	liquid honey	15 mL
Pinch	white pepper	Pinch
	Lime wedges	

Cut halibut into 6 pieces; place in plastic bag. Combine onion, vinegar, honey and pepper; pour over fish. Seal bag and marinate, refrigerated, for 30 minutes, rotating bag occasionally.

Remove steaks from marinade. Grill on greased grill or broil, for 3 to 5 minutes on each side or until fish flakes easily when tested with fork. Garnish with lime wedges.

Makes 6 servings.

Tip: Use a fish basket or grill, which has narrower spaces, to prevent the fish from falling through onto the barbecue.

Dietitian:

Elizabeth McLelan, RDN
Consulting Nutritionist
Campbell River,
British Columbia

Add zest to this fish with a tangy, fat-free marinade.

Per serving:

132 Calories
24 g protein
3 g fat
2 g carbohydrate
trace fibre

Acadian Smothered Salmon with Spinach

The salmon is smothered with seasoning, green onion and minced garlic, then poached in the oven on spinach leaves. Serve with medley of fresh vegetables, if desired.

Chef:

Yvonne Levert
Cordon Bleu Chef
Instructor, Hospitality
Administration
University College of
Cape Breton Island
Sydney, Nova Scotia

12	large spinach leaves	12
2 lb	whole salmon	1 kg
1 tbsp	chopped fresh dill (or 1 tsp/5 mL dried dillweed)	15 mL
1/2 tsp	each salt and pepper	2 mL
1 cup	cold water	250 mL
1-1/2 tsp	margarine, melted	7 mL
1	bunch green onions, sliced (about 2/3 cup/150 mL)	1
1	clove garlic, minced	1

Dietitian:

Nanette Porter-
MacDonald, P.Dt.
Clinical Dietitian
Glace Bay Healthcare
Corporation
Glace Bay, Nova Scotia

Salmon has a bit more fat than other fish, but is still a good choice served with lots of vegetables and rice.

Arrange spinach leaves on bottom of 13- x 9-inch (3.5 L) baking dish. Top with salmon; sprinkle with dill, salt and pepper. Pour water and margarine over salmon. Top with green onions and garlic. Cover tightly with foil.

Bake at 325°F (160°C) for 25 to 30 minutes or until salmon flakes easily when tested with fork, basting twice. Arrange salmon with spinach on serving platter with pan juices.

Makes 8 servings.

Per serving:

157 Calories
21 g protein
7 g fat
1 g carbohydrate
trace fibre

Grilled Chicken Breast with Mediterranean Dried Fruit Salsa (page 161)

Pan-Seared Mahi Mahi with Fresh Papaya Mint Relish

Despite the name of this dish, you can substitute sea bass if mahi mahi is not available, and if papaya is not in season, use pineapple instead.

Chef:

Alfred Fan
Executive Chef
Bridges Restaurant
Vancouver,
British Columbia

Dietitian:

Leah Hawirko, RDN
Leah Hawirko Nutrition
Consulting and
The Vancouver Health
Department
Vancouver,
British Columbia

This is a quick and easy dish with an exotic tropical flavor. The colorful, festive relish, high in beta-carotene, can be made ahead of time.

2 tbsp	all-purpose flour	25 mL
Pinch	each salt and pepper	Pinch
4	mahi mahi fillets (3 oz/90 g each)	4
1 tbsp	extra virgin olive oil	15 mL

	Papaya Mint Relish:	
1-1/2 cups	diced peeled papaya (1 large)	375 mL
1/3 cup	finely diced shallots or green onions	75 rnL
3 tbsp	finely chopped fresh mint	50 mL
2 tbsp	lime juice	25 mL
Pinch	each salt, pepper and granulated sugar	Pinch

Papaya Mint Relish: In small bowl, mix papaya, shallots, mint, lime juice, salt, pepper and sugar; set aside.

Mix flour, salt and pepper; dip fish fillets into flour to coat both sides. In nonstick pan, heat oil over medium-high heat; cook fish 1-1/2 to 3 minutes on each side or until fish flakes easily when tested with fork. Serve topped with Papaya Mint Relish.

Makes 4 servings.

Per serving:

149 Calories
17 g protein
4 g fat
11 g carbohydrate
1 g fibre

Monster Quesadilla (page 214)

Atlantic Salmon Medallions with Two Purées

Two vegetable purées—cherry tomato and beet—are easily made in the food processor or blender, and can be made in advance then chilled. The slices of salmon are quickly fried in a small amount of oil. Serve with asparagus.

Chef:

John Cordeaux
Chef Executif des
Cuisines
Hôtel le Reine Elizabeth
Montréal, Québec

Dietitian:

Kim Arrey, P.Dt.
Consulting Dietitian
Montréal, Québec

Sauces do not have to be high in fat. The cherry tomato purée and beet purée add color, flavor and nutrients—but no fat!

1-1/4 lb	Atlantic salmon fillets	625 g
	Pepper	
1 tbsp	vegetable oil	15 mL
	Chopped fresh chives	

Cherry Tomato Purée:

10	cherry tomatoes	10
1 tbsp	sliced green onion	15 mL
1-1/2 tsp	soy sauce	7 mL
1/4 tsp	Worcestershire sauce	1 mL
1/4 tsp	salt	1 mL

Beet Purée:

3/4 cup	chopped cooked beets	175 mL
2 tbsp	water	25 mL
1 tbsp	chopped onion	15 mL
1 tbsp	red wine vinegar	15 mL
1/4 tsp	salt	1 mL

Cherry Tomato Purée: In food processor or blender, process tomatoes, green onion, soy sauce, Worcestershire sauce and salt until smooth. Pour into small bowl and chill.

Beet Purée: In food processor or blender, process beets, water, onion, vinegar and salt until smooth. Pour into small bowl and chill.

Place salmon in freezer for 30 minutes to aid slicing. Slice diagonally into 6 thin medallions. Sprinkle with pepper to taste. In skillet, heat oil over medium-high heat; quickly brown salmon, about 1 minute on each side.

To serve, place salmon on plate; spoon purées around salmon. Garnish with chives.

Makes 6 servings.

Per serving:

174 Calories
19 g protein
8 g fat
4 g carbohydrate
1 g fibre

The Narrows Crab Cakes

Crab cakes are a traditional favorite in the Atlantic provinces. Enjoy these as a dinner entrée, or reduce the size of the cakes and serve as an appetizer.

Chef:

Steven Watson
Executive Chef
Hotel Newfoundland
St. John's, Newfoundland

Dietitian:

Jane McDonald, R.Dt.
Grace General Hospital
St. John's, Newfoundland

Egg whites bind the ingredients in this recipe and allow you to enjoy a delicious meal without the fat from the yolk.

1	stalk celery, finely chopped	1
1/4 cup	finely chopped onion	50 mL
1 tbsp	chopped fresh parsley	15 mL
4	egg whites, lightly beaten	4
1 cup	fine dry bread crumbs	250 mL
2 tsp	Worcestershire sauce	10 mL
1 tsp	dry mustard	5 mL
1/2 tsp	salt	2 mL
2	cans (6 oz/170 g each) crabmeat, drained and flaked	2
	Lemon wedges	

In skillet sprayed with nonstick cooking spray, cook celery, onion and parsley over medium heat, stirring, until tender, about 5 minutes.

In bowl, stir together egg whites, 3/4 cup (175 mL) of the bread crumbs, Worcestershire sauce, mustard and salt. Stir in celery mixture and crabmeat, mixing well.

Using about 1/3 cup (75 mL) crab mixture for each, shape into 1/2-inch (1 cm) thick patties. Coat with remaining bread crumbs.

Spray skillet again with cooking spray. Cook patties over medium heat about 3 minutes on each side or until golden. Serve with lemon wedges.

Makes 6 servings.

Per serving:

119 Calories
11 g protein
1 g fat
15 g carbohydrate
trace fibre

Paella Valencia

Paella is a Spanish dish with a little of everything, all cooked in one pot. You can replace the saffron with turmeric, which is less expensive, and if clams are not available, use extra mussels or shrimp.

Chef:

Kris Bauchman
School District # 72
Carihi Secondary School
Campbell River,
British Columbia

Dietitian:

Elizabeth McLelan, RDN
Consulting Nutritionist
Campbell River,
British Columbia

This winning combination of vegetables, rice, chicken and seafood translates into a well-balanced meal. The simple step of skinning chicken helps reduce the fat.

12	clams	12
12	mussels	12
2 tbsp	olive oil	25 mL
6	chicken drumsticks, skinned (about 1-1/4 lb/625 g)	6
1/2 cup	diced onion	125 mL
2	cloves garlic, minced	2
1-1/2 cups	diced mixed sweet peppers (yellow, red or green)	375 mL
2	medium jalapeño peppers, seeded and diced	2
1-1/2 cups	sliced mushrooms	375 mL
2 cups	long grain rice	500 mL
1/4 tsp	crushed saffron	1 mL
3 cups	chicken broth	750 mL
6 to 12	large shrimp, peeled and deveined (4 oz/125 g)	6 to 12
1-1/2 cups	frozen peas	375 mL

Scrub clams and mussels; remove beards from mussels. Discard any open shells.

In 4-quart (4 L) ovenproof saucepan, heat 1 tbsp (15 mL) of the oil over medium heat; brown chicken on both sides and remove.

Add remaining oil; cook onion and garlic, stirring, 2 to 3 minutes or until golden. Add sweet and jalapeño peppers; cook, stirring, until softened. Add mushrooms; cook, stirring, 1 to 2 minutes. Stir in rice and saffron; cook, stirring, 2 to 3 minutes. Add chicken broth; bring to boil.

Return chicken to saucepan; cover and bake at 350°F (180°C) for 8 minutes.

Add clams; bake, covered, for 5 minutes. Nestle mussels and shrimp in rice; cook, covered, 6 to 8 minutes or until shrimp are pink, mussels and clams open and rice is tender. Discard any mussels or clams that haven't opened. Stir in peas; let stand 1 to 2 minutes.

Makes 6 servings.

Per serving:

462 Calories
33 g protein
9 g fat
59 g carbohydrate
3 g fibre

Fish Cakes with Cranberry Chutney

This west coast version of fish cakes will be popular with the whole family. The Cranberry Chutney adds a tart note that adults, in particular, will enjoy.

Chef:

Hubertus Surm, Chef
Isadora's Co-operative
Restaurant
Vancouver,
British Columbia

1 lb	white fish fillets (halibut, haddock, cod)	500 g
2 cups	water	500 mL
	Rind and juice of 1 lemon	
1 tsp	salt	5 mL
3	medium potatoes, peeled	3
1/4 cup	2% milk	50 mL
1/4 tsp	white pepper	1 mL
1/2 cup	finely chopped fresh parsley	125 mL
1	egg, lightly beaten	1
2 tbsp	all-purpose flour	25 mL
	Cranberry Chutney (recipe follows)	

Dietitian:

Jane Thornthwaite, RDN
Nutrition Consultant
Fresh Choice Restaurant
Program
Vancouver,
British Columbia

This dish is not your typical fish cake recipe — very flavorful and surprisingly low in fat.

Cut fish into 4 pieces, removing any bones. In skillet, bring water, lemon rind and juice, and 1/2 tsp (2 mL) of the salt to boil. Add fish; cover and reduce heat to poach until fish flakes easily when tested with fork, about 10 minutes. Drain, let cool and flake.

In saucepan of boiling water, cook potatoes until tender; drain and mash with milk, pepper and remaining salt. Stir in parsley and egg, mixing well. Form into six 1/2-inch (1 cm) thick patties; lightly coat with flour.

In skillet sprayed with nonstick cooking spray, brown fish patties 3 to 5 minutes on each side. Serve hot with Cranberry Chutney.

Makes 6 servings.

Cranberry Chutney:

1 cup	water	250 mL
1 cup	granulated sugar	250 mL
1	pkg (12 oz/340 g) cranberries (3 cups/750 mL)	1
1	medium orange	1
1/2 cup	white vinegar	125 mL
2 tsp	dry mustard	10 mL
1 tsp	ginger	5 mL
1/4 tsp	each cinnamon and ground cloves	1 mL

Per serving with 1/4 cup (50 mL) chutney

241 Calories
19 g protein
3 g fat
36 g carbohydrate
3 g fibre

In medium saucepan, heat water and sugar to dissolve sugar. Stir in cranberries and bring to boil; reduce heat to simmer, covered, for 10 minutes. Uncover and simmer 10 minutes longer.

Wash and seed orange; process with skin in food processor until chopped. Add to saucepan along with vinegar, mustard, ginger, cinnamon and cloves; simmer for 20 minutes, uncovered and stirring often, until slightly thickened. Cool and refrigerate.

Makes 3-1/2 cups (875 mL).

Tips: The fish cakes store well in refrigerator for about 1 week or may be frozen for longer storage. Reserve poaching liquid for soups or chowders.

Shrimp Over Zucchini Ribbons with Buttermilk Sauce

Serve cold as summer lunch, garnished with basil leaf or sprig of dill and accompanied with French baguette.

Chef:

*Judson Simpson, CCC
Executive Chef
House of Commons
Ottawa, Ontario*

	Fish stock or water	
24	shrimp, peeled and deveined	24
2	medium zucchini	2
1/2 cup	buttermilk	125 mL
1/4 cup	light sour cream	50 mL
1/4 cup	1% plain yogurt	50 mL
1 tbsp	each chopped fresh basil, chives and dill	15 mL
Pinch	coarsely ground black pepper	Pinch

Dietitian:

*Violaine Sauvé, RD
General Manager, Food
Services Branch
House of Commons
Ottawa, Ontario*

Many people have the misconception that buttermilk is fattening, but in fact, it has less fat than 2% milk!

In skillet of gently simmering fish stock, poach shrimp until pink; drain and chill.

Cut zucchini in half lengthwise; place flat side down and slice into thin ribbons resembling fettuccine. Steam until just tender-crisp. Chill.

In bowl, combine buttermilk, sour cream, yogurt, basil, chives, dill and pepper; stir in zucchini. Divide among plates; top with shrimp.

Makes 4 servings.

Per serving:

142 Calories
21 g protein
3 g fat
8 g carbohydrate
1 g fibre

South Side Halibut

This citrus-flavored fish dish calls for either steaks or fillets and is ready in less than 15 minutes.

Chef:

Steven Watson
Executive Chef
Hotel Newfoundland
St. John's, Newfoundland

Dietitian:

Jane McDonald, R.Dt.
Grace General Hospital
St. John's, Newfoundland

1	clove garlic, minced	1
1/3 cup	finely chopped onions	75 mL
1 tsp	vegetable oil	5 mL
2 tbsp	chopped fresh parsley	25 mL
1/2 tsp	grated orange rind	2 mL
1/8 tsp	pepper	0.5 mL
1/4 cup	orange juice	50 mL
1 tbsp	lemon juice	15 mL
4	halibut steaks (4 oz/125 g each) or 1 lb (500 g) halibut or Pacific snapper fillets	4

In small skillet, sauté garlic and onions in oil over medium heat until tender. Remove from heat; stir in parsley, orange rind and pepper. Combine orange juice and lemon juice.

Arrange fish in baking dish. Spread onion mixture over fish; pour juice over top. Cover tightly with foil. Bake at 400°F (200°C) 8 to 10 minutes or until fish flakes easily when tested with fork.

Makes 4 servings.

Per serving:

149 Calories
24 g protein
4 g fat
4 g carbohydrate
trace fibre

Grilled Salmon with Warm Cranberry and Caper Vinaigrette

Make the tangy vinaigrette the day before, then heat in the microwave while the salmon fillets are grilling. Serve the salmon on salad greens or with rice and vegetables.

Chef:

Daryle Ryo Nagata
Executive Chef
Waterfront Centre Hotel
Vancouver,
British Columbia

Dietitian:

Jane Thornthwaite, RDN
Nutrition Consultant
Fresh Choice Restaurant
Program
Vancouver,
British Columbia

This vinaigrette adds fabulous flavor but does boost the fat.

1/2 cup	red wine vinegar	125 mL
1/4 cup	vegetable oil	50 mL
1/4 cup	water	50 mL
1/4 cup	sliced cranberries	50 mL
2 tbsp	capers	25 mL
1 tbsp	finely chopped shallots	15 mL
1 tsp	minced fresh or dried chives	5 mL
1 tsp	minced garlic	5 mL
1/2 tsp	pink peppercorns	2 mL
Half	each small lemon and lime, peeled and cut into 4 wedges	Half
1/4 to 1/2 tsp	cayenne pepper	1 to 2 mL
Pinch	dried thyme	Pinch
6	salmon fillets (4 oz/125 g each), skin on	6

In jar, combine vinegar, oil, water, cranberries, capers, shallots, chives, garlic, pink peppercorns, lemon and lime wedges, cayenne and thyme; shake well and let stand 6 to 8 hours.

Broil or grill salmon fillets on medium-high heat 3 to 4 minutes each side or until fish flakes easily when tested with fork.

Warm vinaigrette on stove or in microwave; remove lemon and lime wedges. Remove skin from salmon. Serve with vinaigrette spooned over fillets.

Makes 6 servings.

Per serving:

237 Calories
21 g protein
16 g fat
3 g carbohydrate
trace fibre

Seafood Pot-au-Feu

Substituting meat with fish and shellfish makes this 'pot on fire' fish stew a whole new taste experience! Serve with crusty French bread.

Chef:

Guy Blain, Chef/Owner
Restaurant L'Orée
du bois
Chelsea, Québec

Dietitian:

Debra Reid, Ph.D., RD
Ottawa–Carleton
Health Dept.
Ottawa, Ontario

This is a five star main dish for both nutrition and taste! You'll find generous amounts of green and orange vegetables complementing the low-fat seafood in this fast and elegant recipe.

8 cups	water	2 L
2	medium onions, diced	2
2	large tomatoes, diced	2
1 cup	sliced leeks	250 mL
2/3 cup	diced celery	150 mL
1/2 cup	diced carrots	125 mL
1/4 cup	tomato paste	50 mL
2 tsp	salt	10 mL
1/4 tsp	pepper	1 mL
5 oz	skinless salmon fillet	150 g
5 oz	cod fillet	150 g
5 oz	perch fillet	150 g
5 oz	bay scallops (3/4 cup/175 mL)	150 g
5 oz	medium shrimp, peeled and deveined	150 g
18	mussels, scrubbed and debearded	18
1/4 cup	chopped fresh parsley	50 mL
1 tbsp	minced garlic	15 mL

In large deep saucepan, combine water, onions, tomatoes, leeks, celery, carrots, tomato paste, salt and pepper; bring to boil. Cover and reduce heat; simmer 20 minutes.

Meanwhile, cut salmon, cod and perch into 12 pieces each. Add fish pieces along with scallops, shrimp and mussels to saucepan; cook 3 to 5 minutes or until fish is opaque, shrimp are pink and mussels open. (Do not overcook.) Discard any mussels that do not open. Stir in parsley and garlic.

Makes 6 servings.

Per serving:

201 Calories
29 g protein
4 g fat
13 g carbohydrate
2 g fibre

Poached Fish Jardinière

This wonderful recipe features fish marinated with lemon and wine, then topped after baking with a creamy tomato sauce.

Chef:

Alex Clavel, Chef/Owner
Restaurant Chez
la vigne
Wolfville, Nova Scotia

Dietitian:

Heather Cutler, P.Dt.
Clinical Dietitian
Camp Hill Hospital
Halifax, Nova Scotia

Yogurt provides a creamy base for the sauce in this recipe without adding a lot of fat.

I	small onion, chopped	I
6 to 8	bay leaves	6 to 8
6 to 8	portions (4 oz/125 g each) fresh or frozen halibut or haddock	6 to 8
6 to 8	thin slices lemon	6 to 8
I cup	dry white wine	250 mL
1/2 cup	water	125 mL
	Sauce:	
4	large tomatoes, chopped	4
2	cloves garlic, minced	2
1/4 cup	plain yogurt	50 mL
2 tbsp	olive oil	25 mL
2 tbsp	chopped fresh parsley	25 mL
I tbsp	Dijon mustard	15 mL
2 tsp	each dried chervil and tarragon	10 mL
I tsp	Worcestershire sauce	5 mL
1/4 tsp	salt	I mL
	Pepper	

Spread onion on bottom of large shallow baking dish. Place bay leaves in dish; top each with piece of fish and lemon slice. Pour wine and water over top. Cover and chill at least I hour.

Sauce: In saucepan, combine tomatoes, garlic, yogurt, oil, parsley, mustard, chervil, tarragon, Worcestershire sauce, salt, and pepper to taste; cook over low heat 10 to 15 minutes to blend flavors. (Do not boil.)

Bake fish in 425°F (220°C) oven for 10 to 15 minutes or until fish flakes easily when tested with fork. Remove fish from liquid and arrange on plates, adding some liquid to sauce for desired consistency if necessary. Pour sauce over fish.

Makes 6 to 8 servings.

Per each of 8 servings:

204 Calories
26 g protein
8 g fat
7 g carbohydrate
2 g fibre

Meatless Meals

Vegetable Moussaka

Punjabi Potato and Chick-Pea Curry

Puffed Tofu and Vegetables

Roasted Yam Fajitas

Farmer's Omelette

Stir-Fried Mixed Vegetables

Tostada with Black Bean Chili and Mango Corn Salsa

Vegetable and Bean Ragout with
Roasted Tomato Vinaigrette

Gathers Lighter Pizza

Grilled Vegetable Tofu Lasagna

Garden Path Burger

Monster Quesadilla

Vegetarian Chili

Southwestern Torta

Venturing into Vegetarianism

Vegetarianism has been a dietary option since the dawn of recorded time. For the past decade, the trend has become increasingly popular; each year many Canadians become vegetarian while many others begin to make vegetarian food choices. Whether it's for health, culture or ecology reasons, each day more and more Canadian plates are filled with delicious food of plant origin. Vegetarian convenience foods, meatless restaurant entrées, vegetarian magazines and books and even vegetarian spas abound.

Vegetarianism is generally described according to the foods that are included in the diet. Vegetarians completely avoid animal meat, whether it comes from animals, poultry or fish. There is often some flexibility in the degree to which animal products are left out of the diet.

Vegans eat no meat, fish, poultry, dairy products or eggs. Lacto vegetarians continue to use dairy products, while ovo vegetarians include eggs in their meal plans. Lacto-ovo vegetarians continue to use both. Some "semi-vegetarians" use poultry and fish, but avoid red meat.

A well-planned, balanced vegetarian diet is one option that provides completely adequate nutrition. But there is more to becoming a vegetarian than just eliminating meat from your diet. It's important to include excellent sources of iron, zinc and calcium, and to ensure a source of vitamin B-12. This can usually be accomplished by eating a wide variety of foods, being sure to balance food choices among the food groups, as recommended in "Canada's Food Guide to Healthy Eating."

As with any eating pattern, pregnant and nursing moms, as well as children, will need some additional planning and perhaps nutritional supplements to meet their requirements. A dietitian can help plan a variety of tasty and interesting ways to meet your specific needs.

"Canada's Food Guide to Healthy Eating" recommends that we reduce fat intake while increasing intake of both fibre and complex carbohydrates. People who follow these recommendations are likely to have a reduced risk for some lifestyle diseases such as cancer, diabetes and heart disease. Research indicates that plant foods contain a wide variety of components that help keep us healthy: vitamins such as C, E and beta-carotene, dietary fibre, and newly identified protective substances such as phyto chemicals. A vegetarian eating pattern, by its strong emphasis on plant-based food sources, is one option that not only helps to increase your intake of these nutrients, but also helps you to follow Canada's Guidelines for Healthy Eating.

In a vegetarian style of eating, the majority of food choices come from the the two largest arcs in "Canada's Food Guide to Healthy Eating" rainbow. This guide identifies beans, lentils, nuts, seeds and eggs as alternatives to meat. Eating these foods in combination with grains and vegetables each day provides tasty meals that will fulfil your protein requirements.

What is important, as in any healthy-eating pattern, is planning, balance, variety and meeting nutritional needs, especially for protein and energy.

More and more, Canadians are trying the vegetarian option—a meal at a time, a day at a time or as an on-going pattern of eating.

So, if you find yourself venturing into vegetarianism, welcome to the wonderful, creative realm of cooking without meat! Tasty, nutritious alternatives are here for the asking. Try the Monster Quesadilla or the fabulous Grilled Vegetable Tofu Lasagna to tempt even the most skeptical taste buds. Eat well and enjoy!

Vesanto Melina, RD
Vancouver, British Columbia

Vegetable Moussaka

The rich cream sauce normally used in moussaka has been replaced with a tofu mixture that gives all the taste with a fraction of the fat!

Chef:

Mark Mogensen, Chef
HealthWinds
Therapeutic Spa
Toronto, Ontario

Dietitian:

Marsha Rosen, RD
Consulting Dietitian
HealthWinds
Therapeutic Spa
Toronto, Ontario

This is a great lower fat vegetarian version of a Greek classic.

2	medium eggplants	2
	Salt	
1	medium onion, chopped	1
1	clove garlic, minced	1
1	can (19 oz/540 mL) chick-peas, drained	1
1	can (28 oz/796 mL) tomatoes	1
1 tbsp	each dried oregano and basil	15 mL
1/2 tsp	each cinnamon and pepper	2 mL
1/4 cup	grated Parmesan cheese	50 mL

Topping:		
1 lb	tofu	500 g
1	medium onion, quartered	1
2	egg whites	2
Pinch	nutmeg	Pinch

Slice eggplants lengthwise into 1/4-inch (5 mm) thick slices; sprinkle with 1 tsp (5 mL) salt. Let drain in colander for 30 minutes. Bake on greased baking sheets at 350°F (180°C) for 15 minutes. Turn and bake 15 minutes on other side.

In nonstick skillet sprayed with nonstick cooking spray, cook onion and garlic, stirring, for 2 minutes. Add chick-peas, mashing slightly. Stir in tomatoes, oregano, basil, cinnamon, pepper and 1/2 tsp (2 mL) salt; bring to boil. Reduce heat to simmer, uncovered, for 20 minutes, stirring occasionally. Process in food processor until mixture resembles coarse meal.

In greased 13- x 9-inch (3 L) baking pan, layer half the eggplant, then all of chick-pea mixture, half the Parmesan, then remaining eggplant.

Topping: In food processor, purée tofu, onion, egg whites and nutmeg; spread over moussaka. Sprinkle with remaining cheese. Bake at 350°F (180°C) for 30 minutes.

Makes 8 servings.

Tip: For flavor variation, you can also add grilled peppers and zucchini to the eggplant layer.

Per serving:

187 Calories
12 g protein
5 g fat
26 g carbohydrate
6 g fibre

Punjabi Potato and Chick-Pea Curry

Potatoes and canned chick-peas take on a new flavor dimension in this easy-to-make dish, which can be served with brown rice pilaf and whole wheat chapatis.

Chef:

Stephen Ashton
Head Chef/Instructor
Picasso Café
Vancouver,
British Columbia

Dietitian:

Jane Thornthwaite, RDN
Nutrition Consultant
Fresh Choice Restaurant
Program
Vancouver,
British Columbia

Chick-peas offer lower fat, high-fibre, inexpensive protein. A great-tasting versatile legume, chick-peas are wonderful in anything from spreads, soups or sauces to main-course meals.

2 tbsp	vegetable oil	25 mL
6	cloves garlic, minced	6
1	large onion, diced	1
1 tsp	crushed red pepper flakes	5 mL
1 tsp	each turmeric and ground coriander	5 mL
1 tsp	each cumin seeds and brown or black mustard seeds	5 mL
2 tbsp	tomato paste	25 mL
4 cups	apple juice	1 L
2	large (unpeeled) potatoes, diced	2
1	can (19 oz/540 mL) chick-peas, drained	1
1 tbsp	brown sugar	15 mL
1	bay leaf	1
1 tbsp	lemon juice	15 mL
	Hot pepper sauce	

In large skillet, heat oil over medium-high heat; cook garlic and onion, stirring, for 3 to 4 minutes or until softened. Add red pepper flakes, turmeric, coriander, and cumin and mustard seeds; cook, stirring for 2 to 3 minutes.

Stir in tomato paste; pour in apple juice. Add potatoes, chick-peas, brown sugar, bay leaf and lemon juice; bring to boil. Reduce heat and simmer, uncovered, for 25 to 30 minutes, stirring occasionally, until potatoes are tender and mixture has thickened. Discard bay leaf. Add hot pepper sauce to taste.

Makes 4 servings.

Per serving:

439 Calories
10 g protein
9 g fat
82 g carbohydrate
6 g fibre

Puffed Tofu and Vegetables

Tofu is frequently used in oriental cuisine. In this recipe, it's fried first to give a golden brown color, then stir-fried with garlic and vegetables.

Chef:

Jon Paudler
Chef/Instructor
Culinary Arts
Northern Alberta
Institute of Technology
Edmonton, Alberta

Dietitian:

Leslie Maze, RD
Diabetes Outpatient
Clinic
Royal Alexandra
Hospital
Edmonton, Alberta

Perfect as a side dish or can be served equally well as a totally vegetarian main course.

	Vegetable oil for frying	
1	medium soft tofu cake (about 300 g)	1
1 tbsp	vegetable oil	15 mL
1	clove garlic, crushed	1
1/2 tsp	crushed red pepper flakes	2 mL
1	small carrot, sliced	1
1	medium onion, cut into wedges	1
Half	small cucumber, peeled and sliced	Half
1-1/2 cups	sliced bok choy	375 mL
8	snow peas	8
1/4 cup	water	50 mL
1 tbsp	dry sherry	15 mL

	Sauce:	
1/4 cup	water	50 mL
1 tsp	tamari or soy sauce	5 mL
1 tsp	cornstarch	5 mL
Pinch	granulated sugar	Pinch

Heat 1/4 inch (5 mm) oil in wok or skillet. Cut tofu into 4 slices; fry until light golden brown. Transfer to paper towel-lined plate to drain excess oil. Place in hot water for 5 minutes; drain again on paper towel-lined plate.

In same wok or skillet, heat 1 tbsp (15 mL) oil; stir-fry garlic and tofu pieces. Remove garlic. Sprinkle tofu with red pepper flakes; remove from wok and keep warm.

Stir-fry carrot and onion 2 minutes. Add cucumber, bok choy and snow peas; stir-fry 2 minutes. Add water and sherry; cover and cook 1 to 2 minutes.

Sauce: Combine water, tamari sauce, cornstarch and sugar; add to wok and cook until thickened.

Transfer to serving dish and top with tofu.

Makes 4 servings.

Per serving:

159 Calories
8 g protein
11 g fat
9 g carbohydrate
3 g fibre

Roasted Yam Fajitas

Yams, or sweet potatoes, are a popular ingredient in southern dishes and take centre stage in this fun-to-eat fajita recipe.

Chef:

Peter Ochitwa
Executive Chef/Owner
Mad Apples Restaurant
Toronto, Ontario

Dietitian:

Susie Langley, M.S., RD
Nutrition Consultant
Toronto, Ontario

Loaded with beta-carotene, this spicy vegetarian entrée adds a touch of the Caribbean!

4	medium yams (1-1/2 lb/750 g)	4
2 tbsp	olive oil	25 mL
	Salt and pepper	
1	each medium sweet red and green pepper, cut into strips	1
1	medium onion, sliced	1
10	7 to 8-inch (19 to 20 cm) flour tortillas	10

Sauce:		
1/3 cup	orange juice	75 mL
1 tsp	grated lime rind	5 mL
2 tbsp	lime juice	25 mL
1 tbsp	olive oil	15 mL
1 tbsp	minced garlic	15 mL
1 tsp	crushed dried oregano	5 mL
1 tsp	ground cumin	5 mL
1/4 tsp	red pepper flakes	1 mL
1/4 tsp	pepper	1 mL

Toppings: Chopped tomatoes, shredded lettuce, shredded cheese, low-fat sour cream

Sauce: In bowl, combine orange juice, lime rind and juice, oil, garlic, oregano, cumin, red pepper flakes and pepper; cover and let stand at least 4 hours at room temperature. (Or refrigerate overnight.)

Peel yams and cut into 1/2-inch (1 cm) cubes; toss with 1 tbsp (15 mL) of the oil. Place on baking sheet; sprinkle with salt and pepper to taste. Bake at 350°F (180°C) for 20 to 25 minutes or until tender but not mushy. Cool completely.

In large skillet, heat remaining oil over medium-high heat; sauté red and green peppers and onions about 5 minutes. Add yams and sauce; heat through (most of sauce will be absorbed).

Meanwhile, wrap tortillas in foil; bake at 350°F (180°C) for 5 to 10 minutes or until heated. (Or, wrap in paper towels and microwave at High for 40 seconds.) Spoon yam mixture into tortillas. Top with desired toppings.

Makes 5 servings.

Per serving (without toppings):

484 Calories
10 g protein
14 g fat
82 g carbohydrate
6 g fibre

Farmer's Omelette

This one-dish omelette is stuffed with vegetables and topped with cheese. To finish it off, the omelette is browned under the broiler, then served in wedges.

Chef:

Tyrone Miller, CCC
Chef
Kitchener-Waterloo
Hospital
Kitchener, Ontario

Dietitian:

Karen Jackson, RD
Patient Food Service
Manager
The Mississauga
Hospital
Mississauga, Ontario

Fresh herbs and
vegetables enhance
the flavor and eye
appeal. Serve with a
light tomato sauce and
a whole wheat roll
for a great meal.

1 tbsp	vegetable oil	15 mL
1	medium onion, chopped	1
1	clove garlic, minced	1
1/2 cup	each chopped red and green pepper	125 mL
1	medium potato, peeled, cooked and diced	1
1	medium tomato, seeded and chopped	1
6	eggs	6
1/3 cup	skim milk	75 mL
1/2 tsp	crushed dried oregano	2 mL
1/2 tsp	salt	2 mL
1/4 tsp	white pepper	1 mL
Pinch	crushed red pepper flakes	Pinch
1 cup	shredded part-skim mozzarella cheese	250 mL

In 9-inch (23 cm) ovenproof skillet, heat oil over medium-high heat; sauté onion, garlic, red and green pepper for 3 to 5 minutes or until softened. Stir in potato and tomato.

Whisk together eggs, milk, oregano, salt, pepper and red pepper flakes; pour into skillet and cook until bottom is set. Lift with spatula to allow uncooked portion to flow underneath; cook until almost set. Sprinkle with cheese. Broil until cheese melts, 2 to 3 minutes.

Makes 4 servings.

Tip: If your skillet has a handle that's not ovenproof, just wrap the handle in foil before running it under the broiler.

Per serving:

285 Calories
19 g protein
16 g fat
16 g carbohydrate
2 g fibre

Stir-Fried Mixed Vegetables

The beauty of a stir-fry is that you can mix and match vegetables. Chinese cabbage—bok choy—is available in most supermarkets. You'll find shiitake mushrooms in produce shops, either fresh or dried in packages.

Chef:

Raymond Colliver, CCC
Chef/Instructor
Southern Alberta
Institute of Technology
Calgary, Alberta

Dietitian:

Dani Flowerday, RD
Consulting Dietitian
Calgary, Alberta

Stir frying with a minimum amount of oil is a quick, easy way to enjoy an abundance of vegetables.

12 oz	Chinese cabbage	375 g
2 tbsp	vegetable oil	25 mL
2	cloves garlic, minced	2
3 to 4 tsp	grated gingerroot	15 to 20 mL
2 cups	carrot, julienned	500 mL
8	black Chinese or shiitake mushrooms, sliced	8
1	can (5-1/2 oz/156 mL) sliced bamboo shoots (optional)	1
1	can (14 oz/398 mL) baby corn cobs, drained and halved	1
4	green onions, sliced diagonally	4
1 cup	chicken or vegetable broth	250 mL
2 tbsp	light soy sauce	25 mL
4 tsp	cornstarch	20 mL
2 tbsp	cold water	25 mL

Trim cabbage, cutting centre rib into 2-inch (5 cm) chunks; slice leaves into strips.

In large wok or skillet, heat oil over medium-high heat; cook garlic and gingerroot, stirring, for 30 seconds. Add cabbage ribs and carrot; stir-fry 2 to 3 minutes.

Add mushrooms, bamboo shoots, if using, corn and green onions; stir-fry 2 minutes. Add sliced cabbage leaves, broth and soy sauce; cook, stirring, 1 to 2 minutes or until vegetables are tender-crisp.

Mix cornstarch with water; slowly add to broth, stirring constantly until thickened.

Makes 6 servings.

Tip: If using dried shiitake mushrooms, reconstitute in hot water according to package directions. Strain the liquid and, if desired, use in place of water in the recipe.

Per serving:

113 Calories
4 g protein
5 g fat
15 g carbohydrate
3 g fibre

Tostada with Black Bean Chili and Mango Corn Salsa

This brightly colored, spicy Mexican-style recipe can be made in stages, then assembled in layers at serving time. Garnish with sour cream and coriander, if desired.

Chef:

Tim Wood
Chef/Instructor,
Culinary Arts
Northern Alberta
Institute of Technology
Edmonton, Alberta

Dietitian:

Leslie Maze, RD
Diabetes Outpatient
Clinic
Royal Alexandra
Hospital
Edmonton, Alberta

This totally vegetarian dish combines all the necessary ingredients to provide quality protein. It is unique in taste and texture.

2 cups	black turtle beans	500 mL
1	bay leaf	1
2 tbsp	cumin seeds	25 mL
2 tbsp	crushed dried oregano	25 mL
2 tbsp	paprika	25 mL
1/2 tsp	cayenne	2 mL
2 tbsp	vegetable oil	25 mL
3	medium red onions, diced	3
4	cloves garlic, minced	4
1	can (28 oz/796 mL) tomatoes	1
2 tbsp	chili powder	25 mL
1/2 tsp	salt	2 mL
1 tbsp	rice wine vinegar	15 mL
1/4 cup	chopped fresh coriander	50 mL
12	corn tortillas	12

	Mango Corn Salsa:	
1	medium sweet red pepper, finely diced	1
1	large tomato, seeded and chopped	1
1	medium mango, peeled and diced	1
1 cup	frozen corn kernels, thawed	250 mL
1 tbsp	chopped fresh coriander	15 mL
1 tbsp	lime juice	15 mL
1/4 tsp	each salt and pepper	1 mL

Per serving:

530 Calories
24 g protein
10 g fat
95 g carbohydrate
17 g fibre

Cover beans in water to soak overnight; drain and rinse. Place in 4-quart (4 L) saucepan; cover with fresh water and add bay leaf. Bring to boil; reduce heat and simmer.

Meanwhile, heat small skillet over medium heat; add cumin seeds and toast until beginning to color; add oregano, shaking pan frequently to avoid scorching; cook until fragrant. Remove from heat; quickly stir in paprika and cayenne and remove from pan to avoid burning. Grind in small food processor or with mortar and pestle.

In large skillet, heat oil over medium heat; cook onions, stirring, for 3 minutes. Add garlic, tomatoes, chili powder, salt and ground spice mixture; bring to boil. Reduce heat and simmer for 15 minutes. Stir into bean mixture. Cook, uncovered, for about 1 hour or until beans are tender. Stir in vinegar and coriander. Remove bay leaf.
On baking sheet, bake tortillas at 350°F (180°C) for 5 to 8 minutes or until crisp.

Mango Corn Salsa: In bowl, combine red pepper, tomato, mango, corn, coriander, lime juice, salt and pepper.

To serve, place 1 tortilla on each plate; top with bean mixture. Repeat layers. Spoon salsa around tortilla layers.

Makes 6 servings.

Tip: The Salsa can be made ahead and refrigerated in airtight container for up to 3 days.

Vegetable and Bean Ragout with Roasted Tomato Vinaigrette

Chef:

David McQuinn, CCC
Executive Chef
Coast Victoria
Harbourside Hotel/
Blue Crab Bar and Grill
Victoria,
British Columbia

The Roasted Tomato Vinaigrette flavors the wilted spinach in this fresh-tasting vegetable stew. The vinaigrette can also be used as a dressing for pasta or salad, or as a sauce for grilled meats or poultry.

Dietitian:

Helen Dubas, RDN
Manager, Nutrition
Services
Victoria General
Hospital
Victoria,
British Columbia

This recipe is rich in protein, fibre and beta-carotene. The vinaigrette adds extra tang and color to the spinach.

I cup	chicken or vegetable broth	250 mL
4	stalks celery, sliced diagonally	4
3	medium carrots, sliced	3
I	small turnip, cut in julienne strips	I
I	medium red onion, cut in julienne strips	I
I	each large sweet red and green pepper, cut in strips	I
I	can (19 oz/540 mL) fava beans or lupini, drained	I
I	clove garlic, minced	I
I tsp	crushed dried thyme	5 mL
1/4 tsp	each salt and pepper	I mL
I	bag (10 oz/284 g) spinach, trimmed	I

Roasted Tomato Vinaigrette:		
10	plum tomatoes, halved lengthwise	10
2 tsp	olive oil	10 mL
1/4 cup	balsamic vinegar	50 mL
1/2 cup	olive oil	125 mL
I tbsp	chopped fresh parsley	15 mL
I tsp	each minced shallot and garlic	5 mL
I tsp	each crushed dried basil and pepper	5 mL

Per each of 4 main course servings:

284 Calories
8 g protein
16 g fat
32 g carbohydrate
9 g fibre

Roasted Tomato Vinaigrette: Place tomato halves on greased baking sheet; drizzle with 2 tsp (10 mL) olive oil. Bake at 350°F (180°C) for 35 minutes. Cool, remove skin and chop. In bowl, combine tomatoes, vinegar, 1/2 cup (125 mL) oil, parsley, shallot, garlic, basil and pepper. Set aside.

In large saucepan, bring broth to boil; add celery, carrots, turnip, onion and red and green peppers. Cover and reduce heat to simmer 8 from heat; quickly stir in paprika and cayenne minutes. Add beans; cook 2 minutes or until all vegetables are tender. Remove vegetables with slotted spoon; toss with garlic, thyme, salt and pepper. Keep warm.

Add spinach to broth in pan; cook just until wilted, about 1 minute. Drain off any broth. Stir in Tomato Vinaigrette and heat through.

Arrange on serving plates; top with vegetable mixture.

Makes 4 main-course servings or 8-side dish servings (beans may be omitted for side dish).

Gathers Lighter Pizza

Here's a terrific lunch pizza that uses whole wheat pita bread for the base and emphasizes vegetables in the topping.

Chef:

*Murray Henderson
CFM,
Foodservice Director
Manulife Financial
Waterloo, Ontario*

1/2 cup	tomato sauce	125 mL
1/2 tsp	each crushed dried basil and oregano	2 mL
Pinch	garlic powder	Pinch
4	8-inch (20 cm) whole wheat pita breads	4
1/2 cup	shredded or crumbled goat cheese (60 g)	125 mL
1/2 cup	shredded part skim mozzarella cheese (60 g)	125 mL
8	medium mushrooms, thinly sliced	8
1/2 cup	each diced sweet red and green peppers	125 mL
4	thin slices onion, separated into rings	4

Dietitian:

*Carole Doucet Love, RD
Public Health
Nutritionist
Waterloo Region
Community Health
Department
Waterloo, Ontario*

Vegetable toppings and lower fat cheese make this pizza a tasty treat.

Whisk tomato sauce with basil, oregano and garlic powder. Place pitas on large baking sheet; spread sauce evenly over each.

Combine goat and mozzarella cheeses; sprinkle half of the mixture over sauce. Divide mushrooms, red and green peppers and onion rings over cheese; top with remaining cheese. Bake at 350°F (180°C) for 5 to 6 minutes or until cheese melts.

Makes 4 servings.

Per serving:

266 Calories
13 g protein
7 g fat
40 g carbohydrate
6 g fibre

Grilled Vegetable Tofu Lasagna

Two simple changes give this lasagna a whole new flavor—the vegetables are grilled first and tofu is used as a layer with the cheese.

Chef:

Bernard Casavant, CCC
Executive Chef
Chateau Whistler Resort
Whistler,
British Columbia

Dietitian:

Jane Thornthwaite, RDN
Nutrition Consultant
Fresh Choice Restaurant
Program
Vancouver
British Columbia

This vegetarian lasagna provides an abundance of vegetables and is loaded with calcium from the tofu and cheeses.

1	small onion, chopped	1
1 tbsp	vegetable oil	15 mL
3	cloves garlic, chopped	3
1	medium carrot, diced	1
1	stalk celery, diced	1
2 cups	sliced mushrooms	500 mL
1	can (19 oz/540 mL) tomatoes	1
1	can (7-1/2 oz/213 mL) tomato sauce	1
1 tsp	each crushed dried basil and oregano	5 mL
1/2 tsp	salt	2 mL
1/4 tsp	pepper	1 mL
1	pkg (700 g) herb or plain tofu	1
2	medium zucchini, sliced lengthwise and grilled	2
Half	medium eggplant, sliced and grilled	Half
1	sweet red pepper, quartered, grilled and peeled	1
1 cup	2% cottage cheese	250 mL
3 cups	shredded part-skim mozzarella cheese	750 mL
1/3 cup	grated Parmesan cheese	75 mL

In Dutch oven, sauté onion in oil until tender. Stir in garlic, carrot, celery and mushrooms; sauté 5 minutes. Add tomatoes, breaking up with fork; add tomato sauce, basil and oregano. Simmer, uncovered, for 15 to 20 minutes or until thickened and reduced to about 2-1/2 cups (625 mL). Season with salt and pepper.

Spray 13- x 9-inch (3.5 L) baking pan with vegetable oil spray. Cut half of the tofu into 1/4-inch (5 mm) thick slices; line bottom of pan. Spread with half of sauce.

Cut zucchini, eggplant and red peppers into bite-sized pieces; sprinkle half over sauce. Sprinkle with half the cottage cheese and half the mozzarella cheese.

Slice remaining tofu and arrange in layer over cheese. Top with remaining sauce, vegetables and cottage cheese. Blend remaining mozzarella with Parmesan; sprinkle over top. Cover tightly with foil. Bake at 350°F (180°C) for 15 minutes. Uncover and bake until heated through and golden, 15 to 20 minutes. Let stand 5 to 10 minutes before serving.

Makes 8 servings.

Per serving:

298 Calories
27 g protein
15 g fat
16 g carbohydrate
4 g fibre

Garden Path Burger

This vegetarian version of the hamburger gets its flavor from the variety of ingredients—a combination of lentils, grains, beans and vegetables.

Chef:

Daryle Ryo Nagata
Executive Chef
Waterfront Centre Hotel
Vancouver,
British Columbia

Dietitian:

Jane Thornthwaite, RDN
Nutrition Consultant
Fresh Choice Restaurant
Program
Vancouver,
British Columbia

Tofu, lentils, walnuts and grains provide a great meat substitute in these delicious burgers with no cholesterol, little fat, and extra fibre.

1/4 cup	dried lentils	50 mL
1/4 cup	quinoa	50 mL
3 cups	fine dry bread crumbs	750 mL
1/4 cup	quick-cooking rolled oats	50 mL
1/4 cup	chopped walnuts	50 mL
1 cup	coarsely chopped canned chick-peas	250 mL
2/3 cup	each finely chopped carrot, celery and Spanish onion	150 mL
1/2	each finely chopped sweet red and green pepper	125 mL
1/2 cup	grated extra firm tofu	125 mL
1/4 cup	sliced green onions	50 mL
1/4 cup	toasted pepitas (pumpkin seeds)	50 mL
1 tbsp	coarsely cracked black pepper	15 mL
12	onion or vegetable kaiser buns, split and toasted	12

Toppings: Light mayonnaise, bean sprouts, sliced tomato, fresh coriander, shredded lettuce

In medium saucepan, combine lentils, quinoa and 1-1/2 cups (375 mL) water; bring to boil. Reduce heat and simmer 10 minutes; drain.

In large bowl, mix together lentil combination, bread crumbs, rolled oats, walnuts, chick-peas, carrot, celery, onion, red and green peppers, tofu, green onions, pepitas and black pepper. Using 1 cup (250 mL) for each, form into 1/2-inch (1 cm) thick patties about 3 inches (8 cm) diameter.

Bake on baking sheet at 375°F (190°C) for about 20 minutes or until hot and golden brown. Serve on buns with favorite toppings.

Makes 12 servings.

Per serving:

408 Calories
15 g protein
7 g fat
71 g carbohydrate
4 g fibre

Monster Quesadilla

Layer upon layer of seasoned cheese with spinach, refried beans and salsa, topped with sliced tomatoes and mozzarella cheese, make this spectacular recipe a stand-out for taste and appearance. Serve with extra salsa and low-fat sour cream.

Chef:

Don Costello, Cook
Oak Bay Beach Hotel
Victoria,
British Columbia

Dietitian:

Lisa Diamond, RDN
Manager of Nutrition
and Food Services
Vancouver Island
Housing Association for
the
Physically Disabled
Victoria,
British Columbia

This fabulous dish offers a serving from each of the four food groups in every portion.

2 cups	1% cottage cheese	500 mL
2	cloves garlic, minced	2
2 tbsp	grated Parmesan cheese	25 mL
1/4 tsp	pepper	1 mL
1	pkg (10 oz/300 g) frozen chopped spinach, thawed	1
12	10-inch (25 cm) flour tortillas (plain or whole wheat)	12
1	can (14 oz/398 mL) refried beans	1
1-1/4 cups	mild, medium or hot salsa	375 mL
2	large tomatoes, sliced	2
1/2 cup	shredded part-skim mozzarella cheese	125 mL

In food processor or bowl, blend cottage cheese, garlic, Parmesan cheese and pepper until smooth. Squeeze out extra moisture from spinach; stir into cheese mixture.

Place 1 tortilla on pizza pan or baking sheet. Spread with about 2/3 cup (150 mL) refried beans; cover with another tortilla. Spread 1/2 cup (125 mL) of salsa on top; cover with another tortilla. Spread 1 cup (250 mL) cheese and spinach mixture on top; cover with another tortilla.

Starting with refried beans, repeat layers two more times. Arrange sliced tomatoes and mozzarella cheese on top.

Bake at 350°F (180°C) for 45 to 60 minutes; cut in pie-shaped wedges to serve.

Makes 5 servings.

Tip: Substitute extra salsa for sliced tomatoes.

Per serving:

613 Calories
34 g protein
12 g fat
95 g carbohydrate
10 g fibre

Vegetarian Chili

Chili experts will tell you that to be authentic, chili is only a mixture of beans, tomatoes and seasonings. This recipe withholds on the meat, but the bulgur provides a similar texture. You can make it in advance and freeze small quantities in airtight containers for later use.

Chef:

Martin Wilkinson, CCC
Executive Chef
Clarion Hotel Grand
Pacific
Victoria,
British Columbia

Dietitian:

Marianna Fiocco, RDN
Consulting Dietitian
Westcoast Dietetics Ltd.
Vancouver,
British Columbia

This meatless version of chili is hearty and low cost, making it a great choice for cold winter nights.

2/3 cup	bulgur (4 oz/125 g)	150 mL
1 tbsp	vegetable oil	15 mL
1	medium onion, diced	1
2	cloves garlic, minced	2
1/2 cup	each diced celery and carrots	125 mL
1/4 cup	diced sweet green pepper	50 mL
1	can (28 oz/796 mL) tomatoes	1
1	can (5-1/2 oz/156 mL) tomato paste	1
2 to 3 tbsp	chili powder	25 to 50 mL
1	can (19 oz/540 mL) kidney beans	1
2 tsp	Worcestershire sauce	10 mL
	Hot pepper sauce	

Cover bulgur with hot water; let stand.

Meanwhile, in large saucepan, heat oil over medium heat: cook onion, garlic, celery, carrots and green pepper, stirring, 3 to 5 minutes or until softened.

Stir in tomatoes, breaking up with spoon; stir in tomato paste, chili powder, beans with liquid and Worcestershire sauce. Cook 10 to 15 minutes, stirring occasionally, until heated through. Stir in bulgur. Season with hot pepper sauce to taste

Makes 4 servings.

Per serving:

350 Calories
16 g protein
6 g fat
66 g carbohydrate
20 g fibre

Southwestern Torta

The popularity of Tex-Mex cuisine means you can find every-thing you need right in the grocery store to make this tasty dinner.

Chefs:

Takaski Ito, CCC, and
Scott Brown, Executive
Sous Chef
Palliser Hotel
Calgary, Alberta

Dietitian:

Mary Sue Waisman, RD
Nutrition Co-ordinator
Nutrition and Food
Services
Calgary Regional Health
Authority
Calgary, Alberta

1	clove garlic, minced	1
Half	medium onion, chopped	Half
1-1/2 tsp	vegetable oil	7 mL
3	medium tomatoes, seeded and diced	3
2 tbsp	chopped fresh coriander	25 mL
1 tsp	chili powder	5 mL
1	can (14 oz/398 mL) black beans, drained and rinsed	1
2 cups	chicken broth	500 mL
1	pkg (85 g) sun-dried tomatoes, diced (about 1-1/4 cups/300 mL)	1
1/2 cup	yellow cornmeal	125 mL
2 tbsp	chopped fresh basil (or 2 tsp/ 10 mL dried)	25 mL
4	10-inch (25 cm) tortillas	4
1	each medium sweet red, yellow and green peppers, cut in julienne strips	1
2 tbsp	vegetable oil	25 mL
2	eggs, lightly beaten	2
2/3 cup	shredded low-fat Monterey Jack cheese	150 mL
2/3 cup	shredded low-fat medium Cheddar-style cheese	150 mL
	Salsa	

In skillet, sauté garlic and onion in oil until tender. Add tomatoes, coriander and chili powder; cook, stirring, 3 to 5 minutes. Stir in beans. Set aside.

In medium saucepan, bring broth to boil; stir in sun-dried tomatoes, cornmeal and basil. Cook, stirring constantly, until mixture leaves side of pot. Cover and let stand 5 minutes.

In 10-inch (25 cm) springform pan sprayed with vegetable oil spray, fit 1 tortilla snugly into pan. Spread with half of cornmeal mixture. Top with second tortilla. Stir half of remaining polenta into bean mixture; spread over tortilla. Cover with third tortilla.

In skillet, sauté red, yellow and green peppers in oil until tender; stir in remaining polenta. Spread over torta. Place fourth tortilla on top.

Per serving:

412 Calories
23 g protein
11 g fat
58 g carbohydrate
8 g fibre

Using paring knife, poke holes through all layers of torta. Slowly pour eggs over torta, allowing to run down through holes. Sprinkle with Monterey Jack and Cheddar-style cheese. Bake at 350°F (180°C) for 25 to 30 minutes or until firm. Remove from pan; serve warm or cooled, accompanied with salsa.

Makes 6 servings.

Tip: Canned beans can be replaced with dried black beans. Soak 3/4 cup (175 mL) dried black beans overnight. Drain; cover with water and bring to boil. Reduce heat and simmer until tender, about 30 minutes. Drain.

Desserts

Strawberries in Phyllo Cups with Peach Yogurt

Lemon Mousse

Blueberry Flan

Autumn Crumble

Fruit Meringues with Cinnamon Crème Fraîche

Baked Alaska Volcano

Blackberry and Yogurt Cheese Crepes

Almond Pastry Shells with Fresh Fruit Melba

White Chocolate Raspberry Pie

Grapefruit Sorbet

Cranberry Honey Granita with Papaya Coulis

Coupe Bircher

Light Tiramisu

Bircher Muesli

Spicy Fruit Compote

Chocolate Ravioli with Fruit Filling

Three-Layered Chocolate Mousse and Lemon Loaf

Poached Pears with Tea Ice Cream (page 241)

Blueberry Semolina Cake

Fruit Brochette and Coulis with Minted Orange Cream

Lemon Tart with Raspberry Coulis

Poached Pears with Tea Ice Cream

A Little Something Extra . . .

Dessert, anyone? Few questions inspire the kind of angst that this one does. Why is it that so many answer with a reluctant "No, thanks"?

Remembering that pleasure, relaxation and a sense of well-being are a big part of a healthy lifestyle, think of dessert as an opportunity to relax and visit, very often to celebrate together, and to linger and savor the pleasure of the meal you have just enjoyed.

Indulging once in a while is perfectly okay, as long as you balance those occasions with times when you choose fruit or sherbet, and times when you choose not to have dessert at all.

Most of the time, you can choose foods from the four food groups for this part of the meal — custard, bread pudding and fresh fruit are great choices. For a change of pace, why not try Spicy Fruit Compote or Autumn Crumble. Dessert is not an afterthought, but rather an opportunity to expand the culinary horizon!

Over time, all foods fit into a healthy lifestyle. In fact, eliminating the foods you enjoy can lead to feelings of deprivation, sometimes leading to eating disorders. Clearly we can't have these foods any time we want, in any quantity we want, and still stay healthy. But with a little planning, we can have that White Chocolate Raspberry Pie when we want to indulge.

By planning ahead, you can balance your food choices to get the nutrients you need, and still control fat and energy intake. Don't deprive yourself of your favorite food just because it may be high in fat. Remember, it's not necessary to balance every meal by choosing foods with low fat and few calories, lots of fibre and high vitamin and mineral content. It is more important that over several days, our total intake should be balanced in this way.

The key, of course, is moderation. And speaking of moderation, what about foods from the "Other Foods" category in "Canada's Food Guide to Healthy Eating"? These foods, although they do not belong to one of the four food groups, are not bad. But when choosing them, you need to be mindful of how they fit into your overall eating pattern. Over any period of time, we need to be choosy about when we enjoy these foods, and in what amount, being careful to select those that are higher in fat and calories in moderation.

Caffeine-containing beverages like coffee and tea and foods containing caffeine like chocolate are often enjoyed at dessert or at the end of our meal. "Canada's Food Guide to Healthy Eating" cautions us to moderate our intake of caffeine. That doesn't mean you have to eliminate it completely, only that you must be mindful of how much caffeine is contained in your overall eating pattern. One option is to choose decaffeinated coffee or tea to moderate caffeine intake.

The same goes for alcohol. Rather than eliminate it completely, watch the amount you consume and don't overdo it. Give your guests a choice — offer them mineral water, juice or soft drinks as well. And in cooking, you can substitute nonalcohol or reduced-alcohol wine or beer.

The fact is, there are no "good" foods or "bad" foods. A healthy diet contains foods that have varying levels of fat, energy, fibre and other nutrients in them. The challenge is to balance all of these foods to achieve an overall pattern of healthy eating.

Whichever way you plan, and planning is the key, next time someone says "Dessert, anyone?", know that you can answer with an enthusiastic "Yes, please!" — and then enjoy without feeling guilty. Dessert is part of the plan, too — and an important part at that!

Mary Margaret Laing, RD
Cambridge, Ontario

Strawberries in Phyllo Cups with Peach Yogurt

The edible cup—made of phyllo pastry—makes an attractive holder for this refreshing dessert. You can substitute mango, papaya, peaches or pears for the strawberries.

Chef:

Robert Warren, CCC
Executive Chef
Runville Catering &
Muskoka Flag Inn
Huntsville, Ontario

Dietitian:

Mary Ellen Deane, RD
Public Health Dietitian
Muskoka-Parry Sound
Health Unit
Bracebridge, Ontario

When choosing yogurt, look for one with less than 2% MF on the label. You'll get lots of flavor without the extra fat.

4 cups	strawberries, cut into quarters	1 L
1/3 cup	peach schnapps or peach juice	75 mL
5	sheets phyllo pastry	5
3 tbsp	soft margarine, melted	50 mL
3/4 cup	low-fat peach yogurt	175 mL
2 tsp	icing sugar	10 mL
	Fresh mint	

In bowl, combine strawberries and peach schnapps; cover and refrigerate for 3 to 4 hours.

Place 1 phyllo sheet on work surface, keeping remaining phyllo covered with damp towel to prevent drying out. Brush with margarine, covering all edges. Top with second sheet; brush with margarine. Repeat with remaining phyllo. Brush top of last sheet. Cut into 8 pieces. Place in muffin tins, margarine side down, forming cup. Bake at 350°F (180°C) for 10 to 12 minutes or until golden brown. Cool in tins, then remove.

At serving time, divide yogurt among 8 dessert plates. Place phyllo cups on top, pressing gently into yogurt so that cup sits firmly. Fill cups with strawberries; sieve icing sugar over top. Garnish with mint. Serve immediately.

Makes 8 servings.

Tip: When using phyllo pastry, work quickly to prevent pastry from drying out. Cover sheets of phyllo with a damp cloth until you are ready to use.

Per serving:

169 Calories
3 g protein
5 g fat
25 g carbohydrate
2 g fibre

Lemon Mousse

Evaporated milk and gelatin replace whipping cream in this unbelievably good lemon mousse.

Chef:

*Chris Klugman
Executive Chef
Wayne Gretzky's
Restaurant
Toronto, Ontario*

1/4 cup	2% evaporated milk	50 mL
1 tsp	unflavored gelatin	5 mL
1 1/2 tsp	grated lemon rind	7 mL
1/3 cup	lemon juice	75 mL
	Yellow food coloring (optional)	
1/2 cup	granulated sugar	125 mL
1/3 cup	water	75 mL
2	egg whites	2
	Fresh berries	
	Mint leaves (optional)	

Dietitian:

*Susie Langley, M.S., RD
Nutrition Consultant
Toronto, Ontario*

This low-fat, melt-in-your-mouth lemon mousse uses an Italian meringue...a little more work, but it's worth it.

Pour evaporated milk into small bowl; chill in freezer along with beaters.

In small saucepan, sprinkle gelatin over lemon rind and juice; heat over low heat until dissolved. Add few drops of food coloring, if desired. Cool.

In small saucepan, cook sugar and water over high heat until candy thermometer reaches 234°F to 240°F (112°C to 116°C) or soft ball stage (syrup dropped into cold water forms soft ball).

In bowl and using electric mixer, beat egg whites until soft peaks form; gradually pour in syrup, beating constantly. Beat until cool and very stiff. Fold in gelatin mixture.

Beat evaporated milk until soft peaks form; fold into egg white mixture. Pour into 5 dessert glasses. Refrigerate for 3 to 4 hours or until set. Serve topped with fresh berries, and mint leaves, if desired.

Makes 5 servings.

Per serving:

101 Calories
3 g protein
trace fat
23 g carbohydrate
trace fibre

Blueberry Flan

The flavors of blueberries, almond, lemon and cinnamon marry in this easy-to-prepare flan. Allow enough time to refrigerate the flan for at least one hour before serving.

Chef:

Pamela Good
Chef de Partie, Pastry
Prince Edward Hotel
Charlottetown,
Prince Edward Island

1-1/2 cups	all-purpose flour	375 mL
1/4 cup	granulated sugar	50 mL
1-1/2 tsp	baking powder	7 mL
1/4 cup	soft margarine	50 mL
2	egg whites	2
1/4 tsp	almond extract	1 mL

	Filling:	
3 cups	fresh blueberries	750 mL
1/3 cup	granulated sugar	75 mL
1 tbsp	all-purpose flour	15 mL
1 tbsp	lemon juice	15 mL
2 tsp	cinnamon	10 mL

Dietitian:

Carrie Roach, P.Dt.
Community Nutritionist
Health and Community
Services
Charlottetown,
Prince Edward Island

This blueberry flan provides a wonderful fruity flavor with a minimal amount of fat.

In bowl, combine flour, sugar and baking powder; stir in margarine, egg whites and almond extract to form dough. Press into 9-inch (23 cm) flan pan with removable bottom. Freeze for 15 minutes.

Filling: In bowl, mix together blueberries, sugar, flour, lemon juice and cinnamon; pour into crust. Bake at 425°F (220°C) for 15 minutes. Reduce temperature to 350°F (180°C); bake for 20 to 25 minutes longer. Cool on rack. Refrigerate for at least 1 hour before serving.
  Makes 8 servings.

Per serving:

233 Calories
4 g protein
6 g fat
42 g carbohydrate
2 g fibre

Autumn Crumble

The secret ingredients in this comforting recipe are acorn squash and carrots. Serve as a dessert with ice milk or frozen yogurt, or as a side dish with pork chops.

Chef:

Don Costello, Cook
Oak Bay Beach Hotel
Victoria,
British Columbia

Dietitian:

Lisa Diamond, RDN
Manager of Nutrition
and Food Services
Vancouver Island
Housing Association for
the
Physically Disabled
Victoria,
British Columbia

This variation on all-fruit crumble delivers all the flavor and more: fibre from the fruit and grains, and beta-carotene from the orange vegetables.

2 cups	mashed cooked acorn squash (1 large)	500 mL
1/3 cup	packed brown sugar	75 mL
1/4 cup	all-purpose or whole wheat flour	50 mL
1	egg	1
1 tbsp	milk	15 mL
1 tsp	vanilla	5 mL
1 tsp	each cinnamon and nutmeg	5 mL
1/4 tsp	ground cloves	1 mL
2	large apples, peeled and chopped	2
1	large carrot, shredded	1
1/2 cup	raisins	125 mL

Topping:		
1/2 cup	quick-cooking rolled oats	125 mL
1/4 cup	natural wheat bran	50 mL
1/4 cup	packed brown sugar	50 mL
2 tbsp	all-purpose or whole wheat flour	25 mL
2 tbsp	soft margarine	25 mL
1 tsp	cinnamon	5 mL

With electric mixer or in food processor, blend squash, brown sugar, flour, egg, milk, vanilla, cinnamon, nutmeg and cloves until smooth; stir in apples, carrot and raisins. Spread in greased 8-inch (2 L) square baking pan.

Topping: Combine rolled oats, wheat bran, sugar, flour, margarine and cinnamon until crumbly; sprinkle over squash mixture. Bake at 350°F (180°C) for 30 to 35 minutes or until golden brown. Serve warm.

Makes 8 servings.

Per serving:

241 Calories
4 g protein
4 g fat
51 g carbohydrate
6 g fibre

Fruit Meringues with Cinnamon Crème Fraîche

Meringue circles may take a little time, but not much effort. They're the perfect 'dish' for sliced fruit topped with crème fraîche: a mixture of sour cream and sugar flavored with cinnamon and vanilla.

Chef:

Larry DeVries
Chef/Instructor
Crocus Plains Secondary
School
Brandon, Manitoba

Dietitians:

Jackie Kopilas, RD
Rachel Barkley, RD
Brandon and Westman
Area Dietitians
Heather Duncan,
P.H.Ec.
Manitoba Association of
Home Economists–
Southwest Branch
Brandon, Manitoba

A tasty and low-fat dessert. You can use a variety of fresh, frozen or canned fruit depending upon availability.

2	large egg whites	2
1/4 tsp	cream of tartar	1 mL
1/2 cup	instant dissolving (fruit or berry) sugar	125 mL
1/4 tsp	vanilla	1 mL

	Fruit Filling:	
2 cups	sliced fruit	500 mL
2 tbsp	granulated sugar	25 mL
2 tbsp	orange liqueur or orange juice	25 mL

	Crème Fraîche:	
2 tbsp	granulated sugar	25 mL
1/2 tsp	cinnamon	2 mL
1/2 cup	light sour cream or 1% plain yogurt	125 mL
1 tsp	vanilla	5 mL

Line baking sheet with parchment paper or foil. In small bowl, beat egg whites with cream of tartar until soft peaks form; gradually beat in sugar, beating until stiff shiny peaks form. Beat in vanilla.

Using piping bag or spoon, pipe meringue into 4 circles on prepared pan, building up sides to form shells. Bake at 275°F (140°C) for 50 to 60 minutes or until lightly brown. Turn off oven and let meringues stand in oven for 1 hour.

Fruit Filling: Toss fruit with sugar and liqueur; chill.

Crème Frâiche: Mix sugar and cinnamon; stir in sour cream and vanilla. Chill.

To serve, place meringues on dessert plates; fill with fruit and top with crème frâiche.

Makes 4 servings.

Per serving:

257 Calories
4 g protein
2 g fat
54 g carbohydrate
2 g fibre

Baked Alaska Volcano

Flambé this dessert when you want something with real flair, or even easier, decorate with sparklers.

Chef:

Ralph Graham
Instructor
Culinary Arts Foundation
of Saskatchewan
Saskatoon,
Saskatchewan

Dietitian:

Rosanne E. Maluk, P.Dt.
Food Focus
Saskatoon Inc.
Saskatoon,
Saskatchewan

The drama of this dessert is definitely worth the effort. You will be enjoying the compliments a long time after the presentation. If you prefer a lower fat treat, replace the ice cream with your favorite frozen yogurt.

4	egg whites	4
1/4 tsp	cream of tartar	1 mL
1/2 cup	granulated sugar	125 mL
1	angel food cake	1
1	carton (2 cups/500 mL) Neapolitan ice cream	1

	Sauce:	
2 cups	fresh or frozen sliced strawberries	500 mL
1/3 cup	granulated sugar	75 mL
1 tbsp	cornstarch	15 mL
2 tbsp	sweet sherry	25 mL
	Red food coloring (optional)	

In medium bowl, beat egg whites with cream of tartar until soft peaks form; gradually beat in sugar until stiff shiny peaks form.

Slice cake in half crosswise. Slice ice cream in 1/4-inch (5 mm) thick slices; cover bottom part of cake. Replace top of cake. Place on baking sheet. Spread egg mixture evenly over entire cake, sealing well. Freeze until serving time.

Sauce: Combine strawberries with 2 tbsp (25 mL) of the sugar; refrigerate overnight. In small saucepan, combine remaining sugar and cornstarch. Drain liquid from strawberries into measuring cup; add enough cold water to measure 1 cup (250 mL). Add to saucepan; cook, stirring, over medium heat until boiling; reduce heat to simmer 1 minute. Remove from heat; stir in sherry. Add food coloring, if desired. Cool and stir into strawberries.

At serving time, bake cake at 450°F (230°C) for 3 to 5 minutes or just until browned. Drizzle some of sauce over edge of cake like lava of volcano. Serve remaining sauce separately with cake.

Makes 12 servings.

Per serving:

209 Calories
5 g protein
3 g fat
42 g carbohydrate
1 g fibre

Blackberry and Yogurt Cheese Crepes

When you allow yogurt to drain overnight, the result is a thicker 'yogurt cheese.' Pre-made crepes are available in the refrigerated produce section of many grocery stores.

Chef:

Stephen Ashton
Head Chef/Instructor
Picasso Café
Vancouver,
British Columbia

Dietitian:

Leah Hawirko, RDN
Leah Hawirko Nutrition
Consulting and
The Vancouver Health
Department
Vancouver,
British Columbia

The yogurt cheese easily replaces higher fat whipping cream. Another option is thick yogurt now available in stores — no draining necessary.

3 cups	1% plain yogurt	750 mL
	Rind and juice of 1 lemon	
1/4 cup	granulated sugar	50 mL
1/4 tsp	nutmeg	1 mL
1/4 tsp	vanilla	1 mL
8	crepes (about 8-inch/20 cm)	8
4 cups	blackberries (or other seasonal berries)	1 L
	Raspberry Coulis (see recipe below)	
	Icing sugar	
	Mint leaves	

In coffee filter-lined strainer placed over bowl, cover and drain yogurt overnight in refrigerator. Discard liquid.

In bowl, combine drained yogurt, lemon rind and juice, sugar, nutmeg and vanilla. Spread over each crepe.

Lightly mash berries with fork; spread evenly over yogurt mixture. Tightly roll up each crepe; place on tray. Cover and refrigerate for several hours.

To serve, slice each crepe into 4 pinwheels. Spoon Raspberry Coulis onto each plate; top with crepes. Sprinkle with icing sugar and garnish with mint.

Makes 8 servings.

Raspberry Coulis:		
1	pkg (300 g) frozen unsweetened raspberries, thawed	1
1/2 cup	icing sugar	125 mL

In food processor or blender, purée raspberries; press through sieve to remove seeds. Stir in icing sugar. Cover and refrigerate until chilled.

Makes 1 cup (250 mL).

Per serving with coulis:

186 Calories
8 g protein
3 g fat
34 g carbohydrate
4 g fibre

Almond Pastry Shells with Fresh Fruit Melba

You can make the crisp Almond Pastry Shells up to two weeks in advance and store in an airtight container until ready to use.

Chef:

Donald Pattie, CCC
Executive Chef
Niakwa Country Club
Winnipeg, Manitoba

Dietitian:

Joan Rew, RD
Co-op Coordinator,
Community Cooking
Nutrition Instructor
Red River Community
College
Winnipeg, Manitoba

This lower fat, light-tasting dessert shell is a great way to dress up mixed fruit.

	Raspberry Coulis (see page 227)	
2-2/3 cups	frozen vanilla yogurt	650 mL
2 cups	diced mixed fresh fruit	500 mL
	Almond Shells:	
1/2 cup	sliced almonds	125 mL
2/3 cup	icing sugar	150 mL
1/4 cup	all-purpose flour	50 mL
1	large egg white	1
3 tbsp	2% milk	50 mL

Almond shells: In food processor with steel blade, pulse almonds until finely chopped. Add sugar and flour; process until very finely chopped. With motor running, add egg white and milk through feed tube, mixing until well blended.

Line baking sheet with parchment paper; draw four 4-inch (10 cm) circles on paper. Place about 4 tsp (20 mL) mixture in each circle, spreading to cover circle. Bake at 350°F (180°C) until light golden and slightly brown at edges, about 10 minutes. Remove immediately with lifter or peel away paper; place each on inverted small custard cup, fruit nappy or glass. Mould slightly with hand or place second dish on top to form fluted edge. Let cool; remove and turn upright. Repeat with remaining mixture.

Spoon Raspberry Coulis onto each plate. Top with almond shell. Spoon frozen yogurt into each shell; arrange fruit on top.

Makes 8 servings.

Tip: Do not make more than 2 or 4 shells at one time since they are fragile and become difficult to mould if too crisp. If too crisp; return to oven for a few seconds to reheat.

Per serving:

247 Calories
5 g protein
7 g fat
41 g carbohydrate
2 g fibre

White Chocolate Raspberry Pie

White chocolate chips, light cream cheese and light sour cream are combined for this decadently good filling, complemented with a chocolate wafer crust and raspberry topping. For a variation, you can use fresh seasonal berries such as strawberries or blueberries.

Chef:

Janice Mitchell, CCC
Janice's Fine Country
Catering
London, Ontario

Dietitian:

Jane Henderson, RD
Consulting Dietitian
Kintore, Ontario

Low-fat yogurt and light sour cream reduce the fat content of this light-tasting dessert, but it is still a very rich choice. The fruit topping adds color and nutrition.

1-1/2 cups	chocolate wafer crumbs	375 mL
1/4 cup	margarine, melted	50 mL
2 tbsp	brown sugar	25 mL

	Filling:	
1 tsp	unflavored gelatin	5 mL
2 tbsp	cold water	25 mL
1 cup	white chocolate chips	250 mL
1	pkg (250 g) light cream cheese, softened	1
1/2 cup	light sour cream or 1% plain yogurt	125 mL
1 tsp	vanilla	5 mL

	Raspberry Topping:	
1	pkg (300 g) frozen unsweetened raspberries, thawed	1
1/3 cup	granulated sugar	75 mL
2 tbsp	cornstarch	25 mL
	Shaved chocolate (optional)	

In bowl, combine chocolate crumbs, margarine and brown sugar; press into 9-inch (23 cm) pie plate. Bake at 350°F (180°C) for 10 to 12 minutes. Cool.

Filling: In small saucepan or glass bowl, sprinkle gelatin over water; heat over low heat until dissolved, or microwave at High for 25 seconds. Melt chocolate chips over hot water.

In bowl, beat cream cheese until smooth; beat in melted chocolate, sour cream, vanilla and gelatin until smooth. Pour into pie shell. Refrigerate until set, about 3 hours.

Raspberry Topping: Drain raspberries, reserving juice. In small saucepan, combine sugar and cornstarch; stir in juice. Cook, stirring, over medium heat until boiling; reduce heat to simmer for 1 minute. Remove from heat; stir in raspberries. Chill. Just before serving, spoon over pie. Garnish with shaved chocolate, if desired.

Makes 8 servings.

Per serving:

423 Calories
7 g protein
25 g fat
45 g carbohydrate
2 g fibre

Grapefruit Sorbet

The citrus tartness of grapefuit and orange is highlighted in this refreshing sorbet. If you like, serve with a variety of seasonal fruit.

Chef:

David Powell
Executive Chef
Ramada Hotel
Downtown
Saskatoon,
Saskatchewan

1 tsp	unflavored gelatin	5 mL
3/4 cup	cold water	175 mL
1/2 cup	granulated sugar	125 mL
1 cup	grapefruit juice	250 mL
1/4 cup	orange juice	50 mL
2 tbsp	lemon juice	25 mL
Pinch	salt	Pinch
1	egg white, lightly beaten	1

Dietitian:

Rosanne E. Maluk, P.Dt.
Food Focus
Saskatchewan Inc.
Saskatoon,
Saskatchewan

Sprinkle gelatin over 1/4 cup (50 mL) of the water; set aside. In small saucepan, combine remaining 1/2 cup (125 mL) water and sugar; bring to boil. Reduce heat and simmer 10 minutes; stir in softened gelatin until dissolved. Remove from heat. Stir in grapefruit, orange and lemon juices and salt.

Pour into 8-inch (2 L) square metal pan. Freeze until slushy, about 1 hour. Pour into food processor or blender along with egg white; process until well blended. Return to pan; cover and freeze until firm. To serve, spoon into dessert glasses.

Makes 8 servings.

Smooth and light—the perfect ending to a rich meal, or simply a treat when you are trying to beat the summer heat.

Per serving:

68 Calories
1 g protein
trace fat
16 g carbohydrate
trace fibre

Cranberry Honey Granita with Papaya Coulis

Cranberries, water, honey and lemon juice are simmered, then puréed and frozen to make this beautiful ice. You'll notice subtle changes in flavor depending on the type of honey you use.

Chef:

Brian Holden
Head Chef
Elora Mill Restaurant
& Inn
Elora, Ontario

1	pkg (12 oz/340 g) cranberries	1
1/2 cup	water	125 mL
1/3 cup	(approx) buckwheat, wild flower or regular liquid honey	75 mL
1 tbsp	lemon juice	15 mL
	Fresh mint	

Coulis:		
1	medium papaya	1
2 tbsp	granulated sugar	25 mL
1 tsp	lemon juice	5 mL

Dietitian:

Jane Curry, RD
Community Dietitian
Woolwich Community
Health Centre
St. Jacobs, Ontario

The puréed fruit in this low-fat "ice" not only supplies your daily need for vitamin C but also presents a refreshing contrast in taste and color.

In saucepan, combine cranberries, water, honey and lemon juice; bring to boil. Reduce heat and simmer 10 minutes; cool slightly. Press through sieve to remove skins. Taste juice and add 2 tbsp (25 mL) honey if sweeter flavor is desired.

Pour into metal loaf pan. Freeze for about 1 hour or until partially frozen. Pour into food processor; process until well blended. Return to pan; cover and freeze until firm, 3 to 4 hours.

Coulis: Peel and seed papaya. In food processor, process papaya, sugar and lemon juice until smooth. Refrigerate until serving time.

To serve, let granita stand at room temperature 10 minutes. Pour coulis onto dessert plates; scoop granita on top. Garnish with fresh mint.

Makes 5 servings.

Per serving:

129 Calories
1 g protein
trace fat
34 g carbohydrate
3 g fibre

Coupe Bircher

This recipe for Coupe Bircher and the one for Bircher Muesli on page 234 have many similarities but are totally different in flavor. Coupe Bircher is the more elegant of the two, and you can use a variety of fruit such as apples, oranges, bananas, raspberries or blueberries.

Chef:

Anton Koch, CCC
Chef/Owner
Rotisserie St. Moritz
Dorval, Québec

Dietitian:

Kim Arrey, P.Dt.
Consulting Dietitian
Montréal, Québec

Oats and fruit are excellent sources of soluble fibre and make this dish a delicious healthy dessert, or a great breakfast or brunch alternative to hot oatmeal.

1/2 cup	quick-cooking rolled oats	125 mL
1/4 cup	raisins	50 mL
1 tbsp	each sliced hazelnuts and almonds	15 mL
1/2 cup	1% milk	125 mL
1-1/4 cups	1% plain yogurt	300 mL
3 tbsp	granulated sugar	50 mL
2 tbsp	liquid honey	25 mL
1 tsp	lemon juice	5 mL
1 tsp	vanilla	5 mL
2 cups	sliced strawberries	500 mL
2 cups	cubed peeled cantaloupe	500 mL
	Mint leaves	

In bowl, soak oats, raisins, hazelnuts and almonds in milk for 1 hour in refrigerator. Stir in yogurt, sugar, honey, lemon juice and vanilla.

Reserve about 1/2 cup (125 mL) each of strawberries and cantaloupe; fold remaining fruit into yogurt mixture. Refrigerate for several hours or overnight.

Serve in dessert glasses topped with reserved fruit and mint leaves, if desired.

Makes 8 servings.

Per serving:

138 Calories
4 g protein
3 g fat
26 g carbohydrate
2 g fibre

Light Tiramisu

Replace expensive mascarpone cheese with an Italian meringue, light cream cheese and yogurt cheese, and the result is this marvelous orange-flavored version of tiramisu. Make it for a crowd and enjoy without guilt! (This dessert is best served the same day it's prepared.)

Chefs:

Mark Mogensen, Chef
HealthWinds
Therapeutic Spa
Toronto, Ontario

Dietitian:

Marsha Rosen, RD
Consulting Dietitian
HealthWinds
Therapeutic Spa
Toronto, Ontario

This recipe is a testimonial to the fact that elegant desserts don't have to be high in fat.

2 tsp	unflavored gelatin	10 mL
2 tbsp	frozen orange juice concentrate, thawed	25 mL
1/2 cup	granulated sugar	125 mL
1/3 cup	water	75 mL
6	egg whites	6
1	pkg (250 g) light cream cheese	1
1 cup	yogurt cheese	250 mL
1/2 tsp	grated orange rind	2 mL
1/2 tsp	vanilla	2 mL
2	pkg (85 g each) soft lady fingers	2
1 cup	cold strong coffee	250 mL
2 tbsp	cocoa powder	25 mL

In small saucepan, sprinkle gelatin over orange juice concentrate; cook, stirring, over low heat until dissolved. Cool.

In small saucepan, combine sugar and water; cook over medium heat until syrup reaches 234 to 240°F (112 to 116°C) or soft ball stage (syrup dropped in cold water forms soft ball).

In bowl, beat egg whites until soft peaks form; gradually pour in syrup, beating constantly until cool and very stiff. Beat in dissolved gelatin, beating for 30 seconds.

In large bowl, beat together cream cheese, yogurt cheese, orange rind and vanilla until smooth and creamy. Fold in meringue, one-third at a time.

Separate lady fingers, drizzle each with coffee and arrange half in bottom of deep 9-inch (23 cm) glass bowl. Cover with half of meringue mixture. Sprinkle with 1 tbsp (15 mL) cocoa. Repeat layers. Cover and refrigerate at least 4 hours until set.

Makes 16 servings.

Tip: To prepare yogurt cheese, line strainer with cheesecloth and place over bowl to catch liquid. Measure 2 cups (500 mL) 1% plain yogurt into strainer. Cover and refrigerate for several hours or overnight. Discard liquid.

Per serving:

124 Calories

6 g protein

4 g fat

16 g carbohydrate

trace fibre

Bircher Muesli

Muesli can be made ahead and it stores well, refrigerated, for two to three days. Garnish with fresh seasonal fruit if desired.

Chefs:

*Blair Woodruff and
Kurt Zwingli
Instructors, Professional
Cook Program
University College of the
Cariboo
Kamloops,
British Columbia*

Dietitian:

*Cathy Thibault, RDN
Co-Manager, Food and
Nutrition Services
Royal Inland Hospital
Kamloops,
British Columbia*

Originating in Switzerland, this recipe has been modified to decrease the fat content. It's popular with athletes — the local running club has requested this recipe many times for their Sunday morning "Run and Brunch" events.

2/3 cup	quick-cooking rolled oats	150 mL
2 cups	2% milk	500 mL
1/4 cup	granulated sugar	50 mL
1/4 tsp	cinnamon	1 mL
1-1/2 cups	1% plain yogurt	375 mL
1-1/2 tsp	lemon juice	7 mL
2	medium (unpeeled) apples	2
2	medium bananas	2

In bowl, stir oats into milk; let stand 15 minutes. Stir in sugar and cinnamon.

Combine yogurt and lemon juice. Dice apples; stir into yogurt mixture. Stir into softened oats. Refrigerate.

At serving time, slice banana and stir into mixture.

Makes 6 servings.

Per serving:

208 Calories
8 g protein
3 g fat
39 g carbohydrate
2 g fibre

Spicy Fruit Compote

Compote may be made in advance, but stir in kiwi, bananas and strawberries at serving time. You can serve the fruit mixture with a scoop of frozen vanilla yogurt or a slice of angel food cake.

Chef:

Margaret Carson
Chef/Instructor/Owner
Bonne Cuisine School of
Cooking
Halifax, Nova Scotia

Dietitians:

Pam Lynch, P.Dt.
Consultant Dietitian-
Nutritionist
Nutrition Counselling
Services & Associates
Judy Fraser-Arsenault,
Research Associate
Mt. St. Vincent University
Halifax, Nova Scotia

A generous blend of different fruit.

3 tbsp	granulated sugar	50 mL
3 tbsp	brown sugar	50 mL
4 tsp	unsalted butter	20 mL
3 tbsp	lemon juice	50 mL
1 cup	orange juice	250 mL
1 tsp	each cinnamon and ginger	5 mL
1/2 tsp	cardamom	2 mL
Pinch	nutmeg	Pinch
1/3 cup	dark rum	75 mL
2	each medium (unpeeled) apples and pears, cut into wedges	2
2	medium peaches, peeled and cut into wedges	2
2	kiwifruit, peeled and cut into wedges	2
2	bananas, sliced	2
2 cups	strawberries, sliced	500 mL
3 tbsp	each lightly toasted sliced almonds and coconut	50 mL

In large skillet, combine granulated and brown sugars, butter, lemon juice, orange juice, cinnamon, ginger, cardamom and nutmeg; heat, stirring constantly, until boiling. Cook until reduced by half and thickened and glossy.

Stir in rum, apples, pears and peaches; simmer until barely tender. Remove from heat. Stir in kiwifruit, bananas and strawberries just until heated. Serve warm in individual dishes, sprinkled with almonds and coconut.

Makes 8 servings.

Per serving:

213 Calories
2 g protein
5 g fat
42 g carbohydrate
5 g fibre

Chocolate Ravioli with Fruit Filling

Pasta for dessert? The answer is 'yes' when you're serving homemade chocolate-flavored ravioli filled with fruit and almonds!

Chef:

Alastair Gray
Executive Chef
The York Club
Toronto, Ontario

Dietitian:

Mary Margaret Laing,
RD
M.M. Laing & Associates
Healthcare Marketing
Services
Cambridge, Ontario

This is a great way to serve fresh seasonal fruit with flair but still control fat, especially if you hold the whipped cream.

1-1/4 cups	all-purpose flour	300 mL
3 tbsp	cocoa powder	50 mL
2	eggs	2
	Icing sugar	
	Raspberry Coulis (see page 227)	
	Whipped cream (optional)	

	Fruit Filling:	
1/4 cup	cottage cheese	50 mL
1 tsp	granulated sugar	5 mL
Pinch	cinnamon	Pinch
1/2 cup	chopped strawberries	125 mL
1/3 cup	chopped bananas	75 mL
2 tbsp	lightly toasted sliced almonds	25 mL

In food processor, blend flour and cocoa. Add eggs; process 30 seconds. Press into 4 small balls. (If mixture is wet to touch, sprinkle in a little flour and process 10 seconds. If mixture is dry and crumbly, sprinkle in 1 tsp/5 mL water and process 10 seconds.)

Fruit Filling: Press cottage cheese through sieve into bowl; stir in sugar and cinnamon. Fold in strawberries, bananas and almonds.

Set pasta machine rollers to widest setting. Working with one dough ball at a time, flatten and pass through machine. Fold in half; pass through machine again. Repeat rolling and folding 6 to 8 times.

Adjust rollers to next smallest setting; feed sheet, without folding, through machine. Continue to reduce thickness and roll sheet until pasta is desired thickness.

Cut dough into 2-1/2 inch (6 cm) squares. Spoon filling into centre of half of squares; moisten edges with water and cover with another pasta square. Press edges to seal; trim edges. Place ravioli on wax paper-lined baking sheets. Repeat with remaining dough.

Drop ravioli into boiling water for 4 to 5 minutes. Drain well and serve hot, sprinkled with icing sugar. Accompany with Raspberry Coulis, and rosette of whipped cream, if desired.

Makes 6 servings.

Per serving with coulis:

209 Calories
7 g protein
4 g fat
37 g carbohydrate
2 g fibre

Three-Layered Chocolate Mousse and Lemon Loaf

You can make your own lemon cake, or if time is short, purchase frozen light pound cake instead. Be sure to chill the assembled cake until it's firm before serving. Garnish with chocolate shavings, slivered almonds or hazelnuts.

Chef:

John Schroder
J.P. Brothers Food
Management Services
Ltd.
Toronto, Ontario

1 cup	1% plain yogurt	250 mL
	Cake:	
3	eggs	3
3/4 cup	granulated sugar	175 mL
1 tbsp	grated lemon rind	15 mL
2 tsp	vanilla	10 mL
1 cup	sifted all-purpose flour	250 mL
	Mousse:	
1 oz	semisweet chocolate	30 g
1/4 cup	cocoa powder	50 mL
3	egg whites	3
1/4 cup	granulated sugar	50 mL

Dietitian:

Susie Langley, M.S., RD
Nutrition Consultant
Toronto, Ontario

This chocolate mousse owes its deceptively decadent taste to the clever combination of low-fat ingredients.

In cheesecloth-lined strainer set over bowl, cover and refrigerate yogurt to drain for at least 4 hours or overnight. Discard liquid in bowl. Let yogurt stand until at room temperature.

Cake: In bowl, beat eggs, sugar, lemon rind and vanilla until pale and slightly thickened; gradually fold in flour. Pour into greased 8- x 4-inch (1.5 L) loaf pan. Bake at 375°F (190°C) for 25 to 30 minutes or until golden and firm to touch. Cool in pan 10 minutes. Remove from pan and cool on rack.

Mousse: Melt chocolate over hot water or microwave at Medium. In bowl, whisk cocoa into yogurt; stir in melted chocolate. Set aside.

Place egg whites in bowl over saucepan of simmering water; beat with electric mixer until foamy. Gradually beat in sugar until medium-soft peaks form; fold one-third at a time into yogurt mixture.

Trim top off cake; cut cake lengthwise into 3 layers. Clean loaf pan and line with enough plastic wrap to extend over sides. Pour in one-third of mousse; top with 1 cake layer. Repeat twice. Cover with plastic wrap. Refrigerate until firm, about 3 hours. Turn out onto serving tray; remove plastic wrap carefully.

Makes 8 servings.

Per serving:

233 Calories
7 g protein
4 g fat
42 g carbohydrate
2 g fibre

Blueberry Semolina Cake

This easy-to-make cake is best served warm. You can also substitute your favorite fruit for blueberries.

Chef:

Alain Mercier, CCC
Independent Chef
Canadian Forces
BFC Valcartier
Courcelette, Québec

Dietitian:

Fabiola Masri, P.Dt.
Présidente
Santé à la Carte
Québec City, Québec

Talk about low fat! This is a great way to serve your favorite fruit and still satisfy your sweet tooth.

1-1/2 cups	small semolina	375 mL
1 tsp	baking soda	5 mL
1 cup	1% plain yogurt	250 mL
1 cup	fresh or frozen blueberries	250 mL
1 tsp	vanilla	5 mL
1/2 cup	maple syrup	125 mL

In medium bowl, mix semolina and baking soda. Combine yogurt, blueberries and vanilla; stir into dry ingredients just until moistened. Do not overmix.

Spoon into lightly greased 8-inch (2 L) square baking pan. Bake at 325°F (160°C) for 45 to 50 minutes or until toothpick inserted into centre comes out clean. Remove cake from oven; pour syrup on top. Serve warm.

Makes 12 servings.

Tip: If you reheat the cake a day later or after freezing, drizzle or brush 1/4 cup (50 mL) more maple syrup over it to glaze.

Per serving:

136 Calories
4 g protein
1 g fat
29 g carbohydrate
1 g fibre

Fruit Brochette and Coulis with Minted Orange Cream

Here's fruit salad made exciting for the 1990s! Use any seasonal fresh fruit to maximize flavor. You'll need eight wooden skewers for lemon grass stalks for the brochettes.

Chef:

John Higgins
Executive Chef
King Edward Hotel
Toronto, Ontario

Dietitian:

Susan Iantorno, M.H.Sc.,
RD
Food and Nutrition
Communications
Specialist
NutriQuest
Toronto, Ontario

This is an appealing way to add fruit to the diet. It's perfect for a romantic summer picnic.

8	medium whole strawberries (or 4 halved large)	8
8	cubes each peeled cantaloupe, honeydew melon and pineapple	
24	seedless grapes	24
	Mint springs	

	Fruit Coulis:	
1 cup	fresh or thawed berries	250 mL
1/4 cup	apple juice	50 mL
Pinch	freshly crushed black or white peppercorns	Pinch

	Minted Orange Cream:	
1/4 cup	1% plain yogurt	50 mL
2 tbsp	finely chopped fresh mint	25 mL
1-1/2 tsp	liquid honey	7 mL
1 tsp	frozen orange juice concentrate, thawed	5 mL

Alternately thread strawberries, cantaloupe, honeydew melon, pineapple and grapes onto 8 wooden skewers; cover or place in plastic bag and chill.

Fruit Coulis: In food processor or blender, purée berries, apple juice and pepper; cover and chill.

Minted Orange Cream: In bowl, mix yogurt, mint, honey and orange juice concentrate; cover and chill.

To serve, spoon 1/4 cup (50 mL) fruit coulis on each of 4 dessert plates; spoon about 1 tbsp (15 mL) minted orange cream into middle of coulis and swirl with point of knife. Top with 2 fruit brochettes; garnish with mint sprigs.

Makes 4 servings.

Tip: Cut fruit into cubes about the same size as strawberries.

Per serving:

106 Calories
2 g protein
1 g fat
25 g carbohydrate
3 g fibre

Lemon Tart with Raspberry Coulis

Lemon lovers will really appreciate this intensely flavored dessert. The dough is made in a food processor and the crust is baked before filling.

Chef:

Antony Nuth
Chef/Owner
Herbs Restaurant
Toronto, Ontario

Dietitian:

Lynda Chadwick, RD
National Medical
Manager
Nestlé Canada Inc.
Toronto, Ontario

A refreshing ending to a meal, but this one is definitely a higher fat choice.

I tsp	grated lemon rind	5 mL
3/4 cup	lemon juice	175 mL
5	eggs	5
I cup	granulated sugar	250 mL
2/3 cup	whipping cream	150 mL
	Raspberry Coulis (see page 227)	

	Pastry:	
I cup	all-purpose flour	250 mL
1/2 cup	icing sugar	125 mL
1/3 cup	cold unsalted butter, cut in 1-inch (2.5 cm) cubes	75 mL
I	egg	I
2 tbsp	whipping cream	25 mL

Pastry: In food processor, combine flour and icing sugar; add butter and process until mixture resembles coarse crumbs. Lightly beat egg and whipping cream; add to flour mixture with machine running and process just until dough starts to clump together. Gather into ball; wrap with plastic wrap and chill 1 hour.

On lightly floured surface, roll pastry to fit 9-inch (23 cm) flan pan, leaving 1-inch (2.5 cm) overhang. Fold overhang inside flan pan and press to make even 1 inch (2.5 cm) thick edge. Line shell neatly with foil large enough to lift out easily; fill evenly with dried beans or rice. Bake at 400°F (200°C) for 15 minutes or until edges are golden. Remove foil with beans; bake for 4 minutes or until uniformly golden. Let cool.

In bowl, whisk together lemon rind and juice, eggs, sugar and whipping cream. Place baked shell in oven; carefully pour in filling right to rim. Bake at 300°F (150°C) until firm around edge and almost set in centre, 20 to 25 minutes. Cool on rack. Cut into wedges. Serve with Raspberry Coulis.

Makes 8 servings.

Per serving with coulis:

420 Calories
7 g protein
20 g fat
55 g carbohydrate
1 g fibre

Poached Pears with Tea Ice Cream

The poached pears are good enough to serve on their own with a seasonal fruit garnish. But, if you've got the time, make the Earl Grey tea ice cream then sit back for the applause!

Chef:

*John Cordeaux
Chef Executif des
Cuisines
Hôtel le Reine Elizabeth
Montréal, Québec*

Dietitian:

*Kim Arrey, P.Dt.
Consulting Dietitian
Montréal, Québec*

Ice cream lovers take heart—this unusual homemade ice cream is great on taste and lower in fat.

2 cups	water	500 mL
1/3 cup	liquid honey	75 mL
2 tbsp	lemon juice	25 mL
1 tsp	vanilla	5 mL
6	medium ripe pears	6
	Seasonal fruit (raspberries, strawberries, orange slices, kiwifruit slices)	

Tea Ice Cream:

2/3 cup	1% milk	150 mL
3 tbsp	Earl Grey tea leaves	50 mL
3/4 cup	granulated sugar	175 mL
1/4 cup	liquid honey	50 mL
2 tbsp	skim milk powder	25 mL
4 oz	light cream cheese	125 g
1 cup	1 or 2% plain yogurt	250 mL
1/2 cup	light sour cream	125 mL

Tea Ice Cream: In small saucepan, slowly heat milk and tea leaves. Add sugar, honey and skim milk powder; heat, stirring, until dissolved. Cool. Strain out tea leaves. Whisk in cream cheese, yogurt and sour cream until smooth. Refrigerate at least 2 hours.

Pour into shallow metal pan; cover and freeze for about 2 hours or until almost firm. Break up mixture and transfer to food processor; purée until smooth. Return to pan; cover and freeze until firm.

In saucepan, combine water, honey, lemon juice and vanilla; bring to boil. Peel pears, leaving stem attached. Add to saucepan, cover and reduce heat to simmer 10 to 12 minutes, turning pears once, until tender. Pour into bowl along with syrup; cover and chill.

To serve, let Tea Ice Cream stand at room temperature for 10 minutes. Place each pear on dessert plate; drizzle with 1 tbsp (15 mL) syrup. Add scoop of ice cream and seasonal fruit.

Makes 6 servings.

Per serving:

376 Calories
7 g protein
7 g fat
77 g carbohydrate
5 g fibre

A Note on Nutrient Analysis

Nutrient analysis of the recipes was performed by Info Access (1988) Inc., using the nutritional accounting component of the CBORD Menu Management System. The nutrient database was the 1991 Canadian Nutrient File supplemented when necessary with documented data from reliable sources. Nutrient values have been rounded to the nearest whole number.

The analysis was carried out using imperial measures except when the practical recipe quantity was metric. Calculations were based on the first ingredient listed when there was a choice and did not include optional ingredients.

Appendix

Health   Santé
Canada   Canada

CANADA'S

Food Guide

TO HEALTHY EATING

Enjoy a variety
of foods from each
group every day.

Choose lower-
fat foods
more often.

Grain Products
Choose whole grain
and enriched
products more
often.

Vegetables & Fruit
Choose dark green and
orange vegetables and
orange fruit more often.

Milk Products
Choose lower-fat
milk products more
often.

Meat & Alternatives
Choose leaner meats,
poultry and fish, as well
as dried peas, beans and
lentils more often.

Canada

Different People Need Different Amounts of Food

The amount of food you need every day from the 4 food groups and other foods depends on your age, body size, activity level, whether you are male or female and if you are pregnant or breast-feeding. That's why the Food Guide gives a lower and higher number of servings for each food group. For example, young children can choose the lower number of servings, while male teenagers can go to the higher number. Most other people can choose servings somewhere in between.

Grain Products
5-12
SERVINGS PER DAY

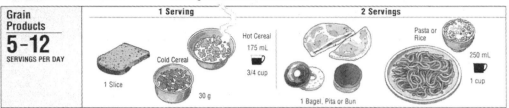

1 Serving

1 Slice

Cold Cereal
30 g

Hot Cereal
175 mL
3/4 cup

2 Servings

1 Bagel, Pita or Bun

Pasta or Rice
250 mL
1 cup

Vegetables & Fruit
5-10
SERVINGS PER DAY

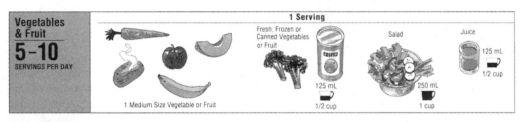

1 Serving

1 Medium Size Vegetable or Fruit

Fresh, Frozen or Canned Vegetables or Fruit
125 mL
1/2 cup

Salad
250 mL
1 cup

Juice
125 mL
1/2 cup

Milk Products
SERVINGS PER DAY
Children 4–9 years: 2–3
Youth 10–16 years: 3–4
Adults: 2–4
Pregnant & Breast-feeding
Women: 3–4

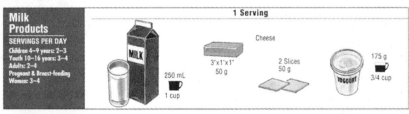

1 Serving

MILK
250 mL
1 cup

Cheese
3"x1"x1"
50 g

2 Slices
50 g

175 g
3/4 cup

Other Foods

Taste and enjoyment can also come from other foods and beverages that are not part of the 4 food groups. Some of these foods are higher in fat or Calories, so use these foods in moderation.

Meat & Alternatives
2-3
SERVINGS PER DAY

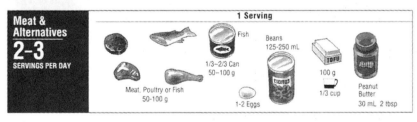

1 Serving

Meat, Poultry or Fish
50-100 g

Fish
1/3–2/3 Can
50–100 g

1-2 Eggs

Beans
125-250 mL

TOFU
100 g
1/3 cup

Peanut Butter
30 mL 2 tbsp

Enjoy eating well, being active and feeling good about yourself. That's VITALITÉ

© Minister of Supply and Services Canada 1992 Cat. No. H39-252/1992E No changes permitted. Reprint permission not required.
ISBN 0-662-19648-1

Chefs and Dietitians

Many thanks to the chefs and dietitians (below) who partnered to create the many nutritious and delicious recipes.

Chefs

Armstrong, Barb
Anderegg, Hans
Ashton, Stephen

Bauchmann, Kris
Blain, Guy
Breares, Trent
Brown, Scott

Carson, Margaret
Casavant, Bernard
Chalmers, Jo-Anne
Charlebois, André
Cipryk, Albert
Clavel, Alex
Colliver, Raymond
Colonerus, Edouard
Cordeaux, John
Costello, Don
Courchesne, Conrad

Davis, Ronald
Dean, Vern
Densmore, Kim
Desjardins, Serge
DeVries, Larry
Dietzel, Thomas

Fagan, Wayne
Fan, Alfred
Fergie, Eric
Franz, Richard

Glass, Samuel
Glover, Ron
Good, Pamela
Graham, Peter
Graham, Ralph
Gray, Alistair
Guiet, Philippe

Halloran, John
Hansen, Chris
Hartmann, Hans
Heaney, Gary
Henderson, Murray
Higgins, John
Holden, Brian

Ito, Takashi

Kennedy, James
Klugman, Chris
King, William
Koch, Anton

LeVert, Yvonne

Marti, Bruno
McQuin, David
McLean, James
Mercier, Alain
Meredith, Darren
Miller, Tyrone
Mitchell, Dean
Mitchell, Janice
Mogensen, Mark

Nagata, Daryle Ryo
Neil, Robert
Nicholson, David
Nuth, Tony

Ochitwa, Peter

Pantel, Leo
Pattie, Don
Paudler, Jon
Peace, Kenneth
Pechey, Ted
Pitt, Thomas
Philippe, Gerald
Pokomandy, Julius
Powell, David

Rodriguez, Louis

Schindler, Rainer
Schroder, John
Scott, John
Selig, Howard
Simpson, Judson
Suriano, Rocco
Surm, Hubertus

Van Arenthals, Beth
Vig, Nanak Chand
Vincent, Yannick

Warren, Robert
Watson, Steven
Wilkinson, Martin
Wood, Tim
Woodruff, Blair

Zwingli, Kurt

Dietitians

Antonishak, Donna
Arrey, Kim
Aucoin, Denise

Barkley, Rachel

Chadwick, Lynda
Cochrane, Tricia
Clarke, Sharlene
Crompton, Renée C.
Cullen, Laura
Curry, Jane
Cutler, Heather

Deane, Mary Ellen
Diamond, Lisa
Doucet Love, Carole
Dubas, Helen
Duffenais, Rosemary

Fiocco, Marianna
Flowerday, Dani

Hamilton, Thomas
Hargrove, Denise
Hawirko, Leah
Henderson, Jane

Iantorno, Susan

Jackson, Karen
Jounault-Hemstock, Suzanne

Kopilas, Jackie

Laing, Mary Margaret
Langley, Susie
Lynch, Pam

Mallette, Connie
Maluk, Rosanne E.
Masri, Fabiola
Maze, Leslie

McDonald, Jane
McLelan, Elizabeth
McNair, Debra
Morency, Sylvie
Musk, Maye

Neuman, Patti

Oro, Kathleen

Palin, Dawn
Paul, Cynthia
Poirier, Vicki
Porter-MacDonald, Nanette

Reid, Debra
Rew, Joan
Richards, Cathy
Roach, Carrie
Rosen, Marsha

Sauvé, Violaine
Scarlett, Pat
Scheuer, Christina
Schwartz, Rosie
Stanton, Monica
Sutherland, Susan

Thériault, Johanne
Thornthwaite, Jane
Turnbull-Bruce, Cheryl

Waisman, Mary Sue
Wright, Kerry

Yeaman, Janice

Index